OXFORD HISTORICAL MONOGRAPHS

Editors

N. GIBBS   J. B. OWEN   R. W. SOUTHERN
R. B. WERNHAM

NOTE

Oxford Historical Monographs will consist of books which would formerly have been published in the Oxford Historical Series. As with the previous series, they will be carefully selected studies which have been submitted, or are based upon theses submitted, for higher degrees in this University. The works listed below are those still in print in the Oxford Historical Series.

THE MINERS AND BRITISH POLITICS

1906–1914

BY

ROY GREGORY

OXFORD UNIVERSITY PRESS

1968

Oxford University Press, Ely House, London W.1

GLASGOW NEW YORK TORONTO MELBOURNE WELLINGTON
CAPE TOWN SALISBURY IBADAN NAIROBI LUSAKA ADDIS ABABA
BOMBAY CALCUTTA MADRAS KARACHI LAHORE DACCA
KUALA LUMPUR HONG KONG TOKYO

PRINTED IN GREAT BRITAIN

TO

MY PARENTS

PREFACE

WHILST a great deal has been written about the coal industry and the men who work in it, there is still surprisingly little that deals specifically and exclusively with the political history of the miners and their trade unions. It is hoped that this book will fill part of the gap. For the miners the decade before the First World War was one of transition. This is a common enough remark among historians about the years they choose to describe, and it is of course true that every period is bound to be transitional; but there are times when a situation changes so strikingly during a particular span of years that the word becomes especially appropriate. It would be an over-simplification to say that between 1906 and 1914 the miners went over to Labour; yet the fact remains that within this short space of time the politics of the British coalfields underwent a change that was swifter and more far-reaching than anything before or since.

Part of this study is devoted to a fairly detailed examination of what actually happened in each of the major coalfields. Bricks are not made without straw, and however assiduous the historian may be he cannot conjure out of thin air materials which do not exist. Some of the mining districts have undoubtedly been much better served by their chroniclers than others. In the North-East, in Yorkshire, and in Derbyshire, for example, the surviving union records are reasonably full and informative; by contrast, the material available for Scotland can only be described as thin. Inevitably, the texture of the narrative differs considerably from one area to another.

For their help and co-operation I am indebted to a variety of individuals and organizations. I am grateful to the Secretary of the Labour Party for permission to consult its correspondence files and the minute-books of the executive committee; to the General Secretary of the National Union of Mineworkers for making available the records of its forerunner the Miners' Federation of Great Britain; to the library staff at the Ministry of Power for their help in unearthing long-discarded colliery maps; and to the staff at the British Museum Newspaper Library for a steady supply of musty and bomb-scarred volumes of provincial newspapers. A number of municipal libraries also went to considerable trouble to find material that was of interest to me. In particular I should like to thank the City Librarians of Leeds, Cardiff, Newcastle upon Tyne, and Sheffield for their assistance. The Secretaries of the Northern Liberal Federation, the Midland Liberal Federation, and the Scottish Liberal Association were kind enough to allow me to look at records in their keeping.

Much of Chapters V, VI, and VII is based on the minute-books of the individual county associations and district federations that constituted the M.F.G.B. The following areas of the N.U.M. kindly permitted me to examine their records: Yorkshire, Derbyshire, Nottinghamshire, Durham, Northumberland, Cumberland, Lancashire, South Wales, North Staffordshire, and Warwickshire. My special thanks are due to Mr. F. Collindridge of Yorkshire, Mr. H. W. Wynn of Derbyshire, and Mr. R. Main of Northumberland for talking to me at some length about mining and the miners. Veterans who were active in politics before the First World War are rare and becoming rarer; among those who gave me the benefit of their recollections in interviews were the Rt. Hon. Wilfrid Paling and the late Lord Lawson of Beamish, the latter in his tiny pitman's cottage and surrounded with the trophies and mementoes of a former Minister of the Crown and Lord Lieutenant of County Durham.

Part of this study was undertaken during a year spent at Nuffield College, Oxford. To the Warden and Fellows I am much indebted for their encouragement and help. For their guidance and sympathy I am particularly grateful to Mr. A. F. Thompson of Wadham College, Oxford, and Professor H. A. Clegg of the University of Warwick, who supervised the thesis upon which this book is based. Mr. Henry Pelling of St. John's College, Cambridge, and Mr. Allan Flanders of Nuffield College, Oxford, were also kind enough to give me a great deal of helpful advice. The responsibility for what follows is, of course, entirely my own.　　　R. G.

CONTENTS

ABBREVIATIONS

A NUMBER of abbreviations have been used in footnotes to refer to frequently quoted sources. These are:

MFGB Miners' Federation of Great Britain
Reports of Executive Committee meetings and annual and special conferences

LPEC Labour Party Executive Committee Minutes

LPLF Labour Party letter files:
incoming and outgoing correspondence of the Labour Party

The following abbreviations refer to the minutes and reports of various miners' unions:

CHAPTER V

DMA Durham Miners' Association

LCMF Lancashire and Cheshire Miners' Federation

CHAPTER VI

YMA Yorkshire Miners' Association

SWMF South Wales Miners' Federation

CHAPTER VII

DMA Derbyshire Miners' Association

NSMF North Staffordshire Miners' Federation

I

THE MINING VOTE

IT would be hard to think of a more steadfast band of
Labour supporters than the coal-miners. For almost fifty
years it has been one of the axioms of British politics
that the miners vote Labour, and since the end of the First
World War the mining constituencies have continuously
provided the party with a high proportion of its safest seats.
When it was overwhelmed at the general election of 1931
and reduced to its hard core, Labour was left with a mere
forty-six Members in the House of Commons: of these no
less than thirty represented constituencies where there was
a sizeable mining vote, and twenty-six of them had actually
been sponsored by the Miners' Federation of Great Britain. A
quarter of a century earlier the infant Labour Party was still
struggling to gain a foothold in the mining districts, and in
most of the coalfields the miners were every bit as solid in
their support for the Liberals as they subsequently became
in their commitment to Labour. True enough, there was
still a long road to tread in 1914, and, indeed, at this stage
the future of the Labour Party itself was by no means
assured; nevertheless, by the outbreak of war the change
was well under way.

The characteristic of the miners that has most impressed
the outside world is their solidarity. Their outlook on life
may be narrow, they may be inarticulate and slow to understand, they can certainly be obstinate and stubborn, but
there is no doubt that they know how to 'stick together'.
Before 1914 they were, as a contemporary observer put it,
'to a great extent a class apart from the rest of the community'.[1] Most of them lived in villages or small towns
where almost everyone was engaged in or dependent upon
the coal industry, and in consequence mining communities
exhibited an exceptional degree of social and occupational

[1] H. S. Jevons, *The British Coal Trade*, 1915, p. 7.

homogeneity. This is familiar ground, and requires no great elaboration; but the census of 1911 does provide some striking examples of concentration. Table 1 shows the percentage of mineworkers in the male working population in a number of urban districts that lay within colliery areas. Whilst these particular districts were certainly not typical, and are in no sense a random sample, it must be remembered that the bulk of the miners lived in small pit villages and hamlets where there was far less occupational diversity than in the kind of built-up area that merited the status of an urban district.

TABLE I

Occupational concentration of the miners

County	Urban districts	Total occupied males	Mine-workers	Per cent
Northumberland	Ashington	8,693	6,864	78
	Bedlingtonshire	8,746	6,389	73
	Earsdon	3,593	2,714	75
Durham	Annfield Plain	5,345	4,073	76
	Tanfield	3,386	2,477	73
	Ryton	4,245	3,049	71
Glamorgan	Rhondda	55,784	41,145	73
Yorkshire	Bolton-upon-Dearne	2,911	2,183	74
	Darfield	1,876	1,505	80
	Featherstone	5,001	3,790	75
	Wombwell	5,805	4,121	70
Derbyshire	Bolsover	3,573	2,536	70

In communities like these there was little of the social stratification and variety of life that is usually found in large industrial conurbations. The typical mining village was a dreary collection of box-like cottages, arranged in monotonous rows, each identical with the next. Almost everyone was related in some degree to everyone else, and physically and psychologically these intensely close-knit societies tended to be cut off from the rest of the world. In Northumberland there was even a special patois, confined to the

colliery districts, known as 'pitmatic'. Far more than most
other industrial workers, miners were bound together by the
peculiar nature of their work; and because they were all
involved in the same discomforts and dangers, and worked
underground either in pairs or in highly disciplined teams,
they developed a unique *camaraderie*.[1] Common memories
of hard times, accidents, and strikes helped to reinforce the
obvious bonds of economic interest that held a mining
community together, and nothing illustrated this unity
better than a pit disaster. In 1909 an explosion in the West
Stanley pit in County Durham killed 168 men and boys;
a local journalist covering the story soon discovered that
every single home in the little town of West Stanley had
suffered the loss of a relative or close friend.[2]

Group loyalty to the chapel and the trade union still further
consolidated a mining community. Nonconformity added a
religious link to all the other common ties; and at the same
time it was the chapel that provided many an up-and-coming
young leader with his first experience of public speaking and
public office. And even more than the chapel, the local
branch of the union was to become the focus of the miners'
attention and the object of their loyalty. The total effect of
all these centripetal forces in the lives of the miners was
summed up by G. D. H. Cole in the early twenties:

> The miner not only works in the pit: he lives in the pit village, and all
> his immediate interests are thus concentrated at one point. The town
> factory worker, on the other hand, lives often far from his place of work
> and mingled with workers of other callings. The townsman's experi-
> ence produces perhaps a broader outlook and quicker response to social
> stimuli coming from without; but the miners' intense solidarity and
> loyalty to their Unions is undoubtedly the result of the conditions
> under which they work and live. They are isolated from the rest of
> the world—even the rest of the Trade Union world; but their isola-
> tion ministers to their own self-sufficiency and loyalty one to another.[3]

Naturally enough, an environment of this kind produced a
similarity of outlook over a wide range of issues; what was

---

[1] In spite of mechanization this aspect of a miner's life and work has changed
little over the years. See Clancy Sigal, *Weekend in Dinlock*, 1960, pp. 172-4.

[2] *Durham Chronicle*, 19 Feb. 1909.

[3] G. D. H. Cole, *Labour in the Coal-Mining Industry (1914-1921)*, 1923, p. 7.

in the interest of one miner was in the interest of every miner, and this went for politics as much as for anything else.[1]

Such is the general picture, and in broad terms it is accurate enough. Yet there are one or two qualifications that ought to be added. As it happens, there were two districts, Lancashire and Staffordshire, where the character of the coalfields was rather out of the ordinary, and where there were probably as many Conservative as Liberal miners. And, of course, the central area of this study is concerned with precisely that period when the newly arrived Labour Party was dividing the miners even in those coalfields which had hitherto been overwhelmingly Liberal in sympathy. Furthermore, to say that districts like Durham and Northumberland, South Wales, Yorkshire, and Derbyshire were overwhelmingly Liberal is not to claim that in areas such as these there were no Conservative miners at all. That would obviously be absurd. Indeed, there is no entirely satisfactory way of demonstrating that even the great majority of the miners were Liberals, because obviously sample surveys cannot be carried out among voters long since dead. The smallest electoral unit for which voting figures are available in Britain is the parliamentary constituency, and, except for the few constituencies whose boundaries happened to coincide with those of county boroughs or administrative counties, there exist no statistics to show how many men were employed in a particular occupation within a constituency. Even if such figures were available the population of most constituencies was too large, and the number of workers in any one trade too small, for reliable conclusions to be drawn from election results about the political allegiance of any individual occupational group.[2]

[1] Recent inquiries suggest that once established within a group a political loyalty tends to become self-perpetuating and self-reinforcing: 'the knowledge of agreement with fellow members of his group, whether family, circle, or friends, or colleagues at work, further strengthens a person's already strong inclination to stand by his established convictions'. M. Benney, A. P. Gray, and R. H. Pear, *How People Vote: A Study of Electoral Behaviour in Greenwich*, 1956, p. 185.

[2] Until recently the electoral geography of this period received little detailed attention. One interesting, but over-simplified and sometimes inaccurate attempt to relate occupation and political allegiance is to be found in E. Krehbiel, 'Geographic Influences in British Elections', *The Geographical Review*, vol. ii, 1916.

By using the laborious method described in Appendix A,[1] however, it has proved possible to estimate the strength of the mining vote in all the constituencies where the miners were to be found in substantial numbers; and clearly where the Liberals consistently enjoyed large majorities in Parliamentary divisions in which 50 per cent, or more, of the electors were miners it is not unreasonable to suppose that the bulk of them did vote Liberal. The same line of reasoning would not necessarily apply to constituencies where there was, say, a 20 per cent mining vote. But it is hardly necessary to juggle with figures when a mass of circumstantial evidence and contemporary observation exists, all of which points in the same direction. Newspaper accounts of election campaigns in colliery districts, for example, all agree that the mining vote was solidly behind the Liberals, and it seems unlikely that experienced local journalists, trade union leaders, and politicians, all with their ears close to the ground, and all telling the same story, should be wildly mistaken. It is also hard to see how the leaders of so many of the miners' unions could have co-operated with the Liberals as closely as they did in the latter years of the nineteenth century had there been really sizeable Conservative elements among the rank and file.

The main concern of this study is with the years of change in the decade before 1914, and not with the deep-seated Liberalism of the coalfields at the beginning of the period; that is the point of departure rather than the major theme. There is, therefore, no need to dwell at length on the reasons for the miners' original adherence to the Liberal Party, the explanation of which probably lies partly in the general nature of the miners' way of life and partly in the particular circumstances of British politics in the nineteenth century. In every country miners have characteristically taken up a radical or left-wing posture, and they have always tended to support parties advocating change and reform in the established order. In Victorian England the natural home of most radicals was on the left of the Liberal Party, and this is

Since this study was completed a comprehensive survey has appeared in Henry Pelling, *Social Geography of British Elections 1885–1910*, 1967.

[1] See pp. 192–7. By way of illustration, a map of the Durham coalfield showing the distribution of collieries in relation to constituency boundaries is included on p. 103.

certainly where the miners were to be found. It is easy to forget that the middle-aged and elderly Lib-Labs of 1910, so vigorously denounced by the new generation of Socialists, had been well to the left of the political spectrum in their own younger days.

Political sociologists suggest that a left-wing attitude is frequently associated with a sense of deprivation which becomes particularly acute when certain essential needs cannot be satisfied.[1] The most important of these requirements are security of income, rewarding work, and recognition of one's value to the community, and on all these counts the miner in nineteenth-century Britain had ample grounds for discontent. There was not a great deal of total unemployment in the coalfields, but short-time working was common enough; and those districts that supplied overseas markets were especially subject to wide fluctuations in earnings. So far as status went, it is true that the hewers, the men who worked at the coal-face itself, did pride themselves on their physical strength, and, indeed, were something of an élite within their own community. But few miners can really have believed that digging coal was an altogether satisfactory way of making a living, and as time went by still fewer encouraged their sons to follow in their footsteps. Though the attitude of the general public towards the mineworker had certainly changed considerably by the end of the century, many of the older men could doubtless remember a time when the rest of society had looked on them as not much more than dangerous and violent savages.

It is claimed that the likelihood of a group moving strongly to the left is even greater if two further conditions are met. The first of these is that there should be adequate channels of communication amongst the men involved, and in this respect the miners were well served by their network of trade union branches, or 'lodges', which provided the opportunity for airing grievances and for planning collective action. The second condition is a belief that the individual can do little to better himself by his own unaided efforts. Very few miners at this time can have perceived a personal ladder of success stretching above them: they hardly needed to be told

[1] See S. M. Lipset, *Political Man*, 1963 edition, pp. 232 et seq.

that a better life for the individual could be achieved only by
drastic social and economic changes that required collective
action aimed at ameliorating the conditions of the group as
a whole. Even today faint cries of surprise are sometimes
heard when it is a miner's son or daughter who achieves a
position of eminence in the world: sixty or seventy years ago
there were real grounds for astonishment.

In the context of nineteenth-century British politics the
Liberal Party offered more specific attractions for the miners.
There was the personal drawing power of William Gladstone,
a venerated figure in thousands of working-class homes.
Before 1884 it was to the Liberals that the miners in the
counties looked for enfranchisement; after the Third Reform
Act there was a certain amount of gratitude. Most important
of all, there were the links between the Liberal Party and
religious dissent. Except for the Roman Catholics of Irish
origin, who were particularly numerous in Lancashire and
parts of Scotland, most miners who professed any religion
at all were Non-conformists of one brand or another. The
Anglican Church was for the squire, the landowner, and the
well-to-do, and the Conservative Party was for the Anglican
Church; the chapel was for the working man, and, broadly
speaking, both were for the Liberal Party.[1]

The task that the early socialists set themselves was to convince the miners that the Liberal Party had outlived its usefulness and ought to be abandoned. So deeply entrenched were
the Liberals in most of the coalfields that this was a formidable undertaking in any circumstances, and it was made even
more difficult because almost without exception the established and influential union leaders rejected Socialist doctrine
and fiercely resented and resisted the concomitant idea of a
new and independent working-class party. On the other
hand, in one important respect any agitator or propagandist
attacking the existing leadership and its attitudes from the

---

[1] Primitive Methodism was particularly strong in most of the English coalfields. For a long list of miners' leaders who were Methodist preachers or were
brought up in Methodist families, see R. F. Wearmouth, *Methodism and the Struggle
of the Working Classes, 1850–1900*, 1954, pp. 173 et seq. What evidence there is suggests that Nonconformity was markedly stronger in the mining counties than in
the rest of the country. See F. Bealey and H. Pelling, *Labour and Politics 1900–1906*,
1958, pp. 3–5.

left was always at a special advantage in the mining world
because there was always a tendency for a psychological gap
to open between those who became union officials, and perhaps M.P.s into the bargain, and those who continued to work
in the pits. Most of the miners' leaders, it was true, had
themselves been working colliers in their younger days, and
had lived the life of the ordinary miner; many of them had
suffered victimization for their union activities. But as the
unions became richer and more respectable the permanent
official became a white-collar worker and acquired something
akin to middle-class status. It was easy enough for him to lose
touch with the rank and file, and it was equally easy for the
agitator intent on undermining the leadership to make the
most of every grievance and to insinuate that the officials,
now so superior, had succumbed to the blandishments of the
coal-owners and betrayed the interests of the men. A miner
who had watched the process at work put it this way:

There has always been a smouldering fire of antagonism towards the
leaders among the miners. . . . The miner's job is hard, dirty and
disagreeable. This gives him a permanent grouse at the world . . .
when the ex-miner turned Labour leader and fat and heavy for lack of
exercise drives up in a motor to the 'mornin'' meeting at some pit,
the assembled colliers, shivering at the pit gate in the chill of the
morning, never fail to remark unflatteringly on his thick well-cut
coat and his embonpoint. The contrast is too great to be endured.[1]

Once the militancy and integrity of a union leader became
suspect so did his politics. In the twenty years before the First
World War the older miners' leaders, staid Liberals almost to
a man, presented vulnerable targets to a younger and more
belligerent generation of Socialist activists. And no sooner
had the Lib-Labs been ousted than the Socialists themselves
came under fire from Syndicalist and Communist snipers,
arguing that the extremists of yesterday had sold out and
become the selfish reactionaries of the present.

So much for the general character of the mining vote.
Turning now to its dimensions and distribution it is not
difficult to see why it loomed so large on the Edwardian
political scene. In 1911 the size of the United Kingdom

[1] J. D. Macdougall, 'The Scottish Coalminer', *Nineteenth Century*, vol. 102,
Dec. 1927.

electorate amounted to about 7,900,000 registered votes, and, when allowance is made for approximately 500,000 plural voters, this meant that 59 per cent of the total adult male population was enfranchised.[1] A detailed examination of population and electoral statistics for the colliery districts suggests that the proportion of adult mineworkers with the vote was rather smaller than the national average, the actual figure being about 55 per cent. Given a total of about 860,000 adult mineworkers in Britain in 1910 this means that roughly 470,000 of them would have been enfranchised, and that over the country as a whole almost seven voters in every hundred were miners.

For one occupational group this was a sizeable figure, and the miners were, of course, heavily concentrated in certain areas as Table 2 shows. This table also sets out the percentage of mineworkers in each district who were members of their appropriate trade union, and these figures reveal some striking contrasts with other occupations: the only other trades to come anywhere near the density of union organization that the miners had achieved were the ship-building workers, with 46 per cent of the labour force unionized, the cotton workers with 44 per cent, the printing workers with 36 per cent, and the railwaymen with 31 per cent.[2] When the official support of the miners was thrown behind a parliamentary candidate the union was thus in an excellent position to mobilize a very high proportion of the mining vote in the constituency concerned.

Within the counties listed in Table 2 the miners were still further concentrated in particular areas. Before the redistribution of seats that formed part of the Third Reform Act of 1884–5 the Boundary Commissioners had been instructed to try as far as possible to keep together in the same constituencies people following similar pursuits, and this they had done, even where in consequence they were obliged to

[1] For calculations and an examination of the reasons for the very limited extent of the franchise, see Neal Blewett, 'The Franchise in the United Kingdom 1885–1918', *Past and Present*, no. 32, Dec. 1965. For further discussion of this issue, see E. Halevy, *History of the English People in the Nineteenth Century*, vol. vi, 1961 edition, p. 443, and H. A. Clegg, Alan Fox, and A. F. Thompson, *A History of British Trade Unions since 1889*, vol. i, 1964, pp. 269 et seq.

[2] Clegg, Fox, and Thompson, op. cit., p. 468.

recommend considerable inequalities in population and decidedly odd shapes for some of the new constituencies. In Derbyshire, for example, they claimed in their report that they had succeeded in 'aggregating' the mining and manufacturing interests, and in Lanarkshire they pointed out that they had kept the mining communities in the North-West, North-East, and Mid divisions, separating them from the predominantly agricultural and pastoral South Lanarkshire constituency.[1]

TABLE 2

Geographical distribution of the Miners, 1910

District	Mineworkers	Membership of miners' and allied unions	Per cent unionized
South Derbyshire	4,000	3,600	90
Durham	155,100	135,590	86
Nottinghamshire	37,900	32,000	84
Flintshire	15,170	12,400	81
Derbyshire	53,000	38,100	71
Warwickshire	15,700	11,000	70
Somersetshire	6,400	4,450	69
South Wales	212,699	147,600	69
Northumberland	57,200	39,800	69
Cumberland	10,100	6,455	63
Scotland	141,000	86,570	62
Yorkshire	146,900	90,900	61
Gloucestershire	8,400	5,200	61
Lancashire	100,800	59,100	57
Worcestershire, South Staffordshire, and Shropshire	32,900	18,860	57
Leicestershire	10,600	5,500	51
North Staffordshire	28,900	8,100	28

As a result of this policy, after 1885 the miners inevitably formed a very high percentage indeed of the electorates in many of the newly created constituencies. As the coal industry expanded these proportions grew still larger, and at the same time, as new pits and new communities were

[1] *Parliamentary Papers, 1884–5*, vols. lxii and xix.

developed in hitherto rural areas, the number of parliamentary divisions containing a substantial mining vote also
increased. In South Lanarkshire, for example, which in 1884
the Boundary Commissioners had described as a predominantly agricultural division, about a fifth of the electors
were miners by 1910, and three years later the local miners'
union singled it out as a seat worth contesting at a by-
election. A complete picture of the way in which the mining
vote was distributed in about 1910 is set out in Table 3,
which lists all the constituencies where it seems probable
that 10 per cent or more of the electors were miners. In all,
there were eighty-six constituencies where they made up a
tenth or more of the electorate, and of these they constituted
between 10 per cent and 20 per cent of the vote in thirty,
between 20 per cent and 30 per cent in sixteen, between
30 per cent and 40 per cent in seventeen, between 40 per
cent and 50 per cent in eleven, between 50 per cent and
60 per cent in seven, between 60 per cent and 70 per cent in
four, and over 70 per cent in one.[1] This was plainly a vote to
be reckoned with and a vote that was worth winning.

[1] For more detailed estimates of the strength of the mining vote in individual
constituencies, see appendices to Chs V, VI, and VII. In these appendices the estimated number of miners on the register adds up to rather fewer than the figure of
470,000 enfranchised miners cited on p. 9. This is mainly because the appendices
list only those constituencies where the miners made up at least 10 per cent of the
electorate.

TABLE 3

Distribution of the mining vote, c. 1910

County	Constituency over 70%	60–70 per cent	50–60 per cent	40–50 per cent	30–40 per cent	20–30 per cent	10–20 per cent
England							
Cumberland	..	..	..	..	Whitehaven	..	Cockermouth
Northumberland	..	Wansbeck	..	Morpeth	..	Tyneside	Hexham
Durham	..	Mid Durham NW. Durham	Houghton-le-Spring Chester-le-Street	..	Bishop Auckland SE. Durham Barnard Castle	Jarrow	Sunderland (two seats) South Shields Gateshead/Durham City
Yorkshire	..	..	..	Normanton Barnsley Osgoldcross	Doncaster Rotherham Hallamshire Morley	Holmfirth Pontefract	Barkston Ash Wakefield Attercliffe
Derbyshire	..	..	..	Chesterfield Mid Derbyshire	NE. Derbyshire Ilkeston	..	SE. Derbyshire
Nottinghamshire	..	..	..	Mansfield	..	..	Rushcliffe Bassetlaw Nottingham W.
Lancashire	..	..	Wigan Leigh	Newton	..	St. Helens Ince	Chorley Eccles Ashton-under-Lyne Radcliffe
Leicestershire	..	..	..	..	Bosworth	..	
Staffordshire	..	..	..	..	NW. Staffordshire W. Staffordshire	Lichfield	Hanley Newcastle under Lyme Stoke-on-Trent Tamworth
Warwickshire	..	..	..	..	..	Nuneaton	..
Gloucestershire	..	..	..	..	..	Forest of Dean	..
Somersetshire	..	..	..	..	..	..	Frome

County	Constituency over 70%	60–70 per cent	50–60 per cent	40–50 per cent	30–40 per cent	20–30 per cent	10–20 per cent
Wales							
Glamorgan	Rhondda	..	Mid Glamorgan E. Glamorgan	Merthyr Tydfil (two seats)	..	Gower	S. Glamorgan
Monmouthshire	..	W. Monmouthshire	..	..	N. Monmouthshire	S. Monmouthshire	..
Breconshire	..	..	..	..	..	..	Breconshire
Carmarthenshire	..	..	..	..	..	..	E. Carmarthenshire
Flintshire	..	..	..	E. Denbighshire	..	..	Flintshire
Denbighshire	..	..	..		..	..	..
Scotland							
Fife	..	..	W. Fife	..	..	..	..
Lanarkshire	..	..	..	..	NE. Lanarkshire Mid Lanarkshire	S. Lanarkshire	NW. Lanarkshire
The Lothians	..	..	..	..	W. Lothian	Midlothian	E. Lothian
Stirlingshire	..	..	..	..	..	Stirlingshire Falkirk Burghs	..
Ayrshire	..	..	..	..	..	S. Ayrshire	N. Ayrshire

II

LIB-LAB POLITICS: THE BLIND ALLEY

STATE intervention in the coal-mining industry goes back well into the nineteenth century, and from the 1840s onwards there was a steady stream of legislation affecting the pits and the men who worked in them. Among the more important measures were those which prohibited the employment underground of women and girls and boys under ten, compelled management and men to observe strict safety regulations, appointed a mines inspectorate, and gave the hewers, who were paid by the weight of their output, the right to appoint from among their own number a check-weigher to ensure that they were not cheated by unscrupulous employers. The principle of state interference and supervision provoked less of an outcry and less resistance than might have been expected in the *laissez-faire* atmosphere of Victorian Britain because many of the owners, on reflection, were prepared to sacrifice some freedom of action if in return there was the prospect of fewer accidents and fewer strikes; stoppages were expensive, for they meant loss of output, loss of revenue, and expensive capital left standing idle.[1] Since Parliament was prepared to devote a good deal of its time and attention to the industry, the miners had always been concerned to make sure that their voice was heard at Westminster and that their views and wishes were taken into account by the Government of the day. By the 1890s there were two pieces of legislation in which they were particularly interested. Firstly, because of the abnormally high accident rate in their own industry, even more than the rest of the trade union movement they wanted a comprehensive scheme for workmen's compensation.[2] And secondly,

---

[1] In South Wales, for example, when a fatal accident occurred, the whole shift came up and followed the dead man's body to his home, E. H. Phelps Brown, *The Growth of British Industrial Relations*, 1959, p. 73.

[2] See R. Page Arnot, *The Miners: A History of the Miners' Federation of Great Britain*, 1949, pp. 272–80.

with the exception of the miners in the North-East, who for reasons of their own took a different line, they were pressing hard for legislation that would limit the hours of work under-ground to eight a day. From 1889, the year of its formation, the Miners' Federation had one bill after another brought before the House of Commons in its efforts to secure an eight-hour day. It was nearly twenty years before an Eight Hours Act was finally passed in 1908.[1]

Before the Third Reform Act of 1884–5 the miners resorted to the familiar techniques that are part of the stock-in-trade of every pressure group. There were petitions to Parliament, there were deputations to Ministers, and friendly M.P.s were lobbied and asked to help. But when the fran-chise was extended in 1884, and thousands of miners came on to the electoral register for the first time in the new con-stituencies, the miners' unions were in a position to apply a much more direct form of pressure through the ballot-box. They could extract pledges from parliamentary candidates of both major parties, and, where they were forceful enough and insistent enough, they could go further and send repre-sentatives from among their own ranks to Westminster, so that their claims could be pressed not only by sympathetic middle-class Members but by miners themselves, possessing a much more intimate knowledge of the industry and the needs of the men. The coal-owners for their part had always been well represented in Parliament: the unions, so it seemed, were now well placed to challenge the employers, or, indeed, to eliminate them from Parliament altogether, since many of the owners were Liberal Members sitting for mining constituencies.[2]

The miners were clearly in a much better position to secure parliamentary representation than most other workers. They dominated many constituencies by sheer weight of numbers, and their powerful and well-organized unions were able to direct and mobilize the mining vote behind the

---

[1] For a full account of the M.F.G.B.'s efforts to secure an eight-hour day, see Page Arnot, op. cit., and B. McCormick and J. E. Williams, 'The Miners and the Eight-Hour Day, 1863–1910', Econ. Hist. Review, vol. xii, 1959.

[2] Between 1885 and 1910 there were never fewer than 24 coal-owners in the House of Commons. See J. A. Thomas, The House of Commons 1832–1901, 1939, pp. 14–16; and The House of Commons, 1906–1911, 1958, p. 14.

chosen man, as well as providing the financial resources necessary for fighting elections. But political loyalties die hard, and the miners' unions preferred to work in co-opera- tion with the major parties rather than in opposition to them; in practice, given the Liberal predisposition of most miners, this meant that the miners had to persuade local Liberal Associations not to run candidates of their own in mining seats but to leave the field open for union nominees. In preliminary negotiations of this kind the weight of the mining vote certainly gave the unions an impressive bargain- ing counter, and before the general election of 1885, with the new registers coming into operation for the first time, they used their strength to advantage. There was already one miners' M.P. in the House in the person of Thomas Burt, the General Secretary of the Northumberland Miners' Association, who had represented the borough of Morpeth since 1874. At the first election after the 1884–5 Reform Act five more miners were to join him; Ben Pickard, the President of the M.F.G.B., was returned for the Normanton division of Yorkshire, John Wilson and William Crawford for Houghton-le-Spring and Mid Durham, Charles Fenwick for the Wansbeck division of Northumberland, and William Abraham, more usually known by his Welsh nickname of Mabon ('the bard'), for the Rhondda. In Yorkshire and Dur- ham there were informal electoral arrangements between the Liberals and the miners, the Liberals agreeing to support the miners' nominees in return for union endorsement of the Liberal candidates in all the other mining seats in the two counties. This was a promising beginning, and soon after the 1885 election Keir Hardie was calling for a parliamen- tary fund so that more miners could be returned at the next election.[1] With the mining vote growing there seemed every reason to expect more successful candidatures in the future.

Events were to take a very different course. In 1900, fifteen years and four general elections later, the number of miners' M.P.s had actually been reduced, and now there were only five. Burt, Fenwick, Wilson, Pickard, and Mabon were still in the House, but Crawford had died in 1890. The only additional success in all these years was Sam Woods's

[1] *The Miner*, Jan. 1887.

victory at Ince in 1892, and this seat was lost three years later at the next general election. Indeed, during the whole of the period from 1885 to 1900 there were only nine new miners' candidatures. Seeing that from 1889 onwards the M.F.G.B. was so passionately concerned to achieve an eight-hour day (and for that matter the unions in the North-East were just as anxious to block any such measure), it seems odd that the miners did not make greater efforts to return more of their own representatives.

At the outset, it must be admitted that they had little cause for dissatisfaction with the record of those Members who did represent the mining constituencies. Whether these M.P.s spoke and voted in the House of Commons in response to pressure from the miners, or whether it was only politicians already in sympathy with the aims of the miners who sought election for mining seats is immaterial; the fact is that the miners rarely had reason for complaint, as an analysis of the division lists when the various eight-hours bills came before Parliament shows clearly enough. An examination of the voting on the bill on six occasions between 1892 and 1908 reveals that of 342 votes cast by Members representing English and Welsh constituencies in the union districts that were members of the M.F.G.B., 241 were in favour, 34 were against, and there were 67 absences or abstentions. Of the votes against the bill twenty came from Lancashire and South Wales, where there was undoubtedly a good deal of genuine opposition to an eight-hours act, because it was thought that a reduction in hours (which in Lancashire were considerably longer than elsewhere) would reduce earnings; consequently a Member holding a seat in one of these districts who chose to vote against the bill could do so in the knowledge that many of the miners among his constituents would applaud rather than condemn.[1] The rest

[1] D. A. Thomas, the Member for Merthyr Tydfil, who had consistently opposed an eight-hours act, claimed during the debate on the second reading in 1893 that a majority of the South Wales miners were against the bill. He pointed out that at the previous election his majority had actually increased despite his well-known opposition to the bill, *H.C. Debates*, 4th Series, vol. ii, cols. 1846–7. One M.P. in a particularly awkward position was L. Atherley-Jones, who was legal adviser to the M.F.G.B., yet held a Durham mining seat. He seems to have resolved his dilemma by not voting on any of the occasions when an eight-hours bill was before the House.

of the Members for the Federated area, as the figures show, gave overwhelming support to the bill. Similarly, the miners in the North-East had every reason to be satisfied. Until the Durham and Northumberland unions themselves abandoned their opposition to an eight-hour day in 1907, M.P.s for the mining divisions in these two counties voted almost unanimously against it.

Yet, whatever the feelings of the miners, their whole approach to the question of parliamentary representation in these years was such that they could hardly hope for success on any scale, with each union ploughing its own furrow and all of them dependent upon the co-operation and goodwill of the Liberals, which more often than not was simply not forthcoming. At the general election of 1885 most of the mining divisions had returned Liberal Members; from that point onwards, if the miners wanted to put up candidates of their own for any of these seats, three courses were open to them. They could oppose the sitting Member—whose views might well be perfectly acceptable—and risk letting in a Conservative in the ensuing three-cornered contest; they could try to persuade the sitting Liberal to retire and make way for a miners' candidate; or they could wait until the seat fell vacant and then press their claims upon the local Liberals. The long-standing loyalty of the miners and their leaders to the Liberal Party almost always ruled out the first course; the second was hardly a starter, for Liberal M.P.s, understandably, were loath to surrender safe seats just to oblige the miners; and, so far as the third course was concerned, it so happened that comparatively few mining seats did become vacant in the years between 1885 and 1900. Even where suitable vacancies did occur, miners' candidates were not always brought forward, because the only species of miner remotely acceptable to a local Liberal Association was a man of some standing in the community, and he would almost certainly be a leading union official. Even the largest unions had only a limited number of capable officials, and they were often reluctant to spare them for long periods away in London; in any case, in the 1880s and 1890s many of the miners' leaders who were to enter Parliament after 1900 were still making their mark on local boards and councils, and were still pre-occupied in building up their unions.[1] Finance was an additional problem for the smaller and more recently created unions, especially as most of the mining constituencies were county divisions rather than parliamentary boroughs, and therefore more difficult and costly to fight. But even if a vacancy did occur in a suitable seat, and even if a miners' union was ready and able to provide a suitable candidate, there still remained one formidable and often insurmountable obstacle: in most mining areas the Liberals were more enamoured of working-class votes than working-class candidates.

For all of these reasons, by the turn of the century the miners had hardly begun to exploit their undoubted electoral advantages. Then quite suddenly between 1900 and 1902 there was a major change of policy, and the M.F.G.B. embarked upon an ambitious scheme designed to secure parliamentary representation on a much increased scale. At the Federation's annual conference in the autumn of 1900, Ben Pickard, the President, suggested that an election fund should be set up, to which every union in the Federation would contribute in proportion to its membership. A ballot was taken on this proposal, and it was approved by 168,000 votes to 68,000. The details of the scheme were then worked out by the Executive Committee of the M.F.G.B., and were accepted at the annual conference of 1902. The central feature of the new arrangements was the establishment of a Labour political fund, to which all individual members of the Federation were to pay a shilling a year. District unions would not be eligible to nominate candidates and receive Returning Officers' fees and other expenses from the fund unless all their members paid their contributions. Every district with under 10,000 members was to be entitled to one candidate, and those with over 10,000 members could claim expenses for one further candidate for every extra 10,000 members. Under the terms of the scheme only miners or miners' representatives could become candidates, and they

---

[1] This was especially true in the Midlands. J. G. Hancock (Nottinghamshire), J. Haslam and W. E. Harvey (Derbyshire), W. Johnson (Warwickshire), and A. Stanley (Cannock Chase), all leading officials of unions founded in the 1880s, all came into the House of Commons after 1900.

could stand under any political label they chose, so long as
there was a reasonable chance of success. The fund was to
provide election expenses, first-class railway passes, and a
salary of £350 a year for successful candidates; miners'
nominees could stand only in their own districts, and the
scheme was to apply only to constituencies in mining areas.[1]

In practice the adoption of this scheme meant that from
1902 onwards Yorkshire was to be entitled to six candidates,
Lancashire to three, Derbyshire to two, Nottinghamshire to
two, South Wales to twelve, the Midland Federation to two,
Scotland to five, and South Derbyshire, Leicestershire,
Cumberland, Bristol, Somersetshire, North Wales, and the
Forest of Dean to one each, making a total of thirty-nine
possible candidatures. It was envisaged that as the unions
grew so would the fund and so would the number of candidates. Considering that at no time since 1885 had more than
three M.P.s represented unions within the Federated area,
this brave new departure calls for some explanation.

Towards the end of the 1890s the whole trade union
movement had begun to recognize the need for political
action and parliamentary influence. In the past there had
been a tendency to look to the Liberals to protect and
promote the interests of the trade unions; but by now faith
in the Liberal Party was on the wane for a variety of reasons.
For a start it had failed in the first essential, that of winning
elections: since 1886 there had been only one brief and
ineffectual Liberal Ministry, between 1892 and 1895.
Gladstone's growing obsession with the Irish problem had
diverted his party's attention away from pressing social
issues, and of the two younger leaders who were genuinely
interested in social reform Joseph Chamberlain had gone
over to the Unionists because of his disagreement with
Gladstone on the Home Rule question and Charles Dilke
had been politically ruined in a notorious sex scandal. If the
Liberal Party seemed a broken reed, the Conservatives were
an equally unsatisfactory alternative, for there was little in
their record of social legislation during their long period in
office to impress the trade unions, or hold out much hope for
the future. True, they did pass a Workmen's Compensation

[1] See Page Arnot, op. cit., pp. 352–62.

Act in 1897; but its scope was far too narrow to satisfy the unions. Throughout the history of the trade union movement the emphasis has always oscillated between political and industrial activity, and, faced with this unpromising political situation, there was for a while the chance that the unions might pin their faith on direct action. But when the engineers, in full cry for an eight-hour day and a share in management decisions, were conclusively beaten in the great lock-out of 1897–8, it began to look as though political action was after all the safer bet.

It was during these years that the confused and vulnerable legal status of the trade unions was being exposed in a series of court cases. There is no need to go into the intricacies of trade union law or the significance of decisions reached in individual cases; it is enough to say that many trade unionists were driven to the conclusion that the judiciary was biased in favour of the employers and that the judges were deliberately and systematically interpreting the law in as detrimental a way as possible to the interests of the unions. As industrial tensions heightened at the turn of the century, the attitude of the courts towards picketing came to be of crucial importance. Strikes could usually be broken provided that the employers could lay hands on enough non-union, or, as it was called, 'free', labour, and provided that these recruits could be kept away from dissuaders and protected from intimidation. So long as the unions were able to picket, violence was always a possibility, and, as imported blacklegs were not usually the most highly principled or determined of men, there was always the chance that the sight of a menacing line of pickets would lead them to revise their views on the virtues of working-class solidarity. Picketing, then, was the point of attack for the employers, and with the celebrated Taff Vale judgement they seemed to be well on their way to subjugating the unions. This was a decisive victory (perhaps too decisive), for not only did the Taff Vale Railway Company secure an injunction (upheld on appeal to the House of Lords in 1901) restraining the Railway Servants from picketing, but also, in December 1902, it successfully sued the union for heavy damages arising out of the strike, and, to rub salt into the wound, relieved the

Railway Servants of a substantial sum by way of legal costs too. The implications of Taff Vale were that in future picketing would be illegal, from which it followed that strikes were unlikely to be effective. And, even if by some chance a strike were to be effective, the employer was bound to emerge unscathed because he could then sue the union for whatever the strike had cost him. Deprived of the threat to strike, trade unions would be in no position to bargain on equal terms with employers, and if they were not to engage in collective bargaining what was the point of their existence? The only remedy lay in legislation, and legislation is made only in Parliament. It was against this background that in 1899 the Trades Union Congress accepted a Socialist-inspired resolution calling for a conference that would consider ways and means of securing direct political representation for Labour; the outcome was the famous Farringdon Street Conference in February 1900 at which the Labour Representation Committee, the forerunner of the Labour Party, came into existence.

In some respects the hostility of the courts was of rather less immediate concern to the miners' unions than to many others. Few miners were not members of their union, and in any case, in the atmosphere of a mining village, blacklegging was almost unthinkable. It would have been virtually impossible for the owners to bring unskilled, free labour into the pits, and, indeed, under the Mines Act of 1887 it was illegal for a man to be employed alone at the coal-face until he had worked underground for at least two years under supervision. Yet the right to picket was still important, even for the miners. Outsiders could not work underground, but they could be recruited to move coal that was already at the pit head; and it was the pickets who would customarily inform an oncoming shift that a strike had begun. More important, awards for damages arising out of strikes would hit the miners as much as anyone else, as they soon discovered. In South Wales, for example, it was a regular practice for the union to bring the men out for one day at a time, the so-called 'stop day', in order to restrict output and maintain prices. When the South Wales Miners' Federation employed this device in 1901 it was sued for damages by the Glamorgan

Coal Company, and the claim was eventually upheld in the House of Lords in 1905. And in Yorkshire in 1903 the Denaby Coal Company obtained an injunction preventing the union from disbursing strike benefit to those of its members who were in dispute with the company, and also sought damages for loss caused by the strike, though this claim failed in the Lords in 1905.

The knowledge that strikes involved a legal risk served only to strengthen the miners' leaders in the belief that the way to their long-cherished eight-hour day was through political and not industrial action. The attitude of the M.F.G.B. had been explained at the annual conference of 1898 by Sam Woods, the Vice-President of the union.

Eighty thousand engineers had for six months been fighting by their unions to get the Eight hours day adopted, and their families had been starving and trade had been driven out of the country and yet to all appearances they were no nearer their object than at the beginning. The miners believed they ought to have an Eight hours day, and the best method of getting it was by legislative enactment.[1]

But, as Ben Pickard, the President of the M.F.G.B., pointed out two years later, there was little hope of an eight-hours act under a Conservative Government; the best chance lay with a Liberal Government in office and a much larger number of Labour representatives, including miners, in Parliament to apply the necessary prodding.[2]

Pickard had no sympathy with the newly formed Labour Representation Committee. He was suspicious (quite correctly) of the motives of its instigators and feared that trade union funds would be used to back Socialist candidates; even if L.R.C. candidates were not Socialists, he saw no reason why other unions should be allowed the use of the miners' money to help send their representatives to Parliament.[3] The miners for their part were rich enough, and had their members concentrated in such a way that they could send their candidates to Parliament without the assistance

[1] *The Times*, 5 Jan. 1898.   [2] Ibid., 25 Oct. 1900.

[3] 'I should like to ask', he said, 'why we as a Federation should be called upon to join an Association to find money, time or intellect to focus the weaknesses of other Trade Unionists to do what you are doing for yourselves, and have done for the last fourteen years.' Page Arnot, op. cit., p. 353.

of other unions, or so they thought. The Miners' Federation therefore would have nothing to do with the L.R.C. But if the Federation was not to go into the L.R.C., and, if the district unions were not to be attracted piecemeal into this undesirable organization, some alternative channel was required for their political aspirations. The M.F.G.B.'s answer was the scheme for parliamentary representation already outlined.

As the serious implications of Taff Vale began to sink in, there was a wave of new recruits to the L.R.C. In July 1900 it had only 232,000 affiliated trade union members; by February 1903 it had 843,315.[1] The only miners' union to join the L.R.C. in these early days was the Lancashire and Cheshire Federation, but just as Taff Vale prompted other unions to seek affiliation to the L.R.C. so it also stimulated the miners' district unions to press for more parliamentary representation under the terms of their own scheme. The movement began in 1902, and soon almost all the larger districts had announced their intention of putting up candidates at the next general election or at any by-elections that might occur. The Derbyshire and Nottinghamshire miners at once made it clear that they would nominate candidates as soon as there were vacancies in local mining seats; the South Wales miners scheduled ten seats (in addition to the Rhondda, which they already held) for which they intended to nominate candidates; the Lancashire miners decided to run three candidates at the next election, and in 1904 added a fourth; the North Staffordshire miners reaffirmed an earlier decision to run a candidate; and also in the course of 1902 the Scottish miners made up their mind to put forward four candidates. In the following year the Warwickshire union selected its candidate, and in 1904 the Yorkshire miners announced that they would contest five seats over and above Normanton which they held already. In the North-East too there was a response to Taff Vale, and in 1903 the Durham mineworkers decided to fight two more seats in addition to Mid Durham.

Pickard's scheme remained in operation from 1902 until 1909, when the miners belatedly followed the example of all

[1] Bealey and Pelling, op. cit., p. 95.

the other major unions and joined the Labour Party. The only modification to the scheme in these years occurred in 1907, when it was agreed that each of the district unions should keep a third of the political levy for their own use. It is clear that what Pickard envisaged was a growing number of miners' M.P.s, mostly of the same Liberal turn of mind as himself, and most of them relying upon the co-operation of their local Liberal Association. In other words, the expectation was that they would be 'Lib-Lab' trade unionists, men of working-class origin and outlook, who, though allowed a certain license on labour issues, were to be in all other respects indistinguishable from the main body of Liberal M.P.s. The miners, like the rest of the working class, needed more political representation and were entitled to it; but, the argument ran, it was within the framework of the Liberal Party and not in conjunction with the Socialists that they were to make their influence felt. Pickard was no visionary, and the chances are that he and his fellow Lib-Labs had no grand design for the future.[1] Yet there was an implicit assumption in the Lib-Lab approach to politics that is of some importance: Pickard and his collaborators believed, though they may never have spelt it out in so many words, that the working class had more to gain by permeating and eventually dominating the Liberal Party than from trying to establish a new, separate, and Socialist Party of their own. This is not the place to argue the merits of that proposition, though anyone inclined to brush it aside might reflect that in the sixty-four years that followed its foundation the Labour Party wielded effective power for only five. But, in any case, it was the Liberals themselves who demonstrated to the trade unions that Lib-Lab politics led nowhere.

[1] Keir Hardie was particularly withering in his remarks about Pickard. 'Mr. Pickard', he wrote, 'has several qualities which are useful in a fight. . . . He is tenacious and thick-skinned, and once an idea is by dint of hard knocks, driven home in his cranium it occupies exclusive possession. He has no room for two ideas at once, and this prevents him from being disturbed by other issues or complications about the rights or wrongs of the question . . . a man of few ideas, of a narrow intolerant cast of mind, and altogether lacking in judgement or discretion. His command of language is of the most meagre description, and like all small minded men, he is intensely egoistic.' D. Lowe, *From Pit to Parliament, The Story of the Early Life of James Keir Hardie*, 1923, p. 56. The Lib-Labs' opinion of Keir Hardie was, if anything, even more unflattering.

Though the miners now had a scheme and a fund for returning more of their own numbers, the success of the new arrangement still depended upon the attitude of the local Liberal Associations, and for the most part they remained stubbornly unwilling to adopt miners' candidates in mining seats. After the M.F.G.B. became affiliated to the Labour Party in 1909 the Liberals had some grounds for refusing to support its candidates because now the miners were members of a separate and on occasions hostile political party. But this was certainly not the case in the years between 1885 and 1908, and an analysis of the circumstances under which miners were elected to Parliament in this period brings out clearly enough how reluctant the Liberals were to make concessions.

Of the twenty-two miners who came into the House of Commons in these years, three were actually opposed by the Liberals on the occasion of their first contest; on six occasions the miners first took their seats as a result of electoral pacts which benefited the Liberals more than the unions concerned; on a further six occasions the seats won by the miners were at the time of their adoption in the hands of the Conservatives; and in only eight instances had the miner been adopted, without any electoral bargain, for a seat which the Liberals themselves were almost certain to win. The full list of these candidatures is given in Table 4; only when all three columns contain the word 'No' can it be said that the Liberals had made any real sacrifice or responded at all generously to the claims of Labour.

If the analysis is confined to the years between 1902 and 1908, when the M.F.G.B. scheme was in operation, it is evident that the miners fared only slightly better than over the period as a whole. Of the eleven new candidates put forward by the Federation under Pickard's scheme only five were adopted by the Liberals for seats which they themselves obviously had a good chance of winning. Moreover, these figures refer only to successful miners' candidates; they take no account of the occasions when the unions wanted to sponsor a man but were rebuffed by the Liberals, nor of those miners who did stand but were unsuccessful largely because of Liberal opposition. For all the electoral

TABLE 4

Miners' candidates and the Liberal Associations, 1885–1908

County	Candidate	First elected	Division	Cons. seat	Lib. opposition	Pact
Northumberland	T. Burt	1874	Morpeth	No	No	No
	C. Fenwick	1885	Wansbeck	No	No	No
Durham	W. Crawford	1885	Mid Durham	No	No	Yes
	J. Wilson	1885	Houghton-le-Spring	No	No	Yes
	J. Wilson	1886	Mid Durham	No	No	Yes
	J. Johnson	1904	Gateshead	No	No	No
	J. W. Taylor	1906	Chester-le-Street	No	Yes	No
Yorkshire	B. Pickard	1885	Normanton	No	No	Yes
	W. Parrott	1904	Normanton	No	No	Yes
	F. Hall	1905	Normanton	No	No	Yes
	J. Wadsworth	1906	Hallamshire	No	No	No
Derbyshire	J. Haslam	1906	Chesterfield	No	No	No
	W. E. Harvey	1907	NE. Derbyshire	No	No	No
Warwickshire	W. Johnson	1906	Nuneaton	Yes	No	No
Staffordshire	E. Edwards	1906	Hanley	Yes	No	Yes
	A. Stanley	1907	NW. Staffordshire	No	No	No
South Wales	W. Abraham	1885	Rhondda	No	Yes	No
	T. Richards	1904	W. Monmouthshire	No	No	No
	W. Brace	1906	S. Glamorgan	Yes	No	No
	J. Williams	1906	Gower	No	Yes	No
Lancashire	S. Woods	1892	Ince	Yes	No	No
	S. Walsh	1906	Ince	Yes	No	No
	T. Glover	1906	St. Helens	Yes	No	Yes

advantages enjoyed by the miners, their policy of going it alone was certainly not a striking success. The L.R.C. by contrast, was in secret driving a much better bargain with the Liberals and reaping the benefit in its twenty-nine victories at the general election of 1906.[1] Painfully, the truth was beginning to dawn on the miners that the pursuit of Lib-Lab politics might be leading them up a blind alley, and that perhaps the future lay with a new and independent Labour Party after all.

[1] For an account of the secret negotiations between Ramsay MacDonald and the Liberals before the general election of 1906, see Bealey and Pelling, op. cit., ch. vi.

III

THE MINERS SEE DAYLIGHT

THE M.F.G.B. was the last of the great unions to join the Labour Party. In fact it was not until the Labour Party had been in existence for nine years that the Federation finally became affiliated to it early in 1909. When the L.R.C. was launched in 1900 the reaction of the miners had been to set up a scheme of their own for securing more parliamentary representation, and for several years after the M.F.G.B.'s new arrangements came into operation in 1902 the Lib-Labs fought a dogged rearguard action to keep their scheme intact and to steer the Federation away from the L.R.C. In 1905, however, as a result of mounting pressure from Scotland, South Wales, and Lancashire, three districts where the Socialists were particularly strong, it was agreed that a ballot should be held on the question of joining the L.R.C. in the course of the following year.

In the meantime, of course, there occurred the general election of January 1906, and for the first, and, indeed, the only, time Pickard's scheme was put to the test. The M.F.G.B. sponsored sixteen candidates in all, eleven of them (all successful) in England and Wales, and five (all unsuccessful) in Scotland.[1] Most of the miners had in any case always voted Liberal, and the issues on which the 1906 election was fought probably won back any waverers who had gone Conservative at the 'khaki' election of 1900. The miners naturally shared the general trade union resentment at the Conservative Government's refusal to amend the law after Taff Vale; the outcry over 'Chinese Labour' hurt the Conservatives as much in the coalfields as everywhere

---

[1] The successful M.F.G.B. candidates at the general election of 1906 were: W. Abraham (Rhondda), T. Richards (West Monmouthshire), W. Brace (South Glamorgan), J. Williams (Gower), F. Hall (Normanton), J. Wadsworth (Hallamshire), S. Walsh (Ince), T. Glover (St. Helens), J. Haslam (Chesterfield), E. Edwards (Hanley), W. Johnson (Nuneaton). In the North-East, T. Burt (Morpeth), C. Fenwick (Wansbeck), J. Wilson (Mid Durham), and J. Johnson (Gateshead) also retained their seats.

else; a policy of protection for industry offered no advantages
to the coal trade, and by now an export duty of a shilling
a ton on coal introduced by the Conservative Government in
1901 was arousing a great deal of hostility in the exporting
districts. The result of the 1906 election was a landslide
victory for the Liberals, and in the mining areas there was
a large turnover of seats against the Conservatives. The
general election of 1900 had left the Conservatives and
Unionists in possession of thirty-three mining seats as
against the fifty-three held by Liberal and Labour members;
six years later no less than seventy-seven of the mining constituencies were won by Liberal and Labour candidates, leaving the Conservatives with a handful of nine mining seats.

With the election over, in the summer of 1906 the
M.F.G.B. held its ballot on affiliation to the Labour Party.
Each district union took a vote of its own members, and in
the event affiliation was rejected by 101,714 votes to
92,222 on a poll of about 57 per cent of the Federation's total
membership. Every district made a separate return of its own
figures, and the individual results are set out in Table 5.

TABLE 5

1906 ballot on affiliation to the Labour Party

District	For	Against	Total membership
South Wales	41,843	31,527	121,261
Yorkshire	17,389	12,730	62,182
Scotland	17,801	12,376	52,500
Lancashire	8,265	3,345	55,420
Derbyshire	1,789	11,257	29,480
Nottinghamshire	1,806	11,292	23,774
Midlands Federation	666	13,553	26,100
Cumberland	492	372	4,311
North Wales	295	2,428	9,232
Somerset	1,101	1,527	3,000
South Derbyshire	136	208	1,923
Leicestershire	60	747	3,693
Bristol	570	352	2,197
Totals:	92,222	101,714	
Majority against:		9,492	

The executive of the M.F.G.B. had gone to some pains to make sure that the miners really understood the implications of joining the Labour Party. Each ballot-paper had attached to it a letter setting out the main items in the constitution of the party, including Clause 3, which made it perfectly clear that if the Federation did become affiliated all miners' M.P.s and candidates would be obliged to cut any ties they had with other political parties, a requirement that was to cause a great deal of heart-searching and a great many disputes in the next few years. Although the Labour Party was vitally interested in the outcome of this ballot, Ramsay MacDonald, the party's General Secretary, thought it prudent not to undertake any overt propaganda at the official level; individual Independent Labour Party branches, however, were not so cautious, and many of them did their best to influence the miners, with the result that in some counties, notably Derbyshire and Nottinghamshire, the Lib-Lab officials retaliated by urging their members to vote against affiliation.[1]

The advocates of affiliation in the Federation were not unduly discouraged by this defeat in 1906, and at the next annual conference in October 1907 they returned to the attack, and demanded that the question should be reopened. In the course of the debate the delegation from South Wales revealed that their Federation was considering the possibility of separate affiliation to the Labour Party if the M.F.G.B. as a whole would not join, a disturbing piece of news for the Lib-Labs, because one district, the Lancashire and Cheshire Miners' Federation, had already gone its own way and affiliated separately in 1903. If South Wales were to take the same step, other unions might well follow suit; it would then be only a matter of time before the Federation scheme broke up, because any union that joined the Labour Party, thereby taking on additional financial liabilities, was not

---

[1] In answer to a request for guidance from the chairman of the Nottingham I.L.P., which was thinking of arranging a miners' demonstration, MacDonald wrote: 'My Executive is taking no part in working up opinion regarding these ballots; if it did it would be open to unpleasant attack. I think the localities themselves should take the responsibility for forming opinions. I believe that such a demonstration as you suggest would do good.' Correspondence between MacDonald and T. A. Pierce, *LPLF*, 31 July 1906/2 Aug. 1906.

likely to continue indefinitely to contribute to the M.F.G.B.s political fund as well. A certain amount of tactical manoeuvring followed, in the course of which the Socialists tried to get the question of affiliation settled by means of a block vote there and then, for by now it was apparent that between them South Wales, Scotland, and Lancashire commanded enough card votes to carry the day against the whole of the rest of the Federation put together. In the end, however, it was decided that another individual ballot should be taken in the coalfields.[1]

On this second occasion, in May 1908, the result of the earlier ballot was decisively reversed; this time the voting was 213,137 in favour of affiliation and 168,446 against, on a poll of about 69 per cent of the total Federation membership. The results for each district are set out in Table 6. Thus in less than two years a majority of over 9,000 against affiliation had been converted into a majority of over 44,000 in favour. When Tables 5 and 6 are compared it can be seen that only one small district, Somerset, changed sides; but appreciably larger majorities for joining the Labour Party were recorded in South Wales, Yorkshire, and Lancashire. Northumberland which had not been a member of the Federation in 1906, came down in favour of affiliation, and though the Midland districts were still emphatically hostile to the Labour Party, the majorities against joining were not as large as in 1906.

Unlike many other important unions the miners had not been drawn into the Labour Party as a result of the Taff Vale judgement, for Taff Vale had prompted the miners' unions to put up more candidates under their own scheme, not to join the Labour Party. It is true that between 1902 and 1906 both the South Wales and the Yorkshire miners had been involved in litigation with the coal-owners, but the 1906 Trade Disputes Act had already blunted the employers' attack on the unions long before the miners came round to voting for affiliation in 1908. The favourable impression made by the Parliamentary Labour Party in the period immediately after the 1906 election may have affected the result of the second ballot, but it is hard to resist the

[1] *MFGB*, Oct. 1907.

TABLE 6

1908 ballot on affiliation to the Labour Party

District	For	Against	Total membership
Yorkshire	32,991	20,793	78,300
Lancashire and Cheshire	30,227	13,702	71,500
Midlands Federation	10,772	19,951	38,100
Derbyshire	5,811	16,519	38,475
Nottinghamshire	2,959	5,822	30,753
Leicestershire	194	675	5,000
South Derbyshire	656	1,072	3,500
North Wales	2,467	6,017	13,200
Cumberland	2,816	1,522	4,900
Somerset	2,052	1,291	3,254
Bristol	1,074	474	2,300
Scotland	32,112	25,823	78,000
South Wales	74,675	44,616	144,600
Northumberland	14,331	10,169	34,200
Totals:	213,137	168,446	

Majority for: 44,691

Durham, with 112,800 miners, did not vote. See p. 73.

conclusion that it was the I.L.P. movement in the coalfields
that played a major role in bringing the miners into the
fold. In every district (except Lancashire) where there was
a majority in favour of affiliation—in the North-East, in
Yorkshire, South Wales, Scotland, and Cumberland—the
I.L.P. was active and influential. By contrast, in all the
Midland districts, where there were large majorities against
affiliation, there were comparatively few I.L.P. branches.
It might be argued, of course, that a strong I.L.P. movement and a liking for the Labour Party were both equally
the products of a particular type of political environment,
and that there was no question of cause and effect. It is
certainly true that the I.L.P. could not of itself create a
climate of opinion where the necessary materials were
entirely lacking, nor could it take root and flourish where
conditions were unsuitable. But wherever there was discontent, for whatever reason, energetic and persistent I.L.P.

propagandists were remarkably skilful at intensifying and exploiting it to the advantage of the Labour Party. Among the miners, loyalties, habits, and traditions go deep, and weaning them away from the Liberal Party was an uphill task that on occasions drove the early socialist evangelists close to despair. The exasperation which they must often have felt is admirably conveyed in the words of the Secretary of a local Labour party in Yorkshire, writing to Ramsay MacDonald for literature to distribute among the miners, who, he complained 'are the last to see daylight, and whose thick skulls we must necessarily penetrate because they hold the key to this Division'.[1]

Still, the trick had now been turned, at least to the extent of persuading them to vote to join the Labour Party, and the outcome of the ballot came up for consideration at the M.F.G.B.'s next annual conference, held at Chester in October 1908. In his opening address Enoch Edwards, who had replaced Pickard as President of the Federation and was himself an old-style Lib-Lab, acknowledged that the question of affiliating to the Labour Party was bound to cause a great deal of dissension among the miners; nevertheless he believed that they ought to act on the result of the ballot, because if they went back on it, or tried to wriggle out of it, they would only be laying up more trouble for themselves. The Lib-Labs, however, were not prepared to give way without a fight, and a resolution was put before the conference by the Derbyshire delegation, which pointed out that less than half of the Federation's membership had actually voted in favour of joining the Labour Party, and called for another ballot and a two-thirds majority before the M.F.G.B. affiliated. James Haslam, the Secretary of the Derbyshire Miners' Association, claimed that though he himself had no objection to joining the Labour Party, he was not willing to cut adrift some of the political friendships of half a lifetime; if the Federation did become affiliated then it would be their duty to press for changes in the Labour Party constitution 'in order to keep their friends as they had found them in the past'. Here, indeed, was to be the great stumbling block in the next few years, for Lib-Labs

[1] H. Barker (Holmfirth L.R.C.) to MacDonald, *LPLF*, 12 July 1907.

like Haslam were determined that whatever happened they were not going to dissociate themselves from their old colleagues and helpers in the Liberal Party; the Socialists, on the other hand, were just as determined that this was exactly what the miners and their M.P.s were going to do. The resolution from Derbyshire was heavily defeated on a card vote, and the conference then went on to debate a motion from Scotland, 'that the M.F.G.B. now make formal application for admission to the Labour Party'. Robert Smillie, who moved it, admitted that those miners' M.P.s who had always worked with the Liberals would face difficulties. The Federation, he suggested, had two possible courses open to it: they could either ask the Labour Party to exempt all the miners' Members from signing the constitution until the next general election, or, alternatively, all the M.F.G.B.'s Lib-Lab Members could resign their seats at once and stand again under their new colours as straight Labour candidates. Not surprisingly this second alternative found little favour.

Smillie and his socialist colleagues, sensing that victory was now assured, were prepared to make some concessions to the Lib-Labs; no immediate change of label or style was required of them, but they were to be in no doubt that in future any candidate sponsored by the M.F.G.B. would have to run under the auspices of the Labour Party, and would have to sign and accept the constitution of the Labour Party. At the end of the debate, the conference carried a resolution to the effect that the M.F.G.B. should apply for admission to the Labour Party 'on the understanding that all the present members now representing this Federation be not called upon to sign the constitution of the Labour Party except in the event of a by-election or at the next General Election'.[1] It was on the basis of this 'Chester resolution' that Thomas Ashton, the Secretary of the M.F.G.B., wrote to Ramsay MacDonald later in October, formally requesting that the Federation should be allowed to affiliate, adding that 'it would have given me greater pleasure to have been able to make this application free from conditions, but if the Labour Party will approach this

[1] *MFGB*, Oct. 1908.

question in the same spirit as the Conference did last week, a compromise will be made and the Federation will become affiliated to the Labour Party at once'. MacDonald, of course, was delighted that at last the massive Miners' Federation had seen the light. Even if the Labour Party had realized how much trouble the miners were to cause in the next few years, it could hardly have afforded to be too punctilious or demanding. A few days later MacDonald wrote back to Ashton saying that the Labour Party appreci- ated the Federation's difficulties and would be glad to welcome it into the party on the conditions set out in Ashton's letter.[1]

Final agreement on the financial relationship between the Federation and the Labour Party was reached in December 1908. The M.F.G.B. was to pay an annual affiliation fee of 15s. per thousand members, and with the first payment it was to make its subscription of a penny per member to the Labour Party parliamentary fund. But, as the miners' M.P.s were not going to draw their salaries from the fund until after the next general election, if the election did not take place during the first year of the Federation's membership of the party it was to pay no further subscriptions until a disso- lution did occur. When the election came, miners' candidates would be entitled to a quarter of the Returning Officer's expenses and, if successful, to a yearly salary of £200 from the party.[2] In February 1909 the M.F.G.B. executive decided that the first payment to the Labour Party should be made after the district unions had made their returns to the Federation for the March quarter.

The M.F.G.B.'s decision to join the Labour Party was a major political event, and its significance was not lost on contemporary observers. In June 1908, six months before the terms of affiliation were sealed, *The Times* pointed out, with an air of quiet satisfaction, that the Liberal Party was bound to suffer because it would now be in direct rivalry with Labour candidates in what had formerly been con- sidered some of its safest seats. There were, it had calculated,

---

[1] Correspondence between MacDonald and Ashton, ibid. 13 Oct. and 19 Oct. 1908.
[2] MacDonald to Ashton, ibid. 16 Dec. 1908.

no less than ninety constituencies where the miners made up
so large a proportion of the electorate that they could decide
the question of representation; fifty-nine of these seats were
held by the Liberals, twenty-six by Labour Members, and
only five by the Conservatives. 'If the Labour Party lays
claim to them', it continued, 'the Liberal Party will be
severely weakened in a quarter where it has hitherto considered itself to be unassailable. The Labour Party will not
spend time, money and energy in fighting doubtful battles
in apathetic districts when there are sixty favourable mining
seats occupied by as many Liberal caretakers which can be
occupied with a minimum of money and trouble.'[1]

This vision of easy pickings for the Labour Party and
immediate electoral disaster for the Liberals proved to be
well wide of the mark. The affiliation of the miners did, of
course, bring the Labour Party substantial benefits; the
Federation brought 550,000 new members into the party,
and in its first year contributed £4,583 to the parliamentary
fund in addition to an affiliation fee of £412.[2] And after the
general election of January 1910 the Parliamentary Labour
Party was at once the stronger by sixteen miners' M.P.s.
In the years between 1909 and 1914, however, the presence
of the M.F.G.B. within the party was to prove a mixed
blessing. Moreover, thousands of miners felt themselves to
be under no obligation to vote for Labour candidates simply
because their Federation had joined the Labour Party, even
when, as often happened, these candidates were officials of
their own district union. Indeed, contrary to the predictions
of *The Times*, after 1910 the number of Labour M.P.s
sitting for mining constituencies far from increasing actually
went down.

For a start, not all the M.F.G.B. Members already in
Parliament when the Federation affiliated were prepared to
come into the Labour Party. By September 1909 the
Federation group had reached its maximum strength of

[1] *The Times*, 10 June 1908. The seats were not named; nor did *The Times* reveal
how strong a mining vote was required to settle the outcome of an election. Its
figure of 90 seats, however, is not very different from the author's assessment that
there were 86 seats with a mining vote constituting 10 per cent or more of their
electorate.

[2] *MFGB*, Sept. 1909.

eighteen,[1] but three of the old Lib-Labs from the North-East, Thomas Burt, Charles Fenwick, and John Wilson, refused point-blank to sign the Labour Party constitution and so were never counted as Labour M.P.s A fourth miner from the North-East, John Johnson, was defeated in Gateshead at the general election of January 1910. Against these four losses to the group could be set two gains in Lancashire, where H. Twist was elected for Wigan and J. E. Sutton for East Manchester. From this point onwards the M.F.G.B. had only one further success, when W. Adamson was returned for West Fife at the second general election of 1910. After this there followed a depressing series of defeats, defections, and expulsions. In 1912 the Hanley seat, hitherto held by Enoch Edwards, was lost in a by-election; in 1913 on the death of James Haslam, the Derbyshire miners put up another Lib-Lab for Chesterfield, but as he then refused to sign the Labour Party constitution the M.F.G.B. was obliged to disown him; the death of W. E. Harvey, the Member for NE. Derbyshire, in 1914 led to a three-cornered fight, the outcome of which was that the Conservatives won the seat at the by-election. And, to complete this tale of woe, in 1914 the Labour whip was withdrawn from two of the miners' M.P.s, W. Johnson, the Member for Nuneaton, and J. G. Hancock, the Member for Mid Derbyshire, for persistently flouting the Labour Party constitution. By the end of 1914 the size of the M.F.G.B. group had been reduced to ten, and between 1910 and 1914 the Federation sponsored no less than eighteen unsuccessful candidatures.

This was an uninspiring record, and to make matters worse, in the earlier part of this period, between 1909 and 1912, there was a great deal of ill-tempered bickering between the Labour Party and the Federation. Apart from the three exceptions already mentioned, all the Federation

---

[1] In addition to the eleven Members elected in 1906, there were two further M.F.G.B. successes in 1907, when W. E. Harvey (NE. Derbyshire) and A. Stanley (NW. Staffordshire) were returned at by-elections. The reaffiliation of Northumberland in 1907 and Durham in 1909 brought four more M.P.s from the North-East—Burt, Fenwick, Wilson, and Johnson—into the M.F.G.B. group. The membership of the M.F.G.B. group reached 18 when J. G. Hancock won Mid Derbyshire at a by-election in the summer of 1909.

candidates did indeed sign the Labour Party constitution, as required, before the general election of January 1910. But many of them either failed to understand what it meant, or, more likely, decided to ignore altogether those parts of it that prohibited co-operation with other political parties. Some indignantly refused to break with their local Liberal Associations, and in the years ahead flatly declined to help establish new and separate Labour organizations in their constituencies; for all the difference it made to their behaviour the Federation might never have joined the Labour Party at all. In the first few years after affiliation, despite a constant stream of protests from the Labour Party, the M.F.G.B. itself would do nothing to discipline these M.P.s. The consequence was that their attitude and behaviour began seriously to undermine the morale of party activists in the mining districts, and at the same time infuriated and affronted socialist enthusiasts all over the country.

Yet, looking ahead for one moment, on the eve of the First World War the outlook was beginning to brighten. It is hard to gauge with any certainty how much progress the Labour Party was making among the rank and file in the coalfields; the evidence here is conflicting and this is a question that is discussed more fully at a later stage.[1] But there is no doubt that the Trade Union Act of 1913, which cleared up the legal uncertainties aroused by the Osborne judgement and permitted trade unions to use their funds for political purposes again, did open the way for a rush of new candidatures, and the signs are that the miners' unions were approaching the general election due in 1915 in a mood of some confidence and optimism. In 1912 Robert Smillie, a veteran socialist pioneer among the miners, became President of the M.F.G.B., and from this point onwards there was a marked change for the better in relations between the Federation and the Labour Party. The M.F.G.B. executive now began to take a much more rigorous line with its dwindling band of recalcitrant Lib-Lab M.P.s, and though some of them lingered on even into the inter-war years, by 1914 in the eyes of most of the younger miners they had already outlived their usefulness.

[1] See p. 187 et seq.

W. E. Harvey, in his time one of the most energetic and forceful of the Lib-Labs, had asked that his gravestone should be inscribed with the words, 'He served his day and generation and then fell asleep.'[1] It was a fitting comment on the latter years of all the Lib-Labs.

To return to the period immediately after affiliation, it was an uneasy partnership that came into existence in 1909, and as it happened the Labour Party, the M.F.G.B., and the Liberals almost at once found themselves entangled in a curious situation in Derbyshire. On the death of the Liberal Member for Mid Derbyshire in the summer of 1909, the Nottinghamshire miners decided to put up J. G. Hancock, their General Secretary, as an official Federation candidate. The local Liberals, believing Hancock to be a sound Liberal, which he was, and presumably under the impression that he would stand as a Lib-Lab like every other miners' candidate in the Midlands, agreed to give him their support. Now that the M.F.G.B. had joined the Labour Party, however, Hancock was required to sign the party constitution in accordance with the Chester resolution, and the constitution plainly prohibited any form of co-operation with the Liberals. Hancock signed, was endorsed by the executive of the Labour Party, and then proceeded to rely entirely upon electoral machinery provided by the local Liberal Association. The Labour Party was uncomfortably aware that Hancock's campaign bristled with irregularities; but short of the drastic step of disowning the first miners' candidate to be run under its auspices, there was no alternative but to put the best face it could on the episode. Even the I.L.P., the preserver of the true faith, was inclined to take a charitable view, and in its annual report for 1909 mildly noted that 'some confusion naturally arose owing to the peculiar position of politics in Mid Derby, and it was greatly exaggerated by the inaccurate reports published in the press'.[2]

Yet there could be no denying that Mid Derbyshire was a bad start, and in the autumn of 1909, with a general election in the offing, there were disquieting signs that a

---

[1] J. E. Williams, *The Derbyshire Miners*, 1962, p. 228.
[2] For a fuller account of this by-election, see pp. 147–50.

good many more miners' candidates intended entering into
arrangements with the Liberals that were certainly not
permitted under the party constitution. In December 1909
the M.F.G.B.'s list of approved candidates reached the
Labour Party, and with it came a letter from Ashton coolly
asking if the Labour Party executive had the power to set
aside the constitution in special cases. Conniving at irregularities in Mid Derbyshire was one thing; making open and
explicit exceptions in the letter of the law was another, and
the M.F.G.B.'s request was curtly refused.[1]

Before the previous general election in 1906 Ramsay
MacDonald and Herbert Gladstone had reached a secret
agreement designed to limit the number of contests between
Labour and Liberal candidates. Whether the terms of this
arrangement were still considered binding in 1910 is hard
to say; but it was clearly the policy of the Labour Party to
fight only seats where there seemed to be a good chance of
success. MacDonald himself certainly favoured a cautious
line, and in a memorandum circulated to members of the
Labour Party executive shortly before the election he urged
them not to place two candidates in double-Member constituencies, not to place too many candidates in the same
area, and not to undertake contests just for their propaganda
value in districts where the Labour Party already held seats.[2]
It was advice that fell on receptive ears, because for many
of the Labour leaders it was the fate of Lloyd George's 1909
budget and the veto claimed by the House of Lords that
were the overriding issues at stake at the election of January
1910. Many of them needed little convincing that in the circumstances three-cornered contests ought to be discouraged
so far as possible in order to avoid splitting the radical vote.
There was also the chance that fresh Labour interventions
might provoke Liberal retaliation in constituencies held by
Labour Members. The Labour Party was reminded of this
last possibility by J. A. Pease, the chief Liberal Whip, in
November 1909, when he expressed the hope that both

---

[1] *LPEC*, 17 Dec. 1909.

[2] *The Infancy of Labour*, vol. ii, folio 128 (British Library of Political and Economic Science: two volumes of miscellaneous papers, letters, and executive committee
minutes).

parties would avoid challenging each other's sitting Members, but at the same time made it clear that if Liberal seats were attacked the Liberals would hit back. 'In my opinion', he added, 'and I do not say it as a threat, the Labour Party are more likely to be losers if an uncompromising attitude is adopted and attempts made to win seats held by the Liberals and Radicals.'[1] Whilst Labour leaders went out of their way to deny that there was any general 'arrangement' with the Liberals, there is reason to believe, and, indeed, it was widely believed by contemporaries, that the party was deliberately pruning its candidatures so as to avoid friction with the Liberals. In December 1909, for example, Arthur Henderson was declaring that he was 'strongly desirous of seeing as few three-cornered contests as possible on this occasion',[2] and the Liberal *Daily News* suggested that Labour's forbearance amounted to a tacit offer of co-operation which the Liberals ought to accept. Be this as it may, the fact is that the Labour Party executive endorsed very few candidates for seats where the ground had not already been broken in 1906.[3]

There was no need to dissuade most of the miners' unions from attacking Liberal seats. Many of the miners' officials were themselves still Liberals in all but name, and were not disposed to break up long-standing alliances with the Liberal Party on the outside chance that they might thereby swell the number of independent Labour representatives in the Commons, especially as some of the miners' M.P.s could not hope to hold their own seats in face of Liberal retaliation. For anyone brought up in the Lib-Lab school of thought, to split the ranks of the progressives at this critical moment was little short of criminal lunacy. It is not surprising that both the South Wales and Yorkshire miners shelved their ambitious plans to run more candidates.[4] On the other hand, a

[1] *The Times*, 17 Nov. 1909.
[2] Ibid. 15 Dec. 1909.
[3] The Master of Elibank, who became chief Liberal Whip after the first election of 1910, wrote in a memorandum dated 14 April 1910: 'Throughout this period I was always able to count on the support of the Labour Party and the Miners. . . . I had no difficulty in making arrangements with them of a favourable nature to my own Party whenever the necessity arose.' A. C. Murray, *Master and Brother*, 1945, p. 48.
[4] See pp. 128–30, and 112.

few of the miners' unions were determined to press forward
with additional candidatures, even though this did mean
contests against the Liberals, and there was nothing that the
Labour Party could do to stop them. By the end of 1909
neither the Durham nor the Lancashire miners were in any
mood to compromise; nor were the Scottish miners, who,
in any case, had been pursuing a sturdily independent,
though hopelessly unsuccessful line for many years past.

To avoid unnecessarily antagonizing the Liberals the
Labour Party was prepared to limit the number of candidates it sponsored; but at the same time it was anxious
that all Labour candidates should adhere strictly to the
terms of the party constitution, and now earlier forebodings
about the miners' candidates proved to be only too well
founded. They had all signed the constitution, but for most
of them their signatures made not a scrap of difference to
the way in which they conducted their election campaigns.
If they had worked with their local Liberal Associations
before, they continued to do so now. It is true that they
could claim, as many of them did, that there was no separate
Labour organization in their constituencies to which they
could turn even had they so wished. But, as everyone was
well aware, it was out of inclination rather than necessity
that they stayed with the Liberals.

The result of the first election of 1910 was a considerable
set-back for the Liberals. With only 275 M.P.s, as against
273 Conservatives, the Liberal Government became dependent upon the votes of the eighty-two Irish Nationalists
and the forty Labour Members. Exactly half the Parliamentary Labour Party now sat for mining constituencies;
sixteen of the Labour M.P.s has been sponsored by the
M.F.G.B., and four others represented mining seats. (See
Table 7.)

When the dust of the election had settled, and the Labour
Party was able to take stock of what had happened in the
mining constituencies, it decided to raise with the Federation the numerous irregularities that had come to light. A
deputation, consisting of MacDonald, Keir Hardie, W. C.
Robinson, and Arthur Peters, the national agent, duly met
the M.F.G.B. executive in April 1910 and pointed out that

some of the miners' candidates had not been selected in the proper fashion and had not conducted their campaigns in accordance with the party's rules. The M.F.G.B. executive examined these allegations at its next meeting, and then saw no reason to take any action. Clearly, the Federation was going to be difficult.

TABLE 7

The General Election of January 1910

M.F.G.B. sponsored	Other Labour M.P.s for mining seats
W. Abraham (Rhondda)	J. Keir Hardie (Merthyr Tydfil)
T. Richards (W. Monmouth)	A. Henderson (Barnard Castle)
W. Brace (S. Glamorgan)	J. Pointer (Attercliffe)
J. Williams (Gower)	J. W. Taylor (Chester-le-Street)
F. Hall (Normanton)	
J. Wadsworth (Hallamshire)	Other miners' M.P.s
E. Edwards (Hanley)	T. Burt (Morpeth)
A. Stanley (NW. Stafford)	J. Wilson (Mid Durham)
T. Glover (St. Helens)	C. Fenwick (Wansbeck)
H. Twist (Wigan)	
S. Walsh (Ince)	
J. E. Sutton (E. Manchester)	
J. G. Hancock (Mid Derbys.)	
J. Haslam (Chesterfield)	
W. E. Harvey (NE. Derbys.)	
W. Johnson (Nuneaton)	

There were few changes after the December election of 1910. From the M.F.G.B. list Twist and Glover were defeated, and there was one additional Member, W. Adamson (W. Fife). Other Labour Members for mining seats were T. Richardson (Whitehaven) and F. Goldstone (Sunderland).

As the summer of 1910 wore on, a steady flow of complaints about the continuing association of miners' Members with the Liberals began to reach the Labour Party's head office. At first, MacDonald thought that a discreet and unofficial approach to the erring Member would prove sufficient. In July 1910, for example, it was reported that James Haslam, the Member for Chesterfield, had taken part in a Liberal meeting in his constituency. In answer to a polite request for an explanation Haslam wrote back to MacDonald in great indignation, claiming that he had simply been invited to address a meeting by some of his constituents, and adding truculently, 'May I say that I doubt your right of interrogation, and I would be much obliged if you will tell me who I am to address if not those who returned me to Parliament.'[1] After this MacDonald took to dealing direct with the M.F.G.B. executive.

These complaints and queries from the Labour Party were highly unpopular with the Federation, and at first it was inclined to ignore them altogether. In July 1910 MacDonald sent off another batch of allegations about miners' M.P.s. When October came and there was still no reply he wrote again to Ashton, still in a vein of good-humoured tolerance but with a note of irritation now becoming apparent: 'I am so sorry to bother you about these recalcitrant Members of yours', he wrote, 'but my Executive Committee nearly discharged me at my last meeting for having failed to get a reply from you . . . I really think your men ought to be a little more careful: it really is not the game.'[2] This prod at last brought a reply a month later, when Ashton blandly reported that his executive had looked into the allegations and was satisfied with the explanations given to it. By this time even MacDonald's patience and charm were showing signs of wear. In November 1910, just before he was due to leave London to speak on behalf of J. G. Hancock in Derbyshire, he was informed that only a day or two earlier Hancock himself had been speaking at a Liberal meeting. He promptly cancelled his visit and wrote to Hancock:

I need hardly say that this sort of meeting is quite outside our constitution, and is just the sort of thing that is making our lives here a burden with our members. I shall likely have protests galore in the course of a day or two. I am perfectly willing to defend the reasonable actions of our Members, but it is quite impossible to defend such a meeting and I don't propose to do it.[3]

Predictably enough, the December election of 1910 brought a renewed crop of complaints about the scandalous doings of the miners' candidates, and from now onwards there was a noticeable stiffening in the tone of MacDonald's communications to Ashton. At the end of December he was again

---

[1] Haslam to MacDonald, *LPLF*, 25 June 1910.
[2] MacDonald to Ashton, ibid. 31 Oct. 1910.
[3] MacDonald to Hancock, ibid. 3 Nov. 1910.

writing to the M.F.G.B., giving details about the alleged misdemeanours of miners' candidates. This time there was no gentle reproof, but instead a cold warning that unless the miners' candidates ran in accordance with the rules, they would receive no assistance from the Labour Party fund; the party executive, Ashton was informed, took a very serious view of the miners' behaviour.[1]

It was a typical set of complaints, the commonest allegations being that many of the miners' candidates had not been selected according to the rules at properly convened meetings of all the Labour organizations in their constituencies, and that they had not made it clear in their election addresses that they were now straight Labour candidates. When the miscreants appeared before the M.F.G.B. executive in January 1911 to explain their conduct, their usual line of defence was that the only effective Labour organizations in their constituencies were the miners' lodges, and it was at meetings of the lodges that they had been selected. If any improprieties had crept into the wording of their election addresses, that must have been the fault of their agents, who were perhaps not yet familiar with the verbal refinements of Labour politics. In the accommodating and understanding atmosphere of a Federation executive meeting, pleas of this kind were acceptable enough, and at the close of the proceedings a resolution was carried completely exonerating the accused, and dismissing the allegations against them as 'trifling in their nature, untrue, or not proven'.[2]

The Labour Party, however, could not afford to be brushed aside as easily as that. Every breach of the rules on the part of a miners' M.P. was indignantly reported to MacDonald by sharp-eyed local activists, and every complaint was accompanied by a demand for disciplinary action. These militant vigilantes could not be ignored, because it was upon their efforts that the party depended in its drive to win over the bulk of the miners. There was already disquieting evidence that the party's failure to take a firmer line with the miners was affecting the morale of party workers, and there was also the danger that disheartened

[1] MacDonald to Ashton, ibid. 30 Dec. 1910.   [2] *MFGB*, 25 Jan. 1911.

enthusiasts might leave the Labour Party altogether in order to join more congenial organizations.[1] In some of the mining districts, especially in the Midlands, a curious situation now began to develop: nominal Labour M.P.s, still working surreptitiously with their former Liberal supporters, and with the full support of the miners' unions that had sponsored them, stood at daggers drawn with all the official Labour organizations in their constituencies. More detailed accounts of the complications and difficulties that ensued are given in a later chapter, but in the meantime extracts from a few of the letters received at the Labour Party's head office at this time do convey something of the anger and frustration produced in the minds of dedicated Socialists by the activities of the miners' M.P.s:

I might say that our Member for the Division [J. G. Hancock] has been a great drawback to us by his attitude. He has been asked on several occasions to hold a public meeting in Belper, but has refused to do so ... He has often made statements which hold the I.L.P. up to ridicule, and prevents us being successful in our work.[2]

He [W. E. Harvey] cannot continuously pursue the policy of speaking for Liberalism without seriously injuring the Labour Party and it is for our Executive Committee to show that it will not permit the Party to be injured by enemies within its own ranks. . . . The Sheffield I.L.P. has over a hundred members in Harvey's constituency and they are discontented and their loyalty strained by no action being taken by the Party to deal with disloyalty other than report them to their own Union ... we cannot expect discipline to prevail in our own ranks while we have a few of our M.P.s undisciplined and unconstitutional.[3]

Talk about being loyal to the Labour Party, why, Harvey does just what he likes. Why not let him go to the Liberal Party, and finish deceiving innocent miners?[4]

The Labour Party now found itself in a difficult and delicate position. The M.F.G.B. was a powerful and welcome recruit, and had to be handled with some care. The unconstitutional

---

[1] In April 1912, for example, the Labour Party executive was informed that: 'One of the I.L.P. branches [in the Chesterfield division] which rendered useful assistance has since given up the effort to secure a Labour Party on our lines and has gone over to the British Socialist Party.' *The Infancy of Labour*, vol. ii, folio 272.

[2] H. Jackson (Belper I.L.P.) to Arthur Henderson, *LPLF*, 21 Oct. 1912.

[3] A. Thatcher (Sheffield I.L.P.) to Henderson, ibid. 4 Dec. 1912.

[4] J. Thornhill (Bolsover I.L.P.) to MacDonald, ibid. 15 Jan. 1911.

behaviour of the former Lib-Labs could not be countenanced indefinitely; but, on the other hand, the Federation was inclined to resent what it considered officious meddling in its affairs by the Labour Party. Up to a point it was an understandable reaction, for the M.F.G.B. was first and foremost a trade union, and in the past its political activities had been undertaken chiefly with the limited objective of improving conditions in the mining industry and promoting the interests of the miners. Naturally enough, some of the miners' leaders were unwilling to endanger the hard-won unity of the Federation by enforcing a set of political rules, the real significance and purpose of which they did not understand. In any case, many of the older members of the M.F.G.B. executive still shared the Liberal sympathies of the colleagues they were asked to censure for apparently trivial peccadiloes. Who did these socialist upstarts think they were? For years the M.F.G.B. had stood alone, a self-sufficient colossus, almost a Labour Party in itself; now it had to learn that it was only part of a much larger whole with political aspirations that transcended the particular and sectional interests of the miners.

As time went on, it was the refusal of many of the miners' M.P.s to help in setting up separate Labour organizations in their constituencies that came to be taken most seriously in Labour Party circles. In February 1911 the Labour Party executive told the M.F.G.B. that it was time the Federation used its influence to see that local parties were formed in constituencies where it had Members or proposed to run candidates.[1] It is not difficult to understand the executive's anxiety: sooner or later these miners' M.P.s would die or retire, and when a new Labour candidate arrived on the scene he would find all the previous 'Labour' Member's election machinery in the hands of his Liberal opponent, if, as was likely, the Liberals decided to fight these seats. In June 1911 Ramsay MacDonald was putting this point to W. E. Harvey, who had just been reported for speaking at a Liberal meeting:

. . . this perpetuates the Liberal hold which is so strong in the constituency, and it means that if you were to die, or for any other reason

[1] MacDonald to Ashton, ibid., 8 Feb. 1911.

your seat became vacant, there would not be sufficient Labour
sentiment or sufficient Labour strength to keep the seat for us; the
Liberal Association would simply step in and fill your shoes by a
Liberal candidate whom it would be impossible for us to fight successfully. The Executive Committee has taken the view that you ought
to help in the formation of a Labour Party, associating your miners
with that Party.[1]

There were at least eight miners' seats in this vulnerable
position, and MacDonald was uneasily aware that the Labour
Party would be hard pressed to hold Chesterfield, Mid
Derbyshire, Nuneaton, Hallamshire, South Glamorgan,
North-West Staffordshire, Hanley, and North-East Derbyshire. Hanley and North-East Derbyshire were in fact lost
in by-elections in 1912 and 1913, partly because no propaganda work had been carried out and no Labour organization
established.[2] To the Labour Party the danger was obvious,
and numerous deputations did their best to bring home to
the M.F.G.B. the risks inherent in the situation. By July
1912 there was still no sign of any action, and at this point
the Federation was told that unless it stirred itself the Labour
Party would go ahead and set up these local constituency
parties without reference to the M.F.G.B.[3] Possibly because
of this threat, or perhaps as a result of the Hanley by-election,
the M.F.G.B. finally went so far as to recommend its
constituent unions to help in establishing separate Labour
organizations. It was only a recommendation, and it was
widely ignored; but at least a start had been made, and the
Federation was prepared to acknowledge some responsibility for political organization and education.

The Hanley by-election drew the attention of the Labour
Party to another unsatisfactory feature of the M.F.G.B.'s
political arrangements. Under the rules of the Federation's
scheme, miners' candidates could stand only for seats within
their own districts. This stipulation presented no particular
difficulty in large districts like South Wales, Yorkshire, or
Durham, where there was a ready supply of able men with
political ambitions. But, if a mining seat fell vacant in a
smaller and less politically conscious district, a real problem

[1] MacDonald to Harvey, *LPLF*, 1 June 1911.
[2] See pp. 170–3 and 164–7.   [3] *LPEC*, 2 July 1912.

might well arise. When Enoch Edwards died, and a vacancy occurred at Hanley, the choice of candidate, if he was to be an official M.F.G.B. nominee, was restricted to members of the Midland Federation, with the result that the Labour Party eventually found itself saddled with a candidate who by general consent was totally unsuitable. Anxious to avoid a repetition, the Labour Party raised the question of this 'locality rule' with the M.F.G.B. executive in August 1912, and before the end of the year the Federation had undertaken to revise its rules to permit a wider choice of candidates.

It was from about this point onwards that relations between the M.F.G.B. and the Labour Party began to improve considerably. By now Robert Smillie had become President of the union, and there was a clear majority of Labour Party sympathizers on the Federation's executive. In 1913 a new Trade Union Act finally cleared away the uncertainties aroused by the Osborne judgement and allowed unions to use their funds for political purposes provided that their members gave their approval by ballot. When the miners voted by 261,643 votes to 194,800 in favour of setting up a political fund there was an immediate revival of interest in political action in all the major coalfields. Candidates were selected, plans were laid for establishing election machinery, and funds were earmarked by district unions for propaganda and organizational work. By the spring of 1914 no less than thirty-four miners' candidates had been selected to stand at the next general election.

When the M.F.G.B. took stock of the position, however, it found that it was in no position to finance so many candidatures, and in April 1914 the executive recommended that there should be only ten new candidates, in addition to the eleven existing Members who would stand again. It also proposed that Yorkshire, Durham, Scotland, and South Wales should each be allocated two extra candidates, and that Northumberland and Lancashire should have one extra candidate each. These proposals were put to a special conference in June 1914, when Smillie explained that because of the Osborne judgement the M.F.G.B.'s parliamentary fund had dwindled to nothing in the period between 1910 and 1913. It was true that under the new Trade Union

Act the Federation was allowed to levy all those of its members who had not contracted out (the sum had been fixed at a shilling a year per member), and given time the Federation would be able to finance a reasonable number of candidates. But, as he pointed out, they were faced with a general election either in 1914 or in 1915, and perhaps even several general elections. Whilst the executive was prepared to risk borrowing enough to finance ten new candidatures, it did not feel that the Federation should be burdened with the debt that would be incurred in running any more. He was well aware of the disappointment that this decision would cause, but it was better, he argued, that the districts should know in advance how many, if any, candidates they had been assigned so that there should be no waste of effort and money. Further details of the Federation's financial position were given by the Treasurer. According to his calculations by July 1915, the latest probable date for a general election, the political fund would probably stand at about £37,000; but of this one-third would have to be returned to the districts, so that the fund would really amount to £25,000. If they allowed £1,200 for each contest they could afford twenty-one candidates as proposed. This, of course, was on the assumption that there was no election until July 1915: if it came much sooner they would have to borrow, as Smillie has suggested. The conference accepted the executive's recommendations after a certain amount of wrangling about the distribution of candidatures, and as a result thirteen candidates had to be dropped, though it was made clear that if the districts could raise enough money on their own they could fight as many seats as they wished.[1]

By the outbreak of the war in the summer of 1914 some of the district unions had not decided which of their proposed candidatures should be financed from local funds and which from the M.F.G.B. fund. But altogether it seems likely that twenty-seven miners would have stood under the auspices of the Labour Party at the next general election, and in at least seven further mining seats there would have been Labour candidates who were not miners. In at least twenty-one of these constituencies Labour and Liberal

[1] *MFGB*, June 1914.

TABLE 8

Miners' and other Labour candidates in the coalfields, 1914

District	Constituency	Candidate	M.F.G.B. Sponsored	Liberal Opposition Expected
Lancashire	Ince	S. Walsh	Yes	..
	Manchester East	J. E. Sutton	Yes	..
	Wigan	H. Twist	No decision	..
	Leigh	T. Greenall	No decision	Yes
Yorkshire	Doncaster	S. Roebuck	Yes	Yes
	Holmfirth	W. Lunn	Yes	Yes
	Hallamshire	T. W. Grundy	Yes	Yes
	Normanton	F. Hall	Yes	..
	Barnsley	J. Guest	..	Yes
	Osgoldcross	J. Potts	..	Yes
Staffordshire	NW. Staffordshire	A. Stanley	Yes	..
Derbyshire	NE. Derbyshire	J. Martin	Yes	Yes
Northumberland	Morpeth	J. Cairns	No decision	..
	Wansbeck	W. Straker	No decision	..
Durham	Houghton-le-Spring	W. P. Richardson	Yes	Yes
	South Shields	J. Batey	Yes	Yes
	Chester-le-Street	J. Gilliland	..	..
South Wales	Rhondda	D. Watts Morgan	Yes	..
	Gower	J. Williams	Yes	Yes
	Mid Glamorgan	V. Hartshorn	No decision	Yes
	East Glamorgan	A. Onions	No decision	Yes
	West Monmouthshire	W. Brace	Yes	Yes
	North Monmouthshire	J. Winstone	No decision	Yes
Cumberland	Whitehaven	T. Richardson	..	..
Scotland	West Fife	W. Adamson	Yes	..
	NE. Lanarkshire	J. Robertson	Yes	Yes
	Midlothian	R. Brown	Yes	Yes
Lib-Lab miners' candidates:				
Durham	Mid Durham	J. Wilson		..
Derbyshire	Chesterfield	B. Kenyon		..
	Mid Derbyshire	J. G. Hancock		..
Warwickshire	Nuneaton	W. Johnson		..
Other Labour candidates in mining seats:				
South Wales	Merthyr Tydfil	J. Keir Hardie		Yes
	South Glamorgan	A. Williams		Yes
Lancashire	St. Helens	J. Sexton		..
Durham	Barnard Castle	A. Henderson		Yes
	Bishop Auckland	B. Spoor		Yes
Yorkshire	Rotherham	J. Walker		Yes
	Attercliffe	J. Pointer		..

candidates would have been in opposition to each other. There had been a similar prospect of a large-scale clash between the Liberal and Labour candidates in the mining constituencies immediately before the January election of 1910, and that had come to nothing. On that occasion, however, many of the proposed miners' candidatures had been very tentative, there had been hardly any preparatory work, and the fate of Lloyd George's budget had over-shadowed everything else. By the middle of 1914 the atmo-sphere in most of the coalfields was quite different. The battle lines had hardened; union money was being spent and union prestige committed, and this at least a year before the probable date of the next general election. This time the odds were very much against another retreat.

IV

THE SEED-BEDS OF CHANGE

MINERS the world over have much in common with each other and always have had. The nature of their work, their pattern of life, and the type of community within which they live bind them together, and at the same time set them somewhat apart from the rest of the industrial working class. Yet the miners are not, and never have been, an undifferentiated mass, and before 1914, to an even greater extent than at present, there were important differences between one British coalfield and another and between one set of miners and another. Consequently, generalizations about 'the miners' and their characteristics, particularly in the period before the First World War, may well be meaningless or misleading unless it is made clear exactly which miners are under discussion. Each of the major coalfields has its own political history, with its own distinctive flavour and its own intrinsic interest, and if the drift of events in all of them was in the same direction, with the Labour Party (or its forerunner the Labour Representation Committee) steadily gaining more support, for the most part at the expense of the Liberals, it soon becomes apparent from a more detailed investigation that the rate at which the Labour Party made headway varied considerably from one mining district to another. A comparative approach to the politics of the coalfields helps to explain regional variations of this kind, and also enables the historian to identify the main determinants of political change among the miners during these years of transition.

The socialist gospel and the earliest propaganda for independent Labour representation began to reach all the coalfields at much the same time in the late 1880s and early 1890s; but, whilst some districts were at once receptive to this new political movement, in others little or no impression was to be made for many years to come. Why was it that coalfields reacted in very dissimilar ways? The answer clearly lies in the nature of the ground upon which the seeds were falling, and it is to the significant differences between mining districts that we must now turn.

To begin with, some of the coalfields were a great deal more prosperous than others. Basicallly, the prosperity of a mining district rested on what the hewers could earn, and the hewers' earnings were determined by their output and the price that the coal they produced would fetch in the market. The quantity of coal that a miner could get depended largely on the accidents of geology and the age of the pit in which he worked. There were some districts, Yorkshire, Derbyshire, and Nottinghamshire, for example, where the prevalence of thick and unbroken coal seams made working conditions relatively easy; output per man was high, and the time and money spent on unproductive maintenance and repairs could be kept to a minimum. In coalfields like these the owners were far less prone than in other and less prosperous districts to try to squeeze wages in order to preserve their profit margins. In an older coalfield like Lancashire, on the other hand, conditions were very different. Here the more easily worked seams had been long since exhausted; widespread flooding, excessive faulting, long haulage distances from the coal face to the pit bottom, and the great depths of many of the shafts all tended to increase the costs of production and to reduce output.[1] In an area like this hours were long and earnings were low. This is not to say that the affluence of a mining district was determined entirely by geology; in South Wales there was also a great deal of faulting, seams often petered out without warning, the roads driven through the coal had an alarming tendency to collapse suddenly, and in many pits there was a constant danger of explosions because they were so dry and fiery.[2] Yet in this area earnings and profits remained at a high level because of the persistently buoyant demand for good-quality Welsh steam coal from world shipping companies.

Prosperity cannot be precisely quantified, and it would be a mistake to try to build too much on the figures for miners'

---

[1] N. Simpkin, 'The Lancashire Coalfield', *Institute of Fuel, War-time Bulletin*, Dec. 1945.

[2] E. D. Lewis, *The Rhondda Valleys*, 1959, pp. 9–11.

earnings that are available. In any case, no figures are needed to demonstrate that there was a wide gulf between Derbyshire, where in 1914 a union official could proudly proclaim that five thousand miners in the county owned their own homes and many a few others besides, and Lancashire where the miners were not even permitted the customary privileges of free house coal and an allowance for their explosives. Such was the complexity of the miners' wage structure that it is difficult to make direct comparisons between coalfields; even so Table 9 does indicate that there were sizeable differences in earnings from one mining district to another.

TABLE 9

Hewers' average earning per shift in 1914[1]

	s.	d.		s.	d.
Yorkshire	10	2	Lancashire	8	6
Warwickshire	10	0	Cannock Chase	8	5
Nottinghamshire			Scotland	8	3
and Derbyshire	9	10	Cumberland	8	1
South Wales	9	4	North Wales	8	0
Northumberland	9	1	South Staffordshire	7	1
North Staffordshire	9	0	Leicestershire	7	0
Durham	8	11			

Relations between the miners' unions and the coal-owners also varied considerably from one region to another. Affluence did not necessarily bring industrial harmony—in Yorkshire, for example, masters and men were never on particularly good terms, and in South Wales industrial relations were among the worst in the country. But, other things being equal, a measure of prosperity did at least create the conditions that made a reasonably amicable relationship possible. Nowhere was this better illustrated than in the east Midlands, where the underlying wealth of the coalfield produced a remarkably generous and enlightened

[1] Finlay Gibson, *A Compilation of Statistics of the Coal Mining Industry of the United Kingdom*, 1922, pp. 140–3. In Durham and Northumberland the money earnings of the hewers averaged 8s. 2d. and 8s. 5d. per shift: but in both counties married men received a rent-free house or a money allowance in lieu. This was worth about 4s. a week extra, bringing earnings up to the figures in Table 9. See J. W. F. Rowe, *Wages in the Coal Industry*, 1923, pp. 84–85.

attitude on the part of the owners in Derbyshire and Nottinghamshire. In the years before 1914 some of the colliery companies and individual employers in this area went to considerable expense to provide well-equipped schools, hospitals, convalescent homes, chapels, libraries, and even swimming-baths for their workers. It was here that some of the first pit-head baths in the country were installed, and the model villages being built by one company at this time provided housing that was vastly superior to the squalid cottages to be found in many other mining districts.[1] The owners made no secret of their motives: their purpose was to convince the unions that the interests of capital and labour were identical and to persuade them that the miners would share in the growing wealth of the coalfield. There were few serious industrial disputes in the east Midlands, and in the absence of disputes the unions became rich and respectable, so much so that by 1914 the Derbyshire and Nottinghamshire Miners' Associations were helping to finance a wide range of municipal undertakings in the area. Unions like these had become pillars of society; the class war, bitter and prolonged strikes, the eviction of miners from their homes, and legal battles with the owners all belonged to a different world.[2]

[1] One of the most prominent of the coal magnates in this area, and, indeed, in the whole country, was Arthur Markham, the Liberal Member for Mansfield. He enjoyed immense popularity and respect among the miners, and on one occasion, when his advanced views about the treatment of his employees were questioned by fellow company directors, he wrote to them: 'Why should you think it inevitable that colliers should live in a state of filth and piggery ? If you try and make good clean homes and help social work, this tends to make better men. . . . After all, the theory that each man represents so much money or profit to a company by the amount of coal he gets and that the obligations of the employer ceases when he has paid him his wages is utterly wrong.' Violet Markham, *Friendship's Harvest*, 1956, p. 10.

[2] By 1909 the Nottinghamshire Miners' Association had lent the Nottingham Corporation over £100,000, and by 1914 the Derbyshire Miners' Association had invested over £120,000 in the Chesterfield and Ilkeston Corporations. It is hardly surprising that some of the trade union leaders became men of considerable substance: on his death in 1914, for example, W. E. Harvey of the Derbyshire miners left estate to the gross value of no less than £5,052, a sizeable sum at that time. See J. E. Williams, op. cit., p. 228. An even more striking example of the rewards that could accrue to a prudent and conciliatory trade union leader is provided by Mabon in South Wales. For details of his financial interests and great personal wealth, see E. W. Evans, *Mabon (William Abraham 1842–1922)*, 1959, p. 96.

They belonged to a world like that of the impoverished Lancashire coalfield, where company paternalism on the scale of the east Midlands was out of the question, even had the owners felt generously disposed towards their employees. For the Lancashire coal-owners the only hope of survival lay in keeping production costs, the most important of which were wages, as low as possible, and this was a policy which naturally brought them into conflict with the unions. When the miners over the whole country came out on strike for a minimum wage in 1912, an itinerant correspondent of the *Daily News*, impressed by the contrasts between Lancashire and Derbyshire, wrote:

Wigan, the Lancashire coal centre, and Chesterfield, the Derbyshire coal centre, are only fifty miles apart as the crow flies. They might be five hundred if a difference in spirit depended on geography. In Derbyshire the demand for a minimum wage is based on economic theory supported by a sense of comradeship with less favoured districts. In Lancashire, the men will tell you it is a matter of life and death. For years the history of the Lancashire coal industry has been a history of miserable strikes following strikes in weary and often futile repetition, of lock-outs and actions at law. The cumulative effect is an estrangement between masters and men such as exists nowhere else except in South Wales. For this, the nature of the coalfield even more than human beings is to blame.[1]

In South Wales, as this passage suggests, there was a similar atmosphere of bitterness and conflict, though here it was not poverty that lay at the root of the trouble. In the last quarter of the nineteenth century South Wales had in fact been a fairly quiescent district. But, beginning with a major lock-out in 1898, the character of the coalfield changed dramatically, and from this point onwards South Wales became notorious for its turbulent and militant trade unionism. There were a variety of reasons for the rapid deterioration that took place in industrial relations after the turn of the century.

The first and most pervasive of them was a gradual decline in the influence of Nonconformity at about this time. When the colliery communities had begun to spread along the valley floors in the nineteenth century, the chapel was

---

[1] Quoted in the *Wigan Observer*, 2 Mar. 1913.

never far behind; as the historian of the Rhondda puts it, 'in every mining village, with the appearance of a group of houses, there was built a small, unpretentious but vitally important chapel'.[1] In 1905, in the Rhondda urban district alone, there were no less than 151 chapels with a seating capacity of 85,000,[2] and in 1910 in Glamorgan as a whole there were over 200,000 Nonconformists as against only 61,000 churchmen.[3] Yet despite what was to be a final religious revival in 1904–5 the chapel was undoubtedly losing support in face of rival attractions. With travel becoming easier miners and their families were no longer tied to their own villages: sport, the theatre, and other entertainments were now competing for the time and interest of the younger generation. Life was still hard; but it was growing easier, and as it did so the solace of religion no longer seemed quite so necessary. More important was the rapid anglicization of the coalfield. Between 1871 and 1911 the number of miners in Glamorgan rose from 34,000 to 150,000, and though part of the increase can be attributed to the high birth-rate among the indigenous population it was mainly because of successive waves of immigration from England, particularly from the West Country, that the labour force grew so quickly.[4] The effect of this massive influx of Englishmen was inevitably to dilute the narrow and illiberal brand of Nonconformity so characteristic of nineteenth-century Wales. Indeed, by 1891 the proportion of Welsh-speaking people in Glamorgan had fallen to 49 per cent,[5] and this in itself was a trend that loosened the grip of the chapel, for it was the language barrier that had effectively isolated parts of Wales from new and disturbing

---

[1] Lewis, op. cit., p. 219.

[2] Lewis, op. cit., p. 220.

[3] K. O. Morgan, 'Democratic Politics in Glamorgan, 1884–1914', *Transactions of the Glamorgan Local History Society*, vol. iv, 1960. The number of Church of England attendants at communion in 1910 in the two counties of Monmouthshire and Glamorgan was 193,000; the figure for Nonconformists of all denominations was over 550,000. *Royal Commission on the Church of England and other Religious Bodies in Wales and Monmouthshire*, Cd. 5432, 1910, p. 20.

[4] Brinley Thomas, 'The Migration of Labour into the Glamorganshire Coalfield, (1861–1911)', *Economica*, vol. x, 1930.

[5] J. Parry Lewis, 'The Anglicisation of Glamorgan', *Transactions of the Glamorgan Local History Society*, vol. iv, 1960.

social, economic, and scientific thought.[1] In the eyes of the young especially, Nonconformity seemed to be tired, out of touch, and no longer interested in the pressing problems of the day. Chapel members guilty of excessive enthusiasm for social change risked denunciation and ostracism; in fact, some of the men who later became prominent Socialists had in their younger days been among the most zealous of chapel-goers.[2] The older miners' leaders, reared in the traditions of Nonconformity, had grown up to believe that disputes could always be settled and progress achieved by conciliation and a policy of what was called 'humanitarian gradualism'. But, as the coalfield became less Welsh and less religious, the mood of the miners began to change under the influence of a new generation of union leaders who rejected moderation in favour of a much more aggressive and strident approach towards the employers.[3]

The nature of ownership and management was also changing in a way that tended to worsen industrial relations in South Wales. Throughout British industry the trend in these years was towards amalgamation and combination, and in South Wales the movement developed further and faster than in most of the other coalfields. In the Rhondda Fach valley, to cite but one example, in 1890 six companies had worked twelve pits; by 1914 three companies controlled sixteen pits. At the turn of the century 80 per cent of all Welsh steam coal was produced by only twenty companies.[4] The miners' reaction to this concentration of capital and control was one of alarm and hostility; as an official report

[1] C. R. Williams, 'The Welsh Religious Revival, 1904-5', *The British Journal of Sociology*, vol. iii, 1952.

[2] One of the first Marxists in the Rhondda, Noah Ablett, had once been a Sunday-school teacher; and A. J. Cook, one of the miners' leaders at the time of the general strike of 1926, had in his youth been a Baptist preacher and member of the Band of Hope, Lewis, op. cit., p. 225, and C. L. Mowat, *Britain between the Wars, 1918–1940*, 1956, p. 299.

[3] Besides undermining the influence of the chapel, the arrival of thousands of Englishmen sometimes produced more immediate disturbances. A hauliers' strike in 1893, for example, was an early sign of future trouble, and it was widely believed to have been the work of Englishmen who had recently come from the Forest of Dean, Bristol, and Lancashire. E. W. Evans, *The Miners of South Wales*, 1961, p. 157.

[4] Lewis, op. cit., p. 100. D. J. Williams, *Capitalist Combination in the Coal Industry*, 1924, p. 92.

put it in 1917, 'many regard the combine movement as being directed towards their industrial subjugation'.[1] The new masters, anonymous and sometimes alien Englishmen into the bargain, were never personally involved in the well-being of their employees and in the fortunes of the pit in the same way as their predecessors, who might have been harsh men, but at least had some roots in the area. Insensitive to the feelings of the miners, and too remote to intervene quickly before quarrels turned into serious disputes, 'they', the owners, became symbols of oppression. Matters had come to such a pass that in the years immediately before the First World War miners were actually looking back with some nostalgia to the old days, when there were no 'soul-less combines', and when 'a man who could not get satisfaction over some difficulty in the pit would go over to the owner's house and find it there'.[2] At the lower levels of management, tension between English colliery officials and Welsh miners was adding to the ground-swell of discontent; pit managers who had been trained in English coalfields and were ignorant or impatient of local customs and un-familiar with the Welsh temperament were not readily inclined to make the adjustments and allowances necessary to avoid the friction and ill feeling which are so easily generated among men working underground in conditions of danger and strain.[3]

In an area like this, with resentment and anger often simmering only just beneath the surface, the particularly heavy concentration of miners in South Wales made a dangerous situation even more explosive. Because most industrial workers lived in or near large towns, and mixed with men employed in other trades, they were aware that others, besides themselves, had grievances and problems. Over large areas of South Wales, however, mining was almost the sole occupation for the men, and under these circumstances what has been called a 'reverberation effect' was easily set up.[4] A grievance might at first be a trivial and

[1] *Report of the Commission of Enquiry into Industrial Unrest, No. 7 District*, Cmd. 8668, 1917.
[2] W. J. Edwards, *From the Valley I Came*, 1956, p. 39.
[3] See *Report of the Commission of Enquiry*, 1917.
[4] Phelps Brown, op. cit., p. 156.

localized affair; but in a coalfield like South Wales it could spread like wildfire, for, when a miner could see his own resentment mirrored in the face of almost every other man in his village or valley, it was not long before he was convinced that a major issue of principle was at stake. This is not to say that concentration caused unrest; there were parts of every coalfield, including those that were quiescent, where the miners were just as thick on the ground as in South Wales. But, where industrial relations were already strained for other reasons, a dispute was more likely to become magnified and embittered when almost the entire population was in some degree involved.

Some coalfields, then, were prosperous and some were comparatively poor. In some districts owners and men were on excellent terms, whilst in others relations could hardly have been worse. Differences of this kind were clearly destined to affect the success of the Labour Party, for it could hardly hope to make the same impact in affluent and trouble-free Derbyshire as in an impoverished area like Lancashire with its record of persistent industrial strife. Yet there were also considerations of a much more specifically political character that were to shape the varying fortunes of the Labour Party, and it is to these that we must now turn.

The attitude of the Liberals towards the political claims of the miners varied a great deal from one part of the country to another. From about 1900 onwards, when the miners, like other trade unionists, began to turn to parliamentary action to protect and promote their interests, their first and natural inclination was to look to the Liberals for help. Most mining seats were occupied by Liberal M.P.s, and the Liberals had always professed a special insight into the needs of the miners, and a special concern for the welfare of the working class in general. But if the miners expected local Liberal Associations, grateful for the loyal support of the miners in the past, to stand aside and vacate safe seats for union nominees they were to be rapidly disillusioned and disappointed, for it soon became apparent that in all except a few districts the Liberals were more interested in the working man's vote than the working man's candidate. The outstanding exception to this generalization was the east Midland coalfield, where in Derbyshire and Nottingham-shire the miners' claims were met promptly and in full, largely because the Liberals, and more particularly the coal-owners among them, were satisfied that the union leaders who became M.P.s could be trusted not to use their position to make trouble for the employers.

Everywhere else the Liberals were extremely reluctant to make more seats available for the miners. In Durham and Yorkshire the miners and the Liberals had entered into electoral arrangements immediately after the Third Reform Act in 1885; the miners were left a clear run in one seat in Yorkshire and in two seats in Durham. In return they agreed to support the Liberal candidates in all the other mining seats in the two counties. Arrangements of this kind might have been reasonable enough in 1885, but in the course of the next fifteen years the mining communities grew to such an extent that these pacts had become grossly inequitable by 1900. Yet when the miners began to seek additional parliamentary representation they found the Liberals quite unwilling to strike a fairer balance. Much the same was true in South Wales, for, though the South Wales Miners' Federation did secure grudging Liberal support for two new candidatures, it was perfectly clear that the Liberals had no intention of meeting the miners' claims in full or anything like it. In Scotland the weak and ill-organized miners' unions had had even less success than their English counterparts in persuading the strongly middle-class Scottish Liberal Associations to co-operate in sending working men to Westminster. When Keir Hardie fought his celebrated by-election campaign as an independent Labour candidate in Mid Lanark in 1888, he still considered him-self a Liberal; he broke with the local Liberal party not because his political views were markedly more radical than theirs, but because the Mid Lanark Liberal Association, like many others, could not bring itself to surrender the seat to a working-class trade unionist. A dozen years later the miners were still meeting similar resistance all over the country. Had they been able to channel the mounting pressure for more parliamentary representation through the

Liberal Party, many of the miners' leaders, especially among the older men, would have been only too pleased. But since the Liberals patently were not prepared to co-operate, it could now be argued, and of course it was argued by I.L.P. propagandists, that the only sensible course open to the miners was to sever their traditional links with the Liberals and throw in their lot with the new and separate Labour Party, which was devoted exclusively to the interests of the trade union movement and the working class.

The politics of the Lancashire coalfield set it sharply apart from the rest, for in the north-west there was a strong tradition of working-class Conservatism. In most of the colliery districts the miners tended to live in villages and small towns occupied mainly by other miners; in Lancashire they were much more intermingled with workers employed in other industries, particularly textiles. In 1911 over a third of the Lancashire miners lived in the seven large towns of Manchester, Burnley, Oldham, Bolton, Blackburn, Wigan, and St. Helens, but only in the last two were they the largest single occupational group. Since they were in no sense isolated from other industrial workers, there is no reason to suppose that Conservatism was not as widespread among the miners as among the rest of the Lancashire working class at this time. Indeed, until the coming of the Labour Party, the Conservatives were consistently successful in Wigan and Newton, two of the constituencies where the miners were most heavily concentrated. This is not to suggest that thousands of Lancashire miners did not vote Liberal; as it happens, the Leigh division, where the miners were every bit as numerous as in Wigan and Newton, was held continuously by the Liberals from 1885 to 1914. The truth is that the Lancashire miners were deeply divided between the two major parties and for any union that was anxious to go into politics this was a situation that presented awkward problems. The Lancashire and Cheshire Miners' Federation could hardly work with the Liberals, as did most other miners' unions, or spend its money and usei ts organiza-tion to support candidates bearing a Lib-Lab label, because the substantial body of Lancashire miners with Conservative sympathies would naturally have objected to such a policy.

Very much the same kind of difficulty was encountered by the Lancashire cotton-workers in the 1890s. Their problem was that whilst the weavers in north-east Lancashire were predominantly Liberal, the spinners in the remainder of the county were mainly Conservative. Both sets of workers were covered by one union, the United Textile Factory Workers' Association, and its answer to the problem was a plan to put up two candidates, one to stand as a Liberal and the other as a Conservative. Not surprisingly, a scheme of this kind ran into practical difficulties and was never put into effect, although in 1899 James Mawdsley, the Secretary of the Association, did stand unsuccessfully as a Conservative–Labour candidate at a by-election in Oldham.[1] For unions like the U.T.F.W.A. and the Lancashire miners, anxious to secure parliamentary representation but hamstrung by divisions among their members, a new party, independent of Conservatives and Liberals alike, offered obvious attractions.

In the North-East there was a special combination of political and industrial circumstances that had no exact equivalent elsewhere. First impressions might suggest that Socialism and independent Labour representation were unlikely to make a strong appeal to the miners of Durham and Northumberland. True, insecurity of income was a factor, because this was an exporting district and therefore earnings fluctuated more than in the central coalfields; but the North-East was by no means a poor coalfield in the sense that Lancashire was.[2] In this district there was adequate machinery for collective bargaining and industrial conciliation; localized disagreements went before small joint committees of owners and union representatives and broader wage questions were settled by Conciliation Boards, though

[1] See H. A. Turner, *Trade Union Growth Structure and Policy: A Comparative Study of the Cotton Unions*, 1962, p. 360; and Bealey and Pelling, op. cit., p. 17. Other unions too were likely to run into trouble because of their Conservative membership in Lancashire. When the Amalgamated Society of Railway Servants proposed to put up their Secretary, Edward Harford, as a Lib-Lab in Northampton in 1894 there were immediate protests from seven branches and the District Council of the A.S.R.S. in Lancashire on the grounds that their members were in the habit of voting Conservative and not Liberal. P. S. Bagwell, *The Railwaymen: The History of the National Union of Railwaymen*, 1963, p. 201.

[2] See Table 9, p. 55.

in Northumberland the Board was out of action between 1896 and 1908. Regular meetings at these boards and committees were undoubtedly useful in helping each side to understand the problems of the other and in promoting a certain amount of mutual respect. Furthermore, for many years Socialism was associated with the demand for an eight-hour day, and until after the turn of the century there was little support for a statutory eight-hour day among the miners of Durham and Northumberland. The unions were dominated by the hewers, and the customary system of shift-working in the North-East was such that the hewers already worked less than eight hours a day. This was possible only because the pit-boys worked a much longer shift. It was hard on the boys, but, as the union leaders frequently pointed out, most of the boys were destined to become hewers, and in time the privileges of a hewer would be theirs. An eight-hour day would necessarily reduce the hours of the boys, would upset the two seven-hour shift system operated by the hewers, and would oblige the miners to adopt an inconvenient and highly unpopular three-shift arrangement. A minimum wage as a first charge upon industry was another socialist demand that at first failed to win much approval in the North-East. It was generally accepted that wages were governed by prices, and that the price fetched by coal produced in the North-East was largely beyond the control of the owners, selling as they did in highly competitive overseas markets. A floor to wages, so the argument ran, might make it impossible for the industry to keep its foreign customers when competitors lowered their prices. Fluctuations in earnings were certainly unsettling, but to press for a minimum wage was folly, for if it were saddled with a less flexible cost structure the industry might be completely ruined.

In the 1890s, however, the beginnings of a change in outlook can be discerned, especially among the younger men. Exposed to socialist literature and propaganda in their formative years, they started to look at old arguments in a new light. For them, the miners' standard of living came first, and it was not to be set aside or overridden simply because they were unfortunate enough to live and work in

F

an exporting coalfield. Traditional attitudes in the North-East were further undermined by the rising prestige of the M.F.G.B. From its inception in 1889 the Federation had set itself two main objectives: to establish a wage floor at 30 per cent above the rates operative in 1888 and to secure a legally enforced eight-hour day. Neither of these aims was at first acceptable in the North-East for the reasons already described, and, indeed, most of the older union officials in Durham and Northumberland were on the worst of terms with their counterparts in the M.F.G.B. Yet the pull of the Federation was always there, and in the great lock-out of 1893 the M.F.G.B. proved that it was far better equipped to resist the owners' demands for wage-cuts than Durham and Northumberland. For the miners in the North-East the price of admission to the Federation was to abandon their opposition to the eight-hour day; as time went on a growing body of opinion began to feel that it was a price worth paying.

So it was that a gap began to open between the leadership and the rank and file, presenting the early Socialists with a unique opportunity. In the 1880s and 1890s the established officials in Durham and Northumberland were, like most others, deeply committed to the Liberal Party, and had scant sympathy with the ideals of Socialism or the vision of a new Labour Party devoted to furthering the interests of the working class. John Wilson, the General Secretary of the Durham Miners' Association, once remarked that he would never vote for a working man who represented working-class interests only, and, with a touch of un-conscious humour, added that he did not believe that 'a man should go to Parliament for that and put himself on a level with the landowner and aristocrat'. Political attitudes of this kind were, of course, to be found among Liberal-minded leaders in the Federated area too. But there was a significant difference between them and the miners' leadership in the North-East that provides a clue to the rapid progress made by the I.L.P. in Durham and Northumberland. In the Federated districts it was already official union policy, fully accepted by the Lib-Labs, to fight for objectives that co-incided with the socialist demands for a guaranteed minimum

wage and an eight-hour day. Those who felt strongly about
these issues had no need to agitate outside of the framework of union activity, nor was there any necessity for
them to turn to the Socialists for leadership. In the North-
East, by contrast, miners who became convinced of the
necessity for an eight-hour day and a floor to wages, whether
or not they thought of themselves as Socialists, found themselves confronted with the stubborn hostility of their
official leaders. Unable to channel their aspirations through
their unions, they naturally turned to political action, and
more particularly to the I.L.P. As the Lib-Lab officials lost
touch with the feelings of a growing number of miners on
industrial and economic questions, so they became more and
more vulnerable to attack on political grounds. By 1910 the
Durham and Northumberland coalfields had become hotbeds of socialist activity.

These, then, were some of the general considerations that
shaped the varying fortunes of the Labour Party in the
mining districts. In the three chapters that follow the
political histories of the major coalfields in the decade or so
before 1914 are narrated in greater detail. Chapter V deals
with the group of districts where, by most yardsticks, the
Labour Party fared best, namely Durham, Northumberland,
Lancashire, Cumberland, and Scotland. Chapter VI covers
two coalfields, Yorkshire and South Wales, where the old
guard successfully fought off the socialist challenge for a
little longer. And Chapter VII is concerned with the rest of
the mining districts, Derbyshire, Nottinghamshire, Warwickshire, and Staffordshire, where the Labour Party had made
least headway by 1914.

V

THE FRONT RUNNERS

(i) DURHAM AND NORTHUMBERLAND

RADICAL politics have flourished in the north-east of England since the days of the Chartists and even earlier. And it was here, in the remote coalfields of Durham and Northumberland, far from the London debating societies and middle-class drawing rooms, that the pioneer Socialists first made an impact on the industrial working class. In 1887 a seventeen-week strike of Northumberland miners brought a band of socialist evangelists from the Social-Democratic Federation and the Socialist League to Tyneside and the nearby colliery villages; and after the strike had ended the redoubtable Tom Mann stayed on for a time as the S.D.F.'s organizer.[1] By 1895 there were a number of I.L.P. branches in existence in Durham, and within a year or two they were beginning to plague the Durham Miners' Association with resolutions calling for independent representation for Labour in Parliament and an eight-hour day in the pits.[2]

Yet so far as Durham was concerned the pattern of parliamentary representation established in 1885 was to change little in the twenty years that followed. By arrangement with the Liberals the Durham mineworkers won two seats at the general election of that year, John Wilson and William Crawford being returned for Houghton-le-Spring and Mid Durham respectively. One of these seats was lost almost at once when Wilson was defeated at the 1886 election. However, on the death of Crawford in 1890 Wilson

---

[1] For accounts of this strike and the role of the Socialists, see Dona Torr, *Tom Mann and his Times*, 1956, pp. 239 et seq.; E. P. Thompson, *William Morris, Romantic to Revolutionary*, 1955, pp. 512–24; Tom Mann, *My Memoirs*, 1923, p. 65; H. W. Lee and E. Archbold, *Social-Democracy in Britain*, 1935, pp. 122–3.

[2] E. Welbourne, *The Miners' Unions of Northumberland and Durham*, 1923, p. 294. G. H. Metcalfe, 'A History of the Durham Miners' Association, 1869–1915' (M.A. thesis, University of Durham, 1947).

took his place in Mid Durham and continued to sit for that
constituency for the next twenty-five years. So it was that
throughout the 1890s the sole representative of the Durham
mineworkers in Parliament was the pugnacious and sharp-
tongued John Wilson, a staunch Liberal and a determined
opponent of Socialism. Until the turn of the century his
authority in the union was unchallenged; but very soon
afterwards the radicals of his generation were to be out-
flanked and outmanœuvred by a new left in the shape of the
I.L.P., and by 1905 the North-East was showing enough
promise to be singled out for special attention by the National Administrative Council of the I.L.P. A new and energetic district organizer named Matt Simm was appointed,
and he immediately began to put his own mining background and Northumbrian burr to good effect. In April
1905 there were only four I.L.P. branches of any consequence in Northumberland; a year later there were at least
thirteen and the number was growing. In Durham by 1907
there were sixty branches as compared with sixteen in 1905.
Though events were to demonstrate that there were parts
of the coalfield where even seven or eight years later the
Labour Party had still not made much of an impression, the
I.L.P. Annual Report for 1906 could claim with some
justice that 'the whole area is now covered by branches of
the party, and the county of Durham especially is in the very
van of the movement for Labour and Socialism'.

But it was Taff Vale rather than the activities of the I.L.P.
that goaded the Durham mineworkers into seeking further
parliamentary representation. In 1903 they selected two
new candidates, John Johnson, an agent of the D.M.A.,
and J. W. Taylor, an official of the colliery mechanics' union,
and to the annoyance of the socialist faction in the D.M.A.
Johnson was returned as a Lib-Lab for Gateshead at a by-
election in 1904. Finding a seat for Taylor proved more
difficult, for unlike Johnson he was a member of the I.L.P.
and had made it plain that he had no intention of co-
operating with the Liberals. There was talk of putting him
up against one of the sitting Liberals in Chester-le-Street or
North-West Durham, but eventually, at the end of 1905
and with a general election imminent, the mineworkers

decided that, although his candidature would definitely be on independent Labour lines, he would have to wait until there was a vacancy in a mining division.[1] The problem, it seemed, had been shelved at least until after the election of 1906.

Almost at once a totally unexpected opening did occur when Sir James Joicey, the Liberal Member for Chester-le-Street, was made a peer. Taylor was promptly nominated for the seat by the mineworkers, and the local Liberal Association was asked not to oppose him. On the few occasions when the Liberals had been prepared to help a working man into Parliament, it was only old-style Lib-Labs, like Thomas Burt and Charles Fenwick in Northumberland, and John Wilson and John Johnson in Durham, whose claims they were ready seriously to entertain. J. W. Taylor was a very different proposition, for their largess certainly did not run to trade unionists who were also avowed Socialists. What little chance there was of Liberal support for Taylor vanished when he appeared before the executive of the Chester-le-Street Liberal Association to explain his position. He told them bluntly that he was a member of the I.L.P., that he had resigned from his own local Liberal Party, that under no circumstances would he stand as a Lib-Lab, and that if he was elected he would apply for the Labour whip in the House of Commons. Not surprisingly this was too much for the Liberals to swallow, and they adopted instead a local Congregational minister.[2]

On the face of things, the decision to run Taylor on independent Labour lines seems to show that even as early as 1905 the Durham mineworkers were prepared to break with the Liberals. The event was certainly of some significance, but at the same time it would be wrong to read too much into it, because this was a decision taken on the basis of lodge votes, and lodge votes were notoriously unreliable as guides to the general opinion of the miners, particularly on political questions. When major issues were at stake— a national strike, or whether or not to affiliate to the Labour Party, for example—it was customary for the miners' unions to arrange an individual ballot of their members; on less

---

[1] *Durham Chronicle*, 22 Dec. 1905.   [2] Ibid., 12 Jan. 1906.

important matters, to save time and money, decisions were often reached as a result of what were called 'proxy' votes. Each lodge was entitled to one proxy vote for every fifty members, and all the proxy votes allocated to a lodge were cast in accordance with the majority view as expressed at a single meeting, which might well have been attended by only a handful of miners. It was a system made to order for a dedicated minority movement, permitting as it did an energetic group of I.L.P. members to commit their lodges to the support of resolutions which may well have been quite unacceptable to the thousands of miners who failed to attend meetings. All that Taylor's independent candidature shows for certain is that the I.L.P. was well entrenched among the activists in the lodges.

As it happened, and as the outcome of the election was to show, the Labour Party had more support in Chester-le-Street than in most of the rest of the county. Even before the general election of 1900 there had been a move to invite Keir Hardie to contest the seat,[1] and at Washington and Usworth, in the heart of the division, lay one of the strongest I.L.P. centres in Durham. Votes of confidence in Taylor were carried at every colliery in the constituency, and in the event he polled 46 per cent of the vote, as against 28 per cent for the Conservative and only 26 per cent for the Liberal. As about half the electorate were miners, there is not much doubt that he took the lion's share of their vote. Interestingly enough, the other mining constituency in Durham where Labour had made substantial progress was the Jarrow division, which also adjoined the urban and industrialized ribbon running along the south bank of the Tyne. Standing as an L.R.C. candidate, Pete Curran was defeated here in 1906; but he made a very respectable showing and the bulk of his support was thought to have come from the local miners.[2]

1 Will Thorne, *My Life's Battles*, 1925, p. 203.

2 The sitting Liberal Member was Sir Charles Mark Palmer, a patriarchal figure whose shipyard was the main source of employment in Jarrow town. See Ellen Wilkinson, *The Town that was Murdered: the Life-story of Jarrow*, 1939. On the death of Palmer in 1907 Curran actually won the seat in a four-cornered contest, but was then defeated in January 1910. Election results for all the mining constituencies are given in full in the appendices to Chs. V, VI, and VII.

Further south, and away from Tyneside, the Labour Party had made less headway by 1906. True, Arthur Henderson had been returned as an L.R.C. candidate in Barnard Castle (where about a third of the electors were miners) at a by-election in 1903; but on this occasion socialism and independent Labour representation had been pushed into the background by other issues. Henderson was sounder on free trade than his Liberal opponent, and in fact most of the local Liberal workers abandoned their official candidate and came over to help him. Furthermore, in order to ingratiate himself with the miners, Henderson had been obliged to promise to support their Lib-Lab candidates at the next general election.[1] In two other acknowledged mining divisions, Houghton-le-Spring and North-West Durham, there is nothing to suggest that the miners were dissatisfied with their Liberal Members or were anxious to run Labour candidates against them.

Across the Tyne in Northumberland the I.L.P. movement was also gaining ground, though here it faced a special problem because the Lib-Lab tradition was embodied in two of the most respected figures in British working-class politics, namely Thomas Burt and Charles Fenwick. Burt had been first elected for Morpeth as far back as 1874, and still enjoyed all the prestige of being one of the first two working men ever to sit in the House of Commons. Fenwick had been returned for the newly created Wansbeck division in 1885, and had gone virtually straight from the coal-face to Parliament. For years the Northumberland Miners' Association had worked hand in glove with the Liberals, and the union itself still appeared to be firmly under the control of the Lib-Labs in 1906. The General Secretary was Burt himself, and all the leading officials were closely identified with the Liberal Party. But beneath the surface, with the I.L.P. busily burrowing into the lodges, the mood was changing, and so quickly was the situation transformed in the course of the next few years that by 1910 both Burt and Fenwick very nearly found themselves faced with official Labour opponents sponsored by their own union.

[1] Bealey and Pelling, op. cit., pp. 152–3.

As the Socialists gained control over more and more of the lodges the position of the Lib-Lab leadership in both Durham and Northumberland became increasingly precarious. At the end of 1906 the advocates of independent Labour representation in Durham managed to carry a resolution that committed the D.M.A. to running all its future candidates 'independent of all political parties', a decision that annoyed Wilson intensely, since it meant that if he wished to continue as an official miners' candidate he would be required to break with his Liberal friends in Mid Durham. The Socialists were delighted at this tactical victory, for if the D.M.A. was not yet part of the Labour Party it was at least detached from the Liberals. At the end of 1907 they had even more cause to congratulate themselves when the Durham miners by 47,986 votes to 18,963 decided to join the M.F.G.B. This, of course, was primarily a trade union matter; but there were political overtones, too, because, whereas the Lib-Labs had consistently opposed affiliation, the Socialists for many years had been urging the miners to go into the Federation. When the M.F.G.B. as a whole voted to join the Labour Party in 1908 Durham was carried in with all the other district unions, though the ballot was never held in Durham because of a legal technicality. And at every half-yearly election to the executive of the D.M.A. the number of Socialists steadily increased until by 1910 they were probably in a narrow majority.

There were further signs of change at the Durham miners' annual gala, one of the great events in the miners' year. Although John Burns and Tom Mann had occasionally appeared at these demonstrations, it was not until 1905 that the recognized leaders of the Labour Party, Keir Hardie and Arthur Henderson, were invited to speak, and a speech at the gala provided a magnificent opportunity for socialist propaganda before an audience of thousands of miners and their families. In 1907, for example, Philip Snowden spoke against an official union resolution that pledged the support of the Durham miners to the Liberal Government[1] and in the following year he was again on the platform, this time setting out a form of under-consumption theory and claiming

---

[1] P. Snowden, *Autobiography*, 1934, vol. i, pp. 154–6.

that it was 'idiotic' to reduce wages when trade was bad,
because lower wages reduced demand, which only resulted
in worse trade and still lower wages. Performances of this
kind naturally exasperated John Wilson, and he took to
using his monthly circular to the miners to attack visitors
who would not support the official union line. On one
occasion, no doubt to the delight of the Socialists, he
actually related Snowden's thesis about the folly of reducing
wages at very considerable length, with an air of scandalized
incredulity that befitted an adherent of the sliding-scale basis
for wage settlements.

In Northumberland, too, the I.L.P. movement was
gathering fresh momentum between the general elections of
1906 and 1910. In August 1906 it was able to launch a new
monthly newspaper, the *Northern Democrat*, with Matt
Simm as editor. In the first issue Simm recalled the advice
given him by friends when he took up his appointment as
district organizer: 'Ye monna say nowt agyen Burt and
Fenwick.' At that time, as he pointed out, 'among the older
school, to agree with Burt and Fenwick was apparently a
religious duty accepted by the old and imposed on the
young'.[1] As the years went by they were still treated with
considerable deference and respect by I.L.P. propagandists,
and every attack on their politics was duly prefaced with a
few kindly words in remembrance of their great services in
the past. The tide really started to run against the Lib-Labs
in July 1906 when by a narrow margin the Northumberland
miners voted for an eight-hour day in the county. In the
same month Keir Hardie appeared at the annual demonstration and by general consent scored a personal triumph.[2]
In August 1907, by a majority of nearly five to one, the
miners then voted to affiliate to the M.F.G.B., and their
application for membership was accepted in October. The
final seal seemed to be set upon the I.L.P.'s success in May
1908, when by 14,371 votes to 10,169 the Northumberland
miners plumped for affiliation to the Labour Party.

As it turned out, there was still one more battle to win,
and there now developed a long and complicated wrangle

1 *Northern Democrat*, Aug. 1906.
2 *Morpeth Herald*, 21 July 1906.

about the position of Burt and Fenwick. When the M.F.G.B. joined the Labour Party it was made quite clear to the Federation that all miners' candidates would be required to sign the Party constitution pledging them not to co-operate with any other political party. Neither Burt nor Fenwick ever had the slightest intention of signing or of cutting themselves off from their Liberal friends.[1] If they could not stand as M.F.G.B. candidates they were quite prepared to stand as Liberals, and the Liberals, for their part, were equally willing to adopt them, whether they had the support of their union or not.[2] The Northumberland miners now found themselves in a very difficult situation. They were anxious to run two official Federation candidates under the auspices of the Labour Party, and these two candidates could not be Burt and Fenwick. But, if they were to put up two other miners against Burt and Fenwick, the union would find itself engaged upon the thankless task of trying to unseat Thomas Burt, its own General Secretary and founding father, the mining vote in Morpeth and Wansbeck would be hopelessly split, and there was even a chance that the Conservatives might slip in on minority votes. In desperation they tried to persuade the M.F.G.B. to grant special dispensation for Burt and Fenwick, but the Federation was adamant, and the Northumberland miners were left in no doubt that only candidates who signed the constitution of the Labour Party could be endorsed.[3]

The union was now deeply and unhappily divided. Burt and Fenwick both had strong personal followings, and their supporters argued that the N.M.A. should stick to its two

[1] As early as March 1908 Burt had given notice that he was not going to sign the Labour Party constitution. In his monthly circular he wrote: 'To the candidate who frankly and conscientiously agrees with the Constitution of the L.R.C. no difficulty presents itself. He may accept the position with alacrity and with perfect honour. But to the candidate who differs on essential points, the alternative presented seems to be whether he shall give up his principles, his independent judgement and his convictions, or shall tacitly, tamely and dishonestly accept, or pretend to accept, a constitution and opinions from which he utterly dissents.' The language was a little confused, but the meaning was clear enough: he did not agree with the constitution and therefore he was not going to sign it. Most of the other Lib-Labs among the miners' M.P.s were less scrupulous: they disagreed with the constitution, signed it, and then ignored it.

[2] *Northern Liberal Federation Minutes*, 11 Nov. 1909.

[3] *MFGB*, 18 Nov. 1909.

old Members and ignore the Federation and the Labour Party. But most of the officials, including erstwhile Lib-Labs, feared that if the Northumberland miners decided to stand by Burt and Fenwick, the union would risk expulsion from the M.F.G.B. At this particular time the N.M.A. could ill afford to cut itself off from the Federation, because preliminary negotiations with the coal-owners about the implementation of the Eight Hours Act (which was due to come into force in the North-East on 1 January 1910) suggested that there might well be a fight in the offing.[1] The only way out of the difficulty was for the union to give up the idea of sponsoring two official candidates, thereby leaving the way open for Burt and Fenwick to stand as independents. In the end this was what the N.M.A. was obliged to do, much to the exasperation and disappointment of the more ardent I.L.P. members in Northumberland. It was probably a wise decision. Burt and Fenwick might well have defeated anyone put up against them, and, in any case, the miners and the Labour Party could only have brought discredit upon themselves had they seemed bent upon hounding two immensely respected men out of parliamentary life. This was certainly the view of the national executive of the Labour Party, which refused to provide the Morpeth L.R.C. with a candidate on the curious grounds that it could not encourage them to contest a seat 'held by a nominee of the M.F.G.B.'[2] Nobody knew better than the Labour Party executive that Burt was no longer a nominee of the M.F.G.B.

As expected, Burt and Fenwick had no difficulty in holding their seats in the election of January 1910. A second and somewhat half-hearted attempt to oust them later in the year came to nothing, and by December they were so secure that the local Conservatives did not even trouble to contest their seats at the December election of 1910. In terms of parliamentary representation the Socialists had nothing as yet to show for their efforts. But it was the sentimental attachment of so many miners to two determined veterans more than loyalty to the Liberal Party that had blocked their path and

---

[1] *Newcastle Daily Chronicle*, 30 Oct. 1909.
[2] *LPEC*, 2 Dec. 1909.

masked the real progress made by Labour both within the union hierarchy and among the rank and file.

In Durham there were no personal obstacles of this kind, and here the union was by now taking a much more uncompromising line with the Liberals. Because the main issue at stake in the January election of 1910 seemed to be the 'people's budget', introduced by Lloyd George in the previous year, the Yorkshire and South Wales miners decided not to press for seats to which they had laid claim, so as to avoid creating three-cornered fights that might help the Conservatives. In Durham, however, it was at this election that the final breach in the old alliance between the D.M.A. and the Liberals occurred. The first hostile move had been made by the Liberals in January 1909, when they decided to run a candidate of their own against John Johnson, the D.M.A. agent who represented Gateshead. The Gateshead Liberals never had much affection for Johnson, and once it was established that he was to stand as a Labour rather than a Lib-Lab candidate at the next election they were glad of the excuse to look about for a more congenial representative. Gateshead alone would have been enough to sour relations between the Liberals and the Durham miners. Shortly before the election, however, they found themselves at odds about the Bishop Auckland seat too. In 1907 the miners had come to the conclusion that they could afford to fight only one additional seat at the next election, and the choice had fallen upon South-East Durham, with William House, the President of the D.M.A., as the candidate. It appeared to be an ideal constituency, for the mining community there was growing rapidly (by 1910 about a third of the electorate were miners), and, more important, there seemed to be every chance of a straight fight against the sitting Conservative, since at this stage the Liberals were showing no interest in the seat. In the course of 1908 House began to make himself known in the constituency, and everyone assumed that it was here that the miners would make their effort. In May 1909, however, the Liberal Member for Bishop Auckland announced that he intended to retire before the next election, whereupon the D.M.A. immediately seized the opportunity to transfer House to

Bishop Auckland, claiming that this seat had been promised to the miners under the 1885 agreement, and that ever since they had been patiently waiting for it to fall vacant. It is hard to believe that the D.M.A. really expected the Liberals to surrender a safe seat to a prominent Socialist like House on the strength of an agreement reached twenty-five years earlier under totally different circumstances. If the Durham miners were not spoiling for a fight they were certainly not putting themselves out to avoid one.

This aggressive new posture caused a certain amount of anxiety among the Liberals, the more so since elsewhere the Labour Party and the miners were proving so accommodating. In November 1909 there were hints that if Labour would withdraw Johnson from Gateshead and nominate him for South-East Durham or Durham City, and switch House from Bishop Auckland to whichever seat Johnson did not contest, the Liberals for their part would give Labour a clear run in Chester-le-Street, Barnard Castle, and Jarrow.[1] There was no response from the Labour side, which was as well for the Liberals, because the results of the election were to show that they had seriously underestimated their own strength. In the event, they won Jarrow, Bishop Auckland, and Gateshead in opposition to Labour, and gained South-East Durham from the Conservatives: the Labour Party lost Jarrow and Gateshead, failed to win Bishop Auckland, and missed an excellent chance of gaining South-East Durham.

Any chance that the two miners' candidates, House and Johnson, did have was ruined by a slice of sheer bad luck. In order to bring the Eight Hours Act into effect the D.M.A.'s officials had been obliged to negotiate a new three-shift system with the owners, and these arrangements at first provoked so much hostility in Durham that at one time during January 1910 50,000 miners were idle in protest. Discontent of this order naturally did nothing to improve House's prospects, for he had always been one of the leading advocates of the eight-hour day. In the circumstances he found it necessary to spend much of his time at pit-head meetings trying to pacify angry miners; and when

<hr>

[1] *North Mail*, 18 Nov. 1909.

he did manage to devote a few days to his campaign there were complaints that he had no business to be electioneering at such a time.[1] Not surprisingly, he finished last with well under a third of the votes cast. John Johnson in Gateshead also suffered as a result of the unpopularity of the Eight Hours Act: on polling day 8,000 miners marched through the town, accompanied by their brass bands, and carrying banners that read, 'Down with Johnson, the three-shift candidate'. The loss of Pete Curran's seat in Jarrow and then a second defeat for House at Bishop Auckland in December 1910 made it an unhappy year for the Labour Party in the Durham coalfield. True, the Lib-Labs had lost control of the D.M.A.; but Labour had certainly not yet won over the bulk of the miners.

In the aftermath of these events, the morale of the I.L.P. sagged alarmingly for a while. In Northumberland it was conceded that Burt and Fenwick could continue to represent Morpeth and Wansbeck for as long as they pleased, and such was the general mood of disenchantment that, when Fenwick claimed that the Labour Party now considered him to be one of themselves, a thoroughly depressed Matt Simm could only comment that if this was so it was yet one more sign of the Labour Party's deterioration.[2] But the phase passed, and in 1912 the N.M.A. began to prepare for the day when Burt and Fenwick finally did retire. Two official candidates, William Straker and John Cairns, were selected, and by 1914 the union had agreed to co-operate with the local I.L.P. branches and other trade unions to establish properly constituted divisional L.R.C.s in the Northumberland mining constituencies. Many of the Northumberland miners were still active workers for the Liberal Party even at this late stage, and it was not until the 1920s that Labour could count on their overwhelming support. But by the outbreak of the 1914–18 War the N.M.A. was at the official level at least as much committed to the Labour Party as it had been to the Liberals in 1906.

In Durham too the union leadership was moving ahead of opinion amongst the rank and file. By-elections in Houghton-le-Spring in 1913 and North-West Durham in 1914 were

[1] *North Mail*, Jan. 1910. [2] *Northern Democrat*, June 1911.

to make it painfully clear to the officials that in parts of the
county Liberal sympathies still ran very deep, and that the
older miners particularly were, as the *Labour Leader* put it,
'steeped in Liberalism' and 'unaware of current trends'.
Seeing that over half the electors in Houghton-le-Spring
were miners, when the Liberal Member died in February
1913 the D.M.A. naturally felt that it had some claim to this
seat and some hope of winning it. William House was again
adopted as the Labour candidate, though before his candidature could be endorsed by the M.F.G.B. an embarrassing
difficulty arose when the Federation discovered that as a
result of the Osborne judgement it was so short of funds
that it could not afford to finance the contest. In the end the
problem was solved by arranging a loan from the Labour
Party.[1] The local Liberals selected a commercial traveller
named Tom Wing, and as the campaign developed it
became apparent that thousands of miners preferred even
this unlikely candidate to the president of their own union
running on the Labour ticket. Nearly every lodge in the
constituency was represented at Wing's adoption meeting,
and, according to its chairman, the Houghton-le-Spring
Liberal Association was made up almost entirely of miners.
House, of course, was not without supporters, and very
soon quite unprecedented and extraordinary situations arose.
Every lodge and every village was split from top to bottom,
and on a good many evenings half of a lodge's officials
were to be found speaking from House's platform whilst the
other half were helping Wing. And, now that the miners
were divided and forced to take sides, the extent to which
they had been previously identified with the Liberals came
out even more clearly. In many parts of the constituency the
Liberals had never troubled to set up separate committee-
rooms for election purposes but had relied on the miners to
provide the necessary organization. Consequently where
the officials went over to Labour the Liberals suddenly
found themselves without any electoral machinery at all.
Fortunately for them the Labour organization was in no
better shape, and the result was a comfortable majority for
Tom Wing, with the Conservative second, and the un-

[1] *LPEC*, 24 Feb. 1913.

fortunate House last with only 22 per cent of the vote. Once
again there was no escaping the conclusion that the Liberals
had done at least as well among the miners as the Labour
candidate, and, as Matt Simm pointed out in a letter to the
Labour Leader, this was an absurd state of affairs, for what
they had witnessed was 'the strange spectacle of a trade
union finding the money to run a candidate and the members
using their votes to defeat their own nominee'.[1] The moral
was that until the D.M.A. bestirred itself and accepted
the responsibility for propaganda and organizational work
between as well as during elections, Labour candidates
would continue to suffer humiliations of this kind.

The lessons of Houghton-le-Spring were underlined less
than a year later when North-West Durham fell vacant in
January 1914. House refused to try his luck again, and the
local L.R.C. adopted G. H. Stuart of the postmen's union, a
move that was applauded by the *Labour Leader* as an indication of 'the decline of sectionalism' within the Labour
Party, but which was received with mixed feelings amongst
the miners. As the result showed, it mattered little whether
the candidate was a miner or not, for like House in the
previous year Stuart finished last with only 28 per cent of
the vote, a highly unsatisfactory result for the D.M.A.,
considering that about 60 per cent of the electorate were
miners.[2]

Yet the union seems not to have been unduly discouraged
by these set-backs because in March 1914 it selected five
new candidates, J. Batey, J. Gilliland, W. P. Richardson,
J. Robson, and J. Lawson, to be in readiness for the coming
general election. When the M.F.G.B. decided to allocate
Durham only two candidates at the next election, the
D.M.A. eventually settled in June for Houghton-le-Spring
and South Shields, with Richardson and Batey as the
candidates,[3] although a third member of the D.M.A.,
J. Gilliland, was adopted by the Chester-le-Street L.R.C.
to replace J. W. Taylor.

[1] *Labour Leader*, 3 Apr. 1913. For accounts of the Houghton-le-Spring by-
election, see *Durham Chronicle* and *Newcastle Daily Chronicle*, Mar. 1913.

[2] For the NW. Durham by-election, see *Durham Chronicle* and *Stanley News*, Jan.
and Feb. 1914.

[3] *DMA*, June 1914.

(ii) LANCASHIRE AND CUMBERLAND

For reasons already discussed in Chapter IV, the idea of a new party, representing exclusively the interests of the working class and trade unions, made a special appeal to the Lancashire and Cheshire Miners' Federation. Political divisions among its own members had always prevented it from co-operating wholeheartedly with either of the two major parties, and, indeed, up to 1906 it had been the least successful of all the important miners' unions in England and Wales in securing parliamentary representation. Sam Woods held Wigan for three years from 1892 to 1895 and that was all. After Taff Vale, however, there was great enthusiasm for Labour representation in Lancashire, and, even before the M.F.G.B. scheme had been approved, Thomas Ashton, the cautious Secretary of the L.C.M.F., was trying to curb the growing demands for more candidates. 'I am afraid we are moving too fast', he complained, '. . . there is plenty of time, let other Districts in the Federation move a little before we get too far ahead.'[1] Even so, by the end of 1902, the Lancashire miners had made provisional arrangements to run candidates in Newton, Ince, and Radcliffe, and, of course, they had more scope than most other miners' unions because they had no inhibitions about contesting seats held by the Liberals.

There was a good deal of chopping and changing in the next three years as regards both candidates and seats. At one time Accrington was substituted for Radcliffe, a move which irritated Ramsay MacDonald because he was anxious to be able to promise the Liberals a clear run here under the terms of his electoral pact with Herbert Gladstone; in the end the miners' candidate, Thomas Greenall, stood down when he found that his Liberal opponent was to be a strong supporter of the Eight Hours Act. Sam Woods, who was to have been the L.C.M.F. candidate in Newton, withdrew because of ill health, and his place was taken not by another miners' nominee but by James Seddon of the shop assistants' union. As against this, St. Helens was added to the L.C.M.F.'s list of seats to be contested.

[1] *LCMF*, Jan. 1902.

When the general election came in 1906 there were two
L.C.M.F. candidates, Stephen Walsh in Ince and Thomas
Glover in St. Helens. In neither case was there any opposition from the Liberals, who were well aware that in constituencies like these a trade unionist, standing as a straight
Labour candidate, had a far better chance than any Liberal
of winning over the Conservative working man. Stephen
Walsh had the good fortune to face a Conservative opponent
who owned a colliery that was one of the largest in the
division and where the miners were actually on strike during
the election.[1] In St. Helens Glover's main problem lay in
overcoming a deep-rooted tradition of Conservative paternalism. The sitting Member, Sir Henry Seton-Karr, owed
his seat to a connection by marriage with the Pilkingtons,
the glass-manufacturing family which dominated the district
both politically and industrially. Seton-Karr himself was not
particularly interested in politics; as the historians of the
town of St. Helens remark, 'his chief interest lay in a cattle
ranch in Wyoming and the hunting of wild animals'.[2] But
he had put himself out to encourage the growth of Conservative working men's clubs, and his ability to hold an
industrial seat like St. Helens, especially when he spent so
much time away from it, suggests that his brand of Conservatism had a considerable appeal among the Lancashire
working class. As in a good many other Lancashire constituencies, the Roman Catholic vote was of some importance
in St. Helens, and Glover was fortunate enough to have the
support of Michael Davitt, the Irish Labour leader, in the
campaign.

Walsh and Glover were both successful, and, as the
L.C.M.F. had become affiliated to the L.R.C. in 1903, they
became the first miners' M.P.s to join the Parliamentary
Labour Party. But, in the three Lancashire divisions where
the miners were most heavily concentrated, there were no
union candidates, and the results in these three constituencies present a curious picture of divided and confused
political loyalties. Wigan returned a Conservative in

[1] *Wigan Examiner*, Jan. 1906.
[2] T. C. Barker and J. R. Harris, *A Merseyside Town in the Industrial Revolution—
St. Helens, 1750–1900*, 1954, p. 475.

opposition to a Liberal; Leigh returned a Liberal in opposition to a Conservative; and Newton returned a Labour member in opposition to a Conservative. Wigan had been a Conservative seat since 1885, and oddly enough the Member for all these years, Sir Francis Sharp Powell, had persistently opposed an eight-hour day for miners.[1] His Liberal opponent in 1906 was a former Conservative mayor of the town, who had left the Conservatives so that he could support the eight-hour day, and yet even in this year of the Liberal landslide Powell still managed to cling on to Wigan. By contrast, in the nearby Leigh division, where the miners were just as numerous, it was the Liberals who had been successful ever since 1885, and in 1906 the miners had no qualms in giving their votes to a Liberal industrialist, J. F. L. Brunner of the Brunner Mond Company. In the third of these mining divisions J. A. Seddon, standing under the auspices of the L.R.C., managed to turn out Colonel Pilkington, the sitting Conservative.

The Lancashire miners were spread over an unusually large number of constituencies, and in addition to the five already mentioned there were probably at least another seven where the proportion of miners in the electorate ranged from 5 to 15 per cent. They cannot all be dealt with in detail, but it is worth pausing to look at one of them, the Westhoughton division, because the sequence of events here underlined the weakness of the Liberals in parts of industrial Lancashire. Westhoughton was a mixed agricultural and industrial constituency, with the miners constituting a little under a tenth of the electorate by 1906. The sitting Conservative was the Hon. Edward Stanley, the heir of the Earl of Derby. The Liberals had decided to contest the seat in 1906, but when their candidate dropped out for business reasons the Horwich Trades Council seized the chance of inviting W. T. Wilson of the carpenters' union to stand as an L.R.C. candidate. Wilson was not at all to the taste of the Liberals: he was not, as their local newspaper put it, 'the right calibre of man'.[2] But once a Labour

---

[1] On the other hand, he was firmly in the tradition of Conservative factory reformers and enjoyed a justified reputation for philanthropy. See H. L. P. Hulbert, *Sir Francis Sharp Powell*, 1914.   [2] *Wigan Examiner*, 10 Jan. 1906.

man was in the field they realized that it would be futile to run a candidate of their own, and, overcoming their reservations, the various Liberal clubs and associations in the constituency one by one eventually advised their members to vote Labour. In the event the victory of Wilson, the working carpenter, over the future Earl of Derby caused great astonishment in Lancashire, and there was a touch of irony in the situation, for a large part of the constituency was actually owned by the Derby family.[1] What was more significant was that in constituencies like Ince, St. Helens, Newton, and Westhoughton it was already the Labour Party, and not the Liberals, that was beginning to provide the real alternative to the Conservatives. In a county like Durham Labour could expect to attract little support away from the Conservatives when it challenged the Liberals; but in Lancashire Labour candidates putting up against sitting Conservatives could hope to draw working-class votes from both the Liberals and Conservatives.

After the election of 1906, and the success of Walsh and Glover, enthusiasm for Labour representation continued to grow. In 1908 there was a decisive vote (by 30,227 votes to 13,702) in favour of joining the Labour Party, and in the same year the union decided that at the next general election, besides defending the two seats it already held, it would sponsor three additional candidates, H. Twist, T. Greenall, and J. E. Sutton, in Wigan, Leigh, and East Manchester. When the election came in January 1910 all five candidates went to the poll, and there were no last-minute withdrawals as in Yorkshire and South Wales, so as to avoid three-cornered contests that might let in the Conservatives on minority votes. In Lancashire, of course, the weakness of the Liberals lent some force to the argument that if there was to be only one anti-Conservative candidate it was the Liberal who ought to stand down. And if the Liberals were not prepared to make way for miners' candidates, the L.C.M.F. was perfectly happy to press on with its candidatures, because with a large number of Conservative sympathizers among its members it could not afford to seem to discriminate in favour of the Liberals when it picked the

[1] Randolph Churchill, *Lord Derby*, 1960, pp. 86 et seq.

seats it would fight. In 1906 the miners had won Ince and
St. Helens from the Conservatives; in 1910 two of the seats
they proposed to contest, Leigh and East Manchester, were
held by the Liberals. It soon became apparent, however,
that even in Lancashire the single-minded pursuit of independent Labour representation, free from Liberal entangle-
ments, was far from easy.

To begin with, the Labour Party itself was anxious to
avoid antagonizing the Liberals wherever possible, and early
in 1909 it approached the M.F.G.B. with the suggestion
that the Federation should try to persuade the Lancashire
miners to withdraw Sutton from East Manchester. The
L.C.M.F. would have none of this, and a three-cornered
contest was avoided only because the local Liberals decided
not to fight the seat but to support Sutton instead.[1] In Leigh,
however, the Liberals were not so accommodating; they had
held the seat for twenty-five years and were in no mood now
to surrender it to the Labour Party. Faced with the prospect
of a direct clash with the Liberals, some of the L.C.M.F.
leaders began to show signs of uneasiness. Stephen Walsh,
for example, though never an old-style Lib-Lab, had become
convinced after four years in Parliament that the circumstances of the 1910 election called for a united front against
the Conservatives, and at the union conference of November
1909 he argued that 'it was folly to fight seats where there was
no hope and might assist in jeopardising other seats'.[2] He
named no names, but the implication was that Leigh counted
as hopeless, and if the Liberals there were offended his own
seat, Ince, might be endangered. And as the campaign
developed it became clear that neither of the L.C.M.F.'s
sitting Members, Walsh and Twist, had any intention of
lifting a finger to help Greenall in Leigh. Despite angry
charges that they were deliberately undermining the
chances of a fellow miner in return for Liberal help in their
own constituencies, both remained quite unrepentant, and
pointedly ignored a conference resolution instructing them
to speak in support of Greenall in Leigh. The upshot of all
this was that Walsh and Glover held Ince and St. Helens,

[1] *Yorkshire Post*, 10 Dec. 1909; *Manchester Guardian*, 10 Dec. 1909.
[2] *LCMF*, 27 Nov. 1909.

Twist and Sutton gained Wigan and East Manchester, and the unfortunate Greenall finished last of three in Leigh with only 24 per cent of the vote, a good part of which was thought to have come from the large body of cotton-workers in the division rather than from the miners who constituted over half the electorate.

Like a good many other unions in the course of 1910 the L.C.M.F. felt the consequences of the Osborne judgement when one of its members secured an injunction against it restraining it from using its funds for political purposes. For a union that was as politically active and militant as the L.C.M.F. this was a particularly damaging blow, and after an initial burst of indignation amongst the members, during which even the prudent Stephen Walsh advocated defiance, a more ingenious way of evading the law was devised. A new organization called the 'Lancashire and Cheshire Miners' Association' was set up, to which as many miners as could be persuaded to do so were to continue to pay the political levy.[1] This Association remained in existence until the 1913 Trade Union Act legalized political expenditure, though how successful it was in wheedling subscriptions out of the miners is hard to say. Some branches apparently never contributed a penny; on the other hand, by 1914 the Association had an accumulated fund large enough to enable the Lancashire miners to think of running one of their parliamentary candidates without any financial assistance from the M.F.G.B.

At the December election of 1910 the L.C.M.F. suffered a number of setbacks. Twist and Glover were defeated in Wigan and St. Helens, and Labour lost a third mining seat when Seddon was beaten in Newton. The Lancashire miners, however, were not easily disheartened, and in 1911 it was decided that at the next general election Twist should try to win back Wigan and that Greenall should again contest Leigh. With Walsh and Sutton defending Ince and East Manchester, the L.C.M.F. was thus committed to fighting four seats by the outbreak of war in 1914, and, if their previous record is any guide, far from reducing their list they might well have added to it.

[1] Ibid., 17 Sept. 1910.

A hundred miles to the north of Lancashire lay the isolated Cumberland coalfield. Most of the 10,000 miners here were concentrated in the Whitehaven and Cockermouth constituencies, and it seems that as in Lancashire the Conservatives had a stronger following than in most mining areas. In Whitehaven, at the last open election in 1868—before the days of the secret ballot—the miners were said to have voted Conservative almost to a man. Indeed, between 1885 and 1906 the Liberals won Whitehaven only once at the general election of 1892, and it may well have been that in the latter part of the nineteenth century many of the miners were still inclined to take their lead from the Lowthers, one of the great Conservative families in the north-west, who owned many of the collieries in the district. Andrew Sharp, the General Secretary of the Cumberland Miners' Association, was himself a Liberal, but, as a contemporary observer put it, 'as his Association contains men of all shades of opinion, [he holds] that he has no right to cast his influence on the side of either of the great political parties'.[1] Perhaps it was because the Cumberland miners were not so firmly committed to the Liberal Party as they were elsewhere that the I.L.P. was able to make such rapid headway in the county. By 1910 there were at least thirteen active and flourishing I.L.P. branches in this tiny coalfield, and, because it was situated on the route between two strongly socialist areas like Clydeside and Lancashire, the local leadership was often able to persuade prominent national figures to break their journey and address a meeting or two.[2]

The first Labour candidature in the Cumberland coalfield, however, foundered badly upon the sectional jealousies of the local trade unions. On the death of the Liberal Member for Cockermouth, in July 1906, the Cumberland miners proposed to run Andrew Sharp as a Lib-Lab under the terms of the M.F.G.B. scheme. Most of the other trade unionists in the constituency preferred Robert Smillie, who

---

[1] W. Hallam, *Miners' Leaders*, 1894, p. 86.

[2] Jim Middleton, the Assistant Secretary of the Labour Party, was himself a native of Workington, and from his London vantage-point he took a specially benevolent interest in the fortunes of the Labour Party in Cumberland.

of course was also a miner, but who could not stand or be paid for as an official Federation candidate outside Scotland, his own district. Seeing that they already contributed to the M.F.G.B. political fund, the Cumberland miners were unwilling to put their hands in their pockets again to help some other miner whom the rest of the local Labour organizations happened to fancy more than their General Secretary, and eventually their delegates walked out of the selection conference in a rage. The Cumberland Miners' Association then proceeded to give its blessing to the new Liberal candidate, and the result was that Smillie finished a poor third in the by-election.[1]

By 1909 this petty feud had petered out, and at the first general election of 1910 all the Whitehaven trade unionists felt able to unite behind Andrew Sharp, standing this time as a straight Labour candidate for the borough seat. Even so, he finished at the bottom of the poll, as did J. P. Whitehead of the steel-smelters, the Labour candidate who had succeeded Smillie in Cockermouth. Both seats went to the Conservatives on minority votes, and the signs are that by the time of the second election of 1910 the Labour Party and the Liberals had reached a tacit understanding over Whitehaven and Cockermouth. When it had been established that Sharp was going to fight Whitehaven once more, the national executive committee of the Labour Party strongly advised the local organizations in Cockermouth not to contest the seat again;[2] and on the other side, after a deputation from the Whitehaven Liberal Association had talked over the situation at the Whips' office in London, the Whitehaven Liberals not only decided against running a candidate of their own but also joined forces with the local Labour Party.[3] It was a surprising gesture because by this time Andrew Sharp, the ex-Liberal, was no longer in the field, and in his place, prompted by the Labour Party national executive, the Whitehaven L.R.C. had adopted Tom Richardson, a Durham miner and a well-known member of the I.L.P. The arrangement, if arrangement

[1] *Whitehaven Free Press* and *Whitehaven News*, July 1906.
[2] *LPEC*, 13 Apr. 1910.
[3] *Whitehaven Free Press*, 3 Dec. 1910.

there was, worked admirably. Richardson, with Liberal votes and Liberal assistance, won Whitehaven for Labour; and the Liberals, in the absence of Labour opposition, were successful in Cockermouth.

(iii) SCOTLAND

By contrast with the situation in England and Wales, the Socialists in the Scottish coalfields were able to dominate most of the miners' unions from their very inception. Indeed, most of the county and district unions that came into existence in the 1880s and 1890s in Scotland were actually founded by Socialists like Keir Hardie, Robert Smillie, R. Chisholm Robertson, William Small, and Robert Brown. Only on the east coast, in Fife, was there an older-established county union, led by a prominent and respectable Lib-Lab in the person of its General Secretary, J. G. Weir. In the western and central coalfields, in Ayrshire, Lanarkshire, and the Lothians, it had always been difficult to build up strong unions, mainly because of the continuing influx of Irish labourers, who were notoriously difficult to organize.[1] So slow was the growth of effective trade unionism that of the 70,000 Scots miners idle in the great strike of 1894 only 30,000 were union members, and in Lanarkshire, the most thickly populated and fastest growing of all the mining districts in Scotland, it was not until 1896 that a single county-wide union was set up.[2] To the early Socialists this state of affairs was both a challenge and a stimulus: finding themselves at the head of unstable and ineffective local unions they turned all the more readily to political action to offset their industrial weakness. When the strike of 1894 collapsed in defeat Keir Hardie, writing in the *Labour Leader*, promptly pointed the moral: they must be prepared to carry the fight against the employers into the political field. 'It is foolish', he wrote, 'to form a union to fight the coalmasters and then send one of these masters or his friend

[1] See Robert Haddow, 'The Miners of Scotland', *Nineteenth Century*, vol. xxiv, Sept. 1888; A. J. Youngson Brown, 'Trade Union Policy in the Scots Coalfields, 1855–1885', *Econ. Hist. Review*, vol. vi, 1953.
[2] R. Page Arnot, *A History of the Scottish Miners*, 1955, pp. 70 and 76.

to make laws for you. The class which makes the laws can do as it pleases. . . .'[1]

Parliamentary representation for the working class did not necessarily mean setting up a new political party. Some of the more important of the miners' unions in England and Wales had had representatives at Westminster ever since 1885 and had managed to work quite successfully with the Liberals. But co-operation of this kind was never really possible in Scotland, for, although in some respects the Scottish Liberal Party was more politically radical than its English counterpart, there was an almost unbridgeable social gulf between most of the local Liberal Associations and the typical working-class trade unionist. Nor was there much incentive for the Scottish Liberals to pocket their pride and work with the miners in their own self-interest, as the Lancashire Liberals did when they frequently made way for or supported miners' candidates on the grounds that a trade union nominee stood a better chance of defeating the Conservative. In Scotland the Liberals felt, with some justification, that they could do without the help of the miners, especially as they were so ill organized, and it is noticeable that when Herbert Gladstone and Ramsay MacDonald came to hatch their celebrated electoral plot in 1903 there was little that they could do to avoid Liberal-versus-Labour contests in Scotland.[2]

A weak trade union movement, in combination with Liberal hostility, provided the I.L.P. with the ideal spring-board, and in the years before 1914 the Scots miners displayed a zeal in running parliamentary candidates that was all the more remarkable in view of their almost total lack of success. In his pioneering contest in Mid Lanark in 1888 Keir Hardie polled only 617 votes out of a total of over 7,000, and in 1894, fighting the same seat at another by-election, Robert Smillie was able to push the Labour vote up to only 1,221 out of nearly 9,000 votes cast. In 1892 Chisholm Robertson had fared even worse in Stirlingshire

---

[1] Page Arnot, op. cit., p. 88.

[2] In March 1904 the Scottish Liberals did make a half-hearted attempt to avoid three-cornered contests by setting up a Conciliation Committee to look into disputes between the Liberal and Labour Parties. By June 1905 it had not met once. *Scottish Liberal Association Minutes*, 30 Mar. 1904 and 29 June 1905.

with a miserable 663 votes out of over 10,000. When the miners switched their attention to North-East Lanarkshire after the turn of the century they did a little better, Smillie polling 2,900 votes out of just over 13,000 in a by-election in 1901, and J. Robertson increasing this figure to 3,984 votes out of about 14,000 at another by-election in 1904. In every case the miners found themselves with Liberal opponents, and in every case their candidate was a bad third. Naturally enough, when the M.F.G.B. launched its national scheme for securing more parliamentary representation, the Scots miners responded with great enthusiasm, and at the general election of 1906 they contested no less than five seats, more than any other miners' union in the country. On this occasion their candidates were D. Gilmour in Falkirk Burghs, J. Robertson in North-East Lanarkshire, J. Sullivan in North-West Lanarkshire, J. Brown in North Ayrshire, and Robert Smillie in Paisley (which was by no stretch of the imagination a mining seat); all of them again faced Liberal opponents, and as usual all of them finished bottom of the poll.

Why was it that the Scots miners were able to achieve so little in terms of parliamentary representation? Over most of the coalfield the Liberals and the union leaders disliked each other so heartily that any form of co-operation was unthinkable, and therefore the possibility of Lib-Lab miners' M.P.s on the English model simply did not arise. In Fife, where there had been talk of a miners' candidate ever since 1889, there was an outside chance that the local Liberals might have supported J. G. Weir had the miners pressed their claim hard enough. But they were so half-hearted and divided amongst themselves that when the West Fife seat fell vacant before the general election of 1900 the Liberals were easily able to push in their own man.[1] So there was no Scottish Mabon, Ben Pickard, or John Wilson. If the Scottish Miners' Federation was going to win seats it had to fight the Liberals for them, and what slender hopes there were of electing a miner in opposition to a Liberal at this stage were ruined by religious and racial divisions in the coalfield. Almost all the industrial constituencies in western and

---

[1] *Dunfermline Press,* 11 Aug. 1900.

central Scotland contained large numbers of Irish Catholics, and for most of them Home Rule for Ireland was more important than parliamentary representation for the working class.[1] Anything that might split the Home Rule vote was to be discouraged, and if there were two Home Rule candidates in the field, one Liberal and one Labour, the natural tendency was to support whichever of them seemed to have the better chance. At this stage it was not often the Labour candidate who appeared to be the more likely winner. In consequence, provided that the Liberal candidate was sound on Home Rule, any miners' nominee was likely to find the Irish vote ranged against him. On occasions, as at the North-East Lanarkshire by-election in 1901 and in North-West Lanarkshire at the general election of 1906, the Irish were officially advised to vote Labour; but more often than not it was the Liberals who enjoyed the blessing of the United Irish League. As if this was not bad enough, the position was further complicated by the presence among the Lanarkshire and Ayrshire miners of a sizeable body of immigrant Orangemen from Ulster, who reinforced the much older Covenanting tradition of militant Protestantism in the two counties.[2] Their natural allegiance was to the Unionist Party, pledged as it was to saving Ulster from Catholic rule, and for them too Labour representation in Parliament came second.[3] In Lancashire the Labour Party was able to turn political divisions within the working class to its own advantage; over most of the Scottish coalfield deep-seated religious fears and animosities served only to confirm thousands of miners in their loyalty to the two major parties. It was not surprising that Labour candidates found the going heavy.

Yet, whatever the outcome of parliamentary elections, there was clearly a great deal of sympathy for the Labour

[1] Religion sometimes produced unexpected difficulties for Labour leaders in the west of Scotland. On one occasion Keir Hardie, who should have known better, introduced Alexander MacDonald (one of the first two working men to sit in Parliament) to an audience of Lanarkshire miners and compared his work to that of Martin Luther. Two-thirds of the miners were Irish Roman Catholics and the meeting ended in a riot. W. Stewart, *J. Keir Hardie*, 1921, p. 11.

[2] *The Third Statistical Account of Scotland*, vol. i (Ayrshire), 1951, pp. 40–1, and 254; and vol. viii (Lanarkshire), 1960, p. 127.

[3] See, for example, R. Smillie, *My Life for Labour*, 1924, p. 110.

Party amongst the rank and file. In the two ballots organized by the M.F.G.B. in 1906 and 1908 on the question of joining the Labour Party the Scottish miners came out quite decisively in favour of affiliation, by 17,801 votes to 12,376 on the first occasion, and by 32,112 votes to 25,823 on the second. The problem was to turn general sympathy into support for particular Labour candidates, and, though the difficulties in Scotland were formidable, in 1910 the Scottish Miners' Federation gamely returned to the attack. Once again five candidates were sponsored, this time in West Fife, North Ayrshire, North-East Lanarkshire, North-West Lanarkshire, and Mid Lanarkshire. In West Fife Willie Adamson (who had succeeded Weir as Secretary of the Fife Miners' Association in 1908) did reasonably well and managed to push the Unionist into third place. But everywhere else the results were disappointing. Smillie was at the bottom of the poll in Mid Lanarkshire, and in the other three constituencies the Labour share of the vote was actually down by comparison with 1906. Before the December election of 1910 the Scottish Miners' Federation decided to concentrate on West Fife and Mid Lanarkshire, and, though Smillie, as usual, was beaten in the latter constituency, Adamson at long last won a seat for the Scottish miners in West Fife, in spiet of the usual opposition from the Liberals.

West Fife was the first and only seat that the Scottish Miners' Federation was to capture before 1914. But they certainly showed no lack of persistence, and more often than not when a mining seat fell vacant they doggedly fought the by-election. In 1911 they contested North-East Lanarkshire, James Robertson finishing last in a three-cornered contest. In 1912 a peerage was conferred on the Master of Elibank, and at the subsequent by-election Robert Brown was put up for Midlothian; predictably enough he was a poor third, but at least the miners could draw some satisfaction from depriving the Liberals of enough votes to turn W. E. Gladstone's old seat over to the Unionists; and in 1913 the union broke new ground when Tom Gibb contested South Lanarkshire, finishing last of three, it need hardly be added. Not discouraged by this unparalleled record of defeat, in the spring of 1914 the Scots miners had plans to run no less than six candidates at the forthcoming election. However, when the M.F.G.B. decided to restrict the number of official candidates it was prepared to finance in Scotland to three, the union settled for West Fife, North-East Lanarkshire, and Midlothian, with Adamson, Robertson, and Robert Brown as its nominees.[1]

[1] *Glasgow Herald,* 11 June 1914.

APPENDIX

(i) *The mining vote* c. *1910*

	Constituency	Electorate	Estimated no. of miner voters	Miners as per cent of total vote
Durham	NW. Durham	18,361	11,280	61
	Mid Durham	15,832	9,550	60
	Houghton-le-Spring	17,504	9,930	56
	Chester-le-Street	23,906	13,160	55
	Bishop Auckland	14,552	5,570	38
	SE. Durham	18,880	7,070	37
	Barnard Castle	12,212	4,220	34
	Jarrow	18,292	4,790	26
	Borough constituencies calculated from 1911 census:			
	Durham City	2,698	535	19
	Sunderland	29,071	5,450	18
	South Shields	18,709	2,810	15
	Gateshead	19,373	2,200	11
Northumberland	Wansbeck	18,959	12,060	63
	Morpeth	10,070	4,310	42
	Tyneside	25,667	5,560	21
	Hexham	11,151	1,540	13
Lancashire	Leigh	14,150	7,720	54
	Newton	14,803	6,950	46
	St. Helens	13,068	3,950	27
	Ince	14,283	3,070	21
	Chorley	14,347	2,500	17
	Eccles	18,786	2,260	12
	Ashton-under-Lyne	8,595	1,080	12
	Radcliffe	14,046	1,560	11
	Borough constituency calculated from 1911 census:			
	Wigan	9,662	5,170	53
Cumberland	Cockermouth	11,328	2,130	18
	Borough constituency calculated from 1911 census:			
	Whitehaven	3,050	920	32
Scotland	West Fife	17,267	10,040	58
	West Lothian	11,810	4,260	36
	NE. Lanarkshire	21,811	7,500	34
	Mid Lanarkshire	17,803	6,140	34
	Midlothian	17,141	4,630	27
	Falkirk Burghs	12,889	3,370	26
	South Ayrshire	18,272	4,090	22
	South Lanarkshire	10,618	2,260	21
	Stirlingshire	20,144	4,220	20
	East Lothian	7,961	1,430	17
	NW. Lanarkshire	20,274	2,660	13
	North Ayrshire	16,458	2,030	12

(ii) *Election results, 1906–14: miners' candidates are in italic*

Durham

	1906	1910 (January)	1910 (December)
NW. Durham	L. Atherley-Jones (L) 9,146 Sir R. M. Filmer (C) 3,992	L. Atherley-Jones (L) 10,497 J. Knott (U) 5,227 By-election, 1914: A. Williams (L) 7,241 J. O. Hardicker (U) 5,564 G. H. Stuart (Lab.) 5,026	L. Atherley-Jones (L) 8,998 J. O. Hardicker (U) 4,827
Mid Durham	*J. Wilson* (L-L)	*J. Wilson* (L-L)	*J. Wilson* (L-L)
Houghton-le-Spring	R. Cameron (L) 9,429 R. V. Williams (LU) 3,639	R. Cameron (L) 10,393 H. Streatfeild (U) 4,382 By-election, 1913: T. Wing (L) 6,930 T. Richardson (U) 4,807 *W. House* (Lab.) 4,165	R. Cameron (L)
Chester-le-Street	*J. W. Taylor* (Lab.) 8,085 S. D. Shafto (C) 4,895 A. B. Tebb (L) 4,606	*J. W. Taylor* (Lab.) 12,684 A. D. Shafto (U) 6,891	*J. W. Taylor* (Lab.)
Bishop Auckland	J. M. Paulton (L) 7,430 G. E. Markham (C) 3,956	Sir H. Havelock-Allan (L) 5,391 Sir W. C. Chaytor (U) 3,841 *W. House* (Lab.) 3,579	Sir H. Havelock-Allan (L) 4,531 *W. House* (Lab.) 3,993 G. E. Markham (U) 3,519
SE. Durham	F. W. Lambton (LU)	E. Hayward (L) 9,298 F. W. Lambton (U) 6,860	E. Hayward (L) 8,203 R. Burdon (U) 7,021
Barnard Castle	*A. Henderson* (Lab.) 5,540 E. Bell (C) 3,888	*A. Henderson* (Lab.) 6,136 H. G. Stobart (C) 4,646	*A. Henderson* (Lab.) 5,868 H. G. Stobart (U) 4,423

H

(ii) Election results, 1906–14; miners' candidates are in italic (cont.)

	1906	1910 (January)	1910 (December)
Durham (cont.)			
Jarrow	Sir C. M. Palmer (L) 8,047 P. Curran (Lab.) 5,093	G. M. Palmer (L) 4,885 P. Curran (Lab.) 4,818 J. Kirkley (U) 4,668 By-election, 1907: P. Curran (Lab.) 4,698 P. Rose-Innes (C) 3,930 S. L. Hughes (L) 3,474 J. O'Hanlon (N) 2,122	G. M. Palmer (L) 5,097 J. Kirkley (U) 4,986 A. G. Cameron (Lab.) 4,892
Durham City	J. W. Hills (C) 1,313 A. R. D. Elliot (LU) 880	J. W. Hills (U)	J. W. Hills (U) 1,313 C. A. Cochrane (L) 877
Sunderland (two members)	J. Stuart (L) 13,620 T. Summerbell (Lab.) 13,430 D. H. Haggie (C) 7,879 J. S. Pemberton (C) 7,244	S. Storey (U) 12,334 J. Knott (U) 12,270 J. Stuart (L) 11,529 T. Summerbell (Lab.) 11,058	H. Greenwood (L) 11,997 F. Goldstone (Lab.) 11,291 W. Joynson-Hicks (U) 10,300 S. Samuel (U) 10,132
South Shields	Sir W. S. Robson (L) 9,717 A. R. Chamberlayne (C) 3431	Sir W. S. Robson (L) 9,090 R. Vaughan-Williams (U) 4,854	R. Rea (L)
Northumberland			
Wansbeck	*C. Fenwick* (L-L) 10,836 W. Riddell (C) 3,210	*C. Fenwick* (L-L) 10,872 C. Percy (U) 4,650	*C. Fenwick* (L-L)
Morpeth	*T. Burt* (L-L) 5,518 S. Coats (LU) 1,919	*T. Burt* (L-L) 5,874 J. Ridley (U) 3,009	*T. Burt* (L-L)

	1906	1910 (January)	1910 (December)
Tyneside	J. M. Robertson (L) 11,496 J. Knott (C) 6,885	J. M. Robertson (L) 13,158 A. H. Cochrane (U) 7,807	J. M. Robertson (L) 11,693 H. M. Robertson (U) 6,857
Hexham	W. C. Beaumont (L) 5,632 S. Clayton (C) 3,547 By-election, 1907: R. D. Holt (L) 5,401 C. L. Bates (C) 4,244	R. D. Holt (L) 5,478 C. L. Bates (C) 4,417	R. D. Holt (L) 5,124 A. H. Chaytor (U) 4,334
Lancashire			
Leigh	J. F. L. Brunner (L) 7,175 D. Macmaster (C) 5,169	P. Raffan (L) 5,325 F. C. Smith (U) 4,646 T. Greenall (Lab.) 3,268	P. Raffan (L) 6,790 W. T. Oversby (U) 5,507
Newton	J. A. Seddon (Lab.) 6,434 R. Pilkington (C) 5,893	J. A. Seddon (Lab.) 7,256 Viscount Wolmer (U) 6,504	Viscount Wolmer (U) 6,706 J. A. Seddon (Lab.) 6,562
St. Helens	*T. Glover* (Lab.) 6,088 Sir H. Seton Karr (C) 4,647	*T. Glover* (Lab.) 6,512 R. Swift 5,717	R. Swift (U) 6,016 *T. Glover* (Lab.) 5,752
Ince	*S. Walsh* (Lab.) 8,046 H. Blundell (C) 3,410	*S. Walsh* (Lab.) 7,723 W. G. Lord (U) 5,029	*S. Walsh* (Lab.) 7,117 W. G. Lord (U) 5,332
Chorley	Lord Balcarres (C) 6,803 E. C. Williams (L) 5,416	Lord Balcarres (U) 7,735 W. L. Blease (L) 5,523	Lord Balcarres (U) 7,423 J. P. T. Jackson (U) 4,887
Eccles	G. H. Pollard (L) 5,841 T. Stuttard (C) 5,246 B. Tillett (Lab.) 3,985	Sir G. H. Pollard (L) 7,090 G. F. Assinder (U) 6,682 G. H. Stuart (Lab.) 3,511	Sir G. H. Pollard (L) 8,467 J. G. D. Campbell (U) 7,676

(ii) *Election results, 1906–14; miners' candidates are in italic (cont.)*

	1906	1910 (January)	1910 (December)
Lancashire (cont.)			
Ashton-under-Lyne	A. H. Scott (L) 4,310 H. Whiteley (C) 3,342	A. H. Scott (L) 4,039 H. Whiteley (U) 3,746 W. Gee (Soc.) 413	W. M. Aitken (U) 4,044 A. H. Scott (L) 3,848
Radcliffe-cum-Farnworth	T. C. Taylor (L) 6,719 S. Musgrave (C) 5,117	T. C. Taylor (L) 7,367 E. White (U) 5,827	T. C. Taylor (L) 6,721 E. A. Bagley (U) 5,937
Wigan	Sir F. S. Powell (C) 3,573 T. Smith (Ind. Lab.) 2,205 W. Woods (L) 1,900	*H. Twist* (Lab.) 4,803 R. J. Neville (U) 4,293	R. J. Neville (U) 4,673 *H. Twist* (Lab.) 4,110
Cumberland			
Whitehaven	W. J. Burnyeat (L) 1,507 J. Robertson-Walker (C) 1,194	J. A. Jackson (U) 1,188 W. H. Wandless (L) 852 *A. Sharp* (Lab.) 825	*T. Richardson* (Lab.) 1,414 J. A. Jackson (U) 1,220
Cockermouth	Sir W. Lawson (L) 5,349 Sir J. S. Randles (C) 4,786 By-election, 1906:	Sir J. S. Randles (U) 4,579 Sir W. Lawson (L) 3,638 J. P. Whitehead (Lab.) 1,909	Sir W. Lawson (L) 5,003 Sir J. S. Randles (U) 4,492
	J. S. Randles (U) 4,593 F. Guest (L) 3,903 *R. Smillie* (Lab.) 1,436		
Scotland			
West Fife	J. D. Hope (L) 6,692 N. B. Constable (C) 1,776	J. D. Hope (L) 6,159 *W. Adamson* (Lab.) 4,736 G. W. Ralston (U) 1,994	*W. Adamson* (Lab.) 6,128 J. D. Hope (L) 5,425

	1906	1910 (January)	1910 (December)
West Lothian	A. Ure (L) 5,282 P. Rose-Innes (C) 2,761 By-election, 1913: J. W. Pratt (L) 5,615 J. Kidd (U) 5,094	A. Ure (L) 6,451 W. C. Smith (U) 3,536	A. Ure (L) 5,835 J. Kidd (U) 3,765
NE. Lanarkshire	A. Findlay (L) 6,436 H. F. Elliot (LU) 4,838 *F. Robertson* (Lab.) 4,658 By-election, 1911: J. D. Millar (L) 7,976 P. Goff (U) 6,776 *F. Robertson* (Lab.) 2,876	T. F. Wilson (L) 9,105 J. R. Wilson (U) 7,012 *F. Sullivan* (Lab.) 2,160	T. F. Wilson (L) 9,848 J. Boyd-Carpenter (U) 7,142
Mid Lanarkshire	J. Caldwell (L) 7,246 D. F. Campbell (C) 4,470 A. S. Gibson (Lab.) 758	J. H. Whitehouse (L) 5,792 J. J. Pickering (U) 5,401 *R. Smillie* (Lab.) 3,864	J. H. Whitehouse (L) 6,033 H. S. Keith (U) 5,702 *R. Smillie* (Lab.) 3,847
Midlothian	Lord Dalmeny (L) 8,348 F. J. Usher (C) 5,131 By-election, 1912: J. A. Hope (U) 6,021 A. Shaw (L) 5,989 *R. Brown* (Lab.) 2,413	Master of Elibank (L) 9,062 M. W. Elphinstone (U) 5,427	Master of Elibank (L) 8,837 J. A. Hope (U) 5,680
Falkirk Burghs	J. A. M. Macdonald (L) 5,158 H. Keith (C) 3,176 *D. Gilmour* (Lab.) 1,763	J. A. M. Macdonald (L) 6,524 H. Keith (U) 4,375	J. A. M. Macdonald (L) 6,276 D. H. L. Young (U) 4,245
South Ayrshire	W. P. Beale (L) 7,852 J. J. Bell (C) 6,611	W. P. Beale (L) 8,833 T. W. McIntyre (U) 6,793	W. P. Beale (L) 8,715 T. W. McIntyre (U) 6,835

(ii) *Election results, 1906–14; miners' candidates are in italic (cont.)*

	1906		1910 (January)		1910 (December)	
Scotland (cont.)						
South Lanarkshire	Sir W. Menzies (L)	4,816	Sir W. Menzies (L)	5,346	Sir W. Menzies (L)	5,160
	J. D. Mitchell (C)	3,541	J. D. Mitchell (U)	3,715	C. M. Douglas (U)	3,963
	By-election, 1913:		W. Watson (U)	4,257		
			G. Morton (L)	4,006		
			T. Gibb (Lab.)	1,674		
Stirlingshire	D. M. Smeaton (L)	9,475	A. Chapple (L)	10,122	A. Chapple (L)	9,183
	Marquis of Graham (C)	5,806	R. S. Horne (U)	6,417	R. S. Horne (U)	6,487
East Lothian	R. B. Haldane (L)	3,469	R. B. Haldane (L)	3,771	R. B. Haldane (L)	3,845
	G. Craig Sellar (LU)	2,289	B. H. Blyth (U)	3,026	B. H. Blyth (U)	3,158
			By-election, 1911: J. D. Hope (L)	3,652		
			B. H. Blyth (U)	3,184		
NW. Lanarkshire	W. M. Thomson (C)	5,588	W. M. R. Pringle (L)	8,442	W. M. R. Pringle (L)	9,315
	C. M. Douglas (L)	4,913	W. M. Thomson (U)	7,528	A. S. Pringle (U)	8,486
	J. Sullivan (Lab.)	3,291	*R. Small (Lab.)*	1,718		
North Ayrshire	T. H. Cochrane (LU)	5,603	A. M. Anderson (L)	6,189	A. M. Anderson (L)	7,286
	A. M. Anderson (L)	4,587	T. H. Cochrane (LU)	5,951	D. F. Campbell (U)	6,932
	J. Brown (Lab.)	2,684	*J. Brown (Lab.)*	1,801		
			By-election, 1911: D. F. Campbell (U)	7,318		
			A. M. Anderson (L)	7,047		

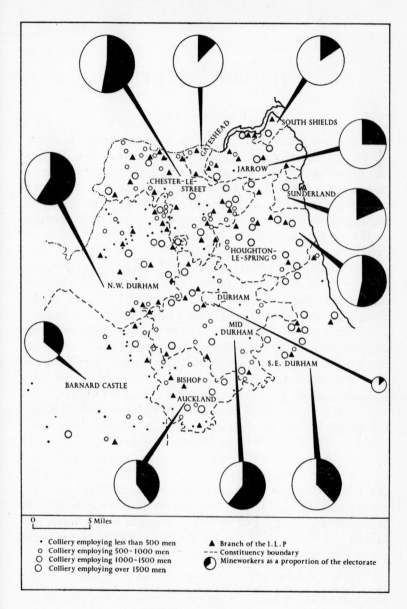

The Durham coalfield *c.* 1910

VI

THE SLOW STARTERS

(i) YORKSHIRE

IN the Yorkshire coalfield there were no early successes for the Socialists; indeed, until the turn of the century almost everything was against them. It was a prosperous and rapidly expanding district,[1] and, because it produced mainly for domestic consumption, earnings were relatively stable and not subject to the violent fluctuations that occurred in the exporting districts. There were no fiercer or more determined opponents of Socialism than Ben Pickard, Ned Cowey, and John Frith, the powerful Lib-Labs who dominated the Y.M.A. in the 1890s, and unlike their counterparts in the North-East, the old school of Lib-Labs in the Federated area had left the I.L.P. no convenient economic levers with which to undermine their political authority. For districts like Yorkshire, which did not compete in overseas markets, a wage-floor and a statutory eight-hour day were desirable and practicable objectives, and the M.F.G.B. had been vigorously pursuing them ever since its foundation in 1889. In adopting these aims the Lib-Labs in Yorkshire and the other Federated districts had appropriated just those items in the Socialist programme that had most popular appeal, and quite unintentionally and unconsciously had succeeded in 'dishing the Socialists'. In the circumstances, the I.L.P.'s failure to break out into the coalfield from its strongholds in the textile districts of the West Riding is scarcely surprising.[2] For twenty years after the Reform Act of 1885 the loyalty of the Yorkshire miners to the Liberal Party remained unshaken and unshakeable.

---

[1] In 1889 there were about 70,000 miners employed in South Yorkshire; by 1914 there were over 164,000, an increase of 133 per cent. Only the relatively unimportant Warwickshire coalfield exceeded this rate of growth. See Finlay Gibson, op. cit., p. 22; and Rowe, op. cit., p. 14.

[2] For I.L.P. activity in the textile areas see E. P. Thompson, 'Homage to Tom Maguire', in *Essays in Labour History*, ed. Asa Briggs and John Saville, 1960.

Yet from about 1900 onwards the mood did begin to change, and now the growing antagonism between capital and labour was brought home to the Yorkshire miners by events in their own backyard. Beginning in 1902 as a comparatively innocuous dispute over payment for bag-dirt at the Denaby and Cadeby Main collieries in the shadow of Conisbrough Castle, there developed a prolonged and bitter struggle between the Yorkshire Miners' Association and the Denaby Colliery Company. There was a strike, miners were evicted from their company-owned houses, and the owners secured an injunction preventing the union from distributing strike pay. The strike itself ended in 1903. But, when the company went on to sue the union for £150,000 for losses incurred as a result of the stoppage, the leaders of the Y.M.A. could only conclude that they were dealing with a vindictive set of owners who were intent on crushing the union.[1] In fact, at the Y.M.A.'s annual demonstration in 1906, one of the miners' agents claimed to be in possession of letters from the Denaby Colliery Company to other companies in Yorkshire urging them to pursue a similarly aggressive policy with the object of reducing the Yorkshire miners in a year or two to an 'undisciplined mob'.[2] In the previous autumn there had been more evictions at Hemsworth near Barnsley, when, after a lock-out lasting nearly a year, the miners and their families had been turned out of their homes and obliged to live under canvas. And by this time the leadership of the Y.M.A. had also undergone a change, for in the three months from December 1903 to February 1904 Pickard, Cowey, and Frith had all died, and, though their successors, John Wadsworth, Fred Hall, and John Dixon, were Lib-Labs, they wielded nothing like the authority of the men they replaced. A rising new I.L.P. man named Herbert Smith had also appeared on the scene, though his interest in politics never matched his industrial militancy.[3]

[1] Bealey and Pelling, op. cit., pp. 223-4.
[2] YMA, June 1906.
[3] See J. J. Lawson, *The Man in the Cap: the Life of Herbert Smith*, 1941, p. 252. For Smith the solidarity and cohesion of the union outweighed any kind of political consideration. At the time of the general election of 1906, for example, he put his name to a circular repudiating I.L.P. criticisms of Wadsworth's Lib-Lab candidature in Hallamshire; and as late as 1914 he was still rebuking a young Socialist,

With the climate becoming more favourable, the number of I.L.P. branches in the Yorkshire coalfield began to grow; seven were set up in the course of 1904,[1] and by 1906 there was at least one branch in all the more important mining centres. Neither in influence nor in numbers did they ever match the I.L.P. movement in the North-East; nevertheless, one or two branches were so successful in exploiting local grievances that they managed to transform the political climate in their district. The Wombwell miners have gone into the history books as the men who stoned Pete Curran, the I.L.P. candidate, at a by-election in Barnsley in 1897.[2] Ten years later this same district was widely regarded as one of the most militantly left-wing areas in the Yorkshire coalfield, and the secretary of the local I.L.P. was writing to Ramsay MacDonald in 1907:

We have the strongest and most advanced Trade Unions connected with the Y.M.A. in this district. The vote for the Miners' Federation was, in seven collieries, 11,000 men, over 5 to 1 for affiliation with the L.R.C. . . . if you came to Wombwell I could find you the biggest crowd of miners you ever spoke to. It is only because we have prepared the ground for you that we invite you down. If there is one place in Yorkshire where an Organiser is wanted, it's in this Division [Barnsley]. It's the backbone of the Y.M.A. and it seems ripe for the plucking.[3]

Yet, as events were now to show only too clearly, the I.L.P. was still a long way off controlling the political policy of the union. In 1885, under the terms of an electoral pact similar to the arrangements in Durham, the Yorkshire Liberals had agreed to leave Ben Pickard a clear run in Normanton in return for the support of the miners in the rest of the Yorkshire mining constituencies. It was a shrewd bargain for the Liberals, and over the next twenty years with the help of the Y.M.A. they were easily able to retain Barnsley, Osgoldcross, Hallamshire, Rotherham, Morley, and Holmfirth.

Wilfrid Paling, for his intemperate attacks on Wadsworth. (Interview with the Rt. Hon. Wilfrid Paling.)

[1] Bealey and Pelling, op. cit., p. 225.
[2] Page Arnot, op. cit., pp. 300–2; Philip P. Poirier, *The Advent of the Labour Party*, 1958, pp. 69–70.
[3] A. J. Poiner to MacDonald, *LPLF*, Jan. 1907.

But, with the mining vote growing so rapidly, the 1885 agreement had become blatantly inequitable by the end of the century, and in 1902 the union nominated William Parrott for the East Leeds seat. When Pickard died in 1904 the Y.M.A. transferred Parrott to Normanton, and, despite angry protests from the advocates of political independence and the I.L.P. faction in the union, he was duly returned as a Lib-Lab at the subsequent by-election. So far the 1885 pact had emerged unscathed. But the problems of preserving it intact were immensely complicated when the M.F.G.B. adopted its scheme for increased parliamentary representation in 1902, for the terms of the scheme entitled the Yorkshire miners to no less than six candidates.

With Parrott installed in Normanton, in March 1904 the Y.M.A. executive recommended that five more candidates should be selected to be in readiness for any vacancies that might occur at the next general election. At the same time, the officials were instructed to take soundings to see which constituencies were 'likely to be available for working men's representatives'.[1] There was clearly no intention of contesting seats against sitting Liberals: only if a seat fell vacant and the Liberals conceded that it was 'available' would the Y.M.A. put forward a candidate. A month later the five candidates, Herbert Smith, Fred Hall, John Wadsworth, James Walsh, and Stephen Jacks, were selected. At this point there were two seats, Osgoldcross and Hallamshire, where the outlook seemed promising, since in both cases it was known that the Liberal Members did not intend to seek re-election.

In Osgoldcross the miners soon ran into difficulties. As it happened, the local Liberal Association had already invited J. Compton-Rickett, a coal-owner, to be their candidate, and he was certainly not inclined to make way for a miner. To make matters worse, the railwaymen and Goole dockyard workers made it quite plain that under no circumstances would they support a miners' nominee.[2] The Y.M.A. council, however, was determined to put up a fight over this seat, and in November 1904 the Osgoldcross branches were

[1] *YMA*, 7 Mar. 1904.
[2] *Penistone Express*, 12 Nov. 1904.

instructed to go ahead and choose their man, which they did in the summer of 1905, selecting Fred Hall. Hallamshire, on the other hand, looked as though it would prove an easier proposition. Here the choice of the local trade unionists fell upon John Wadsworth, and by the summer of 1905 there were signs that the Liberals might be prepared to give him their support.

The situation was given a new twist by the sudden death of Parrott in November 1905. The vacant Normanton seat was a considerable prize, and the competition for it came to represent something of a trial of strength between the Lib-Labs in the union and their I.L.P. challengers. The contest opened with a procedural victory for the Lib-Labs when all five of the original candidates were declared to be eligible for the nomination, even though Hall and Wadsworth had already been put down for Osgoldcross and Hallamshire. From the outset it was understood that the miners were choosing as much between policies as between men; most of the lodges that were under I.L.P. control lined up behind Smith, whilst the Lib-Lab lodges split their vote between Wadsworth and Hall. When Wadsworth dropped out after the first ballot almost all the lodges which had supported him switched to Hall, giving him a clear majority. As the Lib-Lab nominee of the Y.M.A., Hall was then adopted, with some relief, by the Normanton Liberal Association and was returned unopposed at the subsequent by-election.[1]

Hall's election for Normanton in November 1905 extricated the Lib-Labs from a very awkward position and was an even bigger tactical success for them than it appeared. Before Normanton fell vacant there had been no move on the part of the Y.M.A. to withdraw Hall from Osgoldcross, and in fact during the summer of 1905 he was busy making himself known in the constituency. Since Compton-Rickett, the Liberal, had refused to stand down, there seemed to be every prospect of a three-cornered fight and a breach in the long-standing compact with the Liberals. In the circumstances, the death of the unfortunate Parrott, worn out by anxiety over the Denaby and Cadeby Main case, came as something

[1] See *Leeds and Yorkshire Mercury* and *Wakefield Express*, Nov. 1905.

of a godsend to the Lib-Labs, and Hall was only too pleased
to be transferred to the eminently safe miners' seat of
Normanton.[1]

The significance of the move was not lost on the I.L.P.
faction in the union. According to their version of the affair,
it was Hall himself who had taken the initiative in engineer-
ing his move to Normanton, for by means of this manœuvre
the Lib-Labs not only avoided a clash with the Liberals over
Osgoldcross, but also, to the baffled indignation of the I.L.P.,
ensured that Herbert Smith would not be selected for
Normanton.[2] Had the original arrangements remained intact,
Hall and Wadsworth would have stayed in Osgoldcross and
Hallamshire, and the choice of candidate for Normanton
would have been confined to Smith, Walsh, and Jacks, in
which case Herbert Smith would almost certainly have been
selected. And, since Smith would not have consented to stand
as a Lib-Lab, the Normanton Liberals would probably have
put up a candidate of their own to oppose him.[3] The
abandonment of Osgoldcross averted a double breach with
the Liberals—in Osgoldcross, where Hall would have been
obliged to stand against Compton-Rickett, and Normanton, where Smith might well have found himself with a
Liberal opponent.

At the general election of 1906 every effort on the part of
the I.L.P. to disrupt the alliance between the miners and the
Liberals came to nothing. Attacks on Wadsworth and Hall
served only to rally all the union leaders, including known
L.R.C. sympathizers, behind the Y.M.A.'s two Lib-Lab
candidates. A move to secure an independent Labour candidate to stand against the Liberal coal-owner Joseph Walton

---

[1] See Bealey and Pelling, op. cit., p. 226, where the situation is described somewhat misleadingly. According to this account, Hall, 'whose objections had not been
vigorous enough to prevail', was 'deprived' of his candidature. Far from being
deprived, Hall was only too willing to argue that Osgoldcross should be given up.
There is certainly nothing to suggest that he was aggrieved by this turn of events,
because both in 1906 and for some years afterwards he was to be found speaking on
Compton-Rickett's platform in Osgoldcross.

[2] W. O. Bull, letter to the *Wakefield Express*, 20 Jan. 1906.

[3] This possibility was clearly foreseen in Liberal circles where it was hinted that
the Liberals might have to reconsider the 1885 pact if the Y.M.A. nominated a
candidate who was not prepared to act in the spirit of that agreement. *Leeds and
Yorkshire Mercury*, 20 Nov. 1905.

in the increasingly militant Barnsley division was unsuccessful, and everywhere else in the coalfield co-operation between the Y.M.A. and the Liberals was as smooth and
effective as ever. The Liberal candidate in Morley,
A. E. Hutton, was returned unopposed and devoted much
of his time to speaking for Wadsworth in Hallamshire; Sir
William Holland in Rotherham and Compton-Rickett in
Osgoldcross both had the public support of Wadsworth and
Hall; in the Doncaster division, where the mining vote was
growing by leaps and bounds, C. N. Nicholson, the Liberal
candidate, had the backing of the miners' leaders; and
H. J. Wilson, the Liberal Member for Holmfirth, even held
joint meetings with Wadsworth.

For the moment the Socialists had been worsted and outmanœuvred right along the line. Still, their constant sniping
and growing influence were evidently beginning to alarm the
Lib-Labs, for soon after the 1906 election Y.M.A. officials
took to issuing circulars virulently attacking the I.L.P. and
claiming that its object was to capture the union and dictate
its policies. The fiercest criticisms of all were reserved for
Keir Hardie, who was castigated for his 'impertinent attacks'
on the Y.M.A. The views of the Yorkshire miners' leaders
make odd reading today: 'This man Hardie', one of the
circulars roundly proclaimed, 'is no friend to trade unionism . . . you can depend upon it, Hardie will sell anybody if
he can get a hundred members to join his I.L.P.'[1] Their
fears were well grounded, for in 1906 the Yorkshire miners
voted decisively by 17,389 votes to 12,730 to affiliate to the
Labour Party, and in the following year they invited Philip
Snowden, Will Crooks, Stephen Walsh, and (despite the
views of the officials) Keir Hardie himself to speak at the
annual demonstration, where, it seems, they were given a
far more favourable reception than the Lib-Labs. With
evident satisfaction the *Labour Leader* was able to quote the
words of the political correspondent of the Conservative
Sheffield Daily Telegraph: 'Hitherto, the Y.M.A. has been
the obedient servant of the Liberal Party; it is so no longer.
The I.L.P. has captured it.' In the summer of 1907 this was
certainly an exaggeration; but the first breath of the wind of

[1] *YMA*, Jan. 1906.

change had reached the sensitive and hopeful ears of the Yorkshire Conservatives.

In the next few years the tide continued to run strongly for the Socialists, and in the 1908 ballot on joining the Labour Party the 1906 majority was more than doubled, 32,991 votes being cast in favour of affiliation and 20,793 against. But, for all the progress that it had made, the general election of January 1910 was to show that the I.L.P. was still not quite in a position to control the political policy of the union. Under the M.F.G.B. scheme the Y.M.A. was by now entitled to seven candidates, and naturally the Socialists were insistent that the union should contest its full quota, the more so since all these candidates would now be required to run on the straight Labour ticket. The Lib-Labs, for their part, argued that because of the uncertainties aroused by the Osborne judgement it would be most unwise for the Y.M.A. to extend its parliamentary commitments at this stage.[1] For a while it seemed that their opposition had been swept aside, for in November 1909 the Y.M.A. council decided that Wadsworth and Hall were to defend Hallamshire and Normanton, and that five further candidates, Herbert Smith, James Walsh, William Lunn, Stephen Jacks, and Sam Roebuck, were to contest the additional seats, which would be named at the next meeting of the council in December. Thus, on the eve of the election, the stage seemed to be set for a full-scale clash between the Y.M.A. and the Liberals. Hall and Wadsworth had already been obliged to sign the Labour Party constitution, thereby repudiating their connections with the Normanton and Hallamshire Liberals—though as it happened, since they totally ignored the spirit of the constitution, no particular dispute arose with the Liberals in these two divisions. If the Y.M.A. was going to run five fresh candidates in Yorkshire mining constituencies it could hardly avoid challenging sitting Liberals somewhere; and, even in the unlikely event of Liberal M.P.s being persuaded to make way for miners' nominees, the local Liberal Associations concerned could hardly be expected to welcome with open arms these new candidates, running on the straight Labour ticket, in whose selection they had had no voice at all.

[1] William Lunn, letter to the *Northern Democrat*, Oct. 1909.

The clash never came. When the Y.M.A. council met on 13 December it decided that only the Morley division should be contested, with Herbert Smith as the miners' candidate. The four other candidatures to which the union was entitled were to be abandoned so as to avoid three-cornered fights and, as the resolution put it, 'to be quite certain that the Association and its members should be left at liberty to oppose the House of Lords and support the budget'.[1] The Y.M.A.'s caution is understandable enough. Though the I.L.P. faction claimed that the Lib-Labs were merely using the Osborne case as an excuse for inaction, there is no doubt that the uncertain legal position of the unions was a genuine cause for concern. Furthermore, in the year 1909 all but the most deeply committed Socialists really did see the budget as the most important issue to be decided at the coming election; trade unionists, many of whom had only grudgingly and reluctantly broken with the Liberals, and who were only half convinced of the need for an independent Labour Party, were certainly not prepared to risk presenting the Conservatives with safe Liberal seats simply to gratify I.L.P. purists. An exchange at one of Hall's election meetings catches the prevailing mood:

Hall. I have signed the L.R.C. Constitution and I am standing here this evening as a representative of Labour.
Voice. The platform doesn't look like it.
Hall. Never mind the platform. I want to embrace as far as possible all the Progressive forces not only in Normanton but throughout the country, because this is not a time for us to differ on any matter that may be between us.[2]

Hall and Wadsworth, of course, had good reasons of their own for keeping in the good books of the Liberals. Wadsworth was almost entirely dependent on the Liberals for his election machinery, and at his adoption meeting had thought it wise to assure the Hallamshire Liberal Association that he was still just as sound a Liberal as ever. As a local political correspondent wrote:

The signing of the L.R.C. Constitution means very little in the present state of politics, and so far as the miners' Member for Hallamshire goes, the signing is merely to avoid splitting the Progressives . . . labels cannot change men of the Wadsworth type. The campaign is being conducted just as in 1906.[1]

In Normanton, Hall was probably rather less dependent upon the Liberals, because this had been a miners' seat for twenty years and the miners themselves had more control over the electoral machinery than in Hallamshire. In any case, no difficulty arose, because Hall himself was still perfectly acceptable in the eyes of the local Liberals:

In addition to being the best of the miners' leaders, he is a sound Liberal and although he has accepted the L.R.C. ticket his principles have not changed. The supporters of the Liberal cause in the Division hold him in high esteem and they are confident they could not have a better representative.[2]

It need hardly be said that testimonials of this kind did nothing to endear Wadsworth and Hall to Socialists in Yorkshire, and it was precisely press-cuttings like these, accompanied by furious letters of protest, that were beginning to find their way on to Ramsay MacDonald's desk in London.

If the Y.M.A.'s electoral policy seems to have been excessively timid, it must be remembered that the Labour Party itself was hardly striking a militant posture at this point. Whilst the party leaders were often at pains to deny that there was any general arrangement with the Liberals, they clearly saw no reason to invite trouble unnecessarily; and, as it happened, there were a number of friendly understandings in the West Riding from which the Labour Party stood to gain. In East Leeds the Liberal candidate withdrew and allowed James O'Grady a straight fight with the Conservative; the Attercliffe Liberals agreed to support Joseph Pointer; and in West Bradford the local Liberals were advised by their Association to support Fred Jowett.[3] In the circumstances it is not surprising that the Labour Party executive refused to consider the Doncaster L.R.C.'s request for a candidate, and that even Herbert Smith's candidature

[1] *Sheffield Daily Independent*, 1 Jan. 1910.
[2] *Leeds and Yorkshire Mercury*, 4 Jan. 1910.
[3] See *Yorkshire Observer*, Dec. 1909.

821830 I

in Morley was opposed by Arthur Henderson and Stephen Walsh.[1] It is clear, too, that the Labour Party was putting itself out to avoid embarrassing the Y.M.A. in its dealings with former Liberal allies. In Holmfirth, for example, the local L.R.C. was running William Pickles of the painters' union as an official Labour candidate against H. J. Wilson, a Liberal who had always been sympathetic to the cause of Labour representation. When the Holmfirth L.R.C. asked the Labour Party to bring pressure to bear on the Y.M.A. leaders to support Pickles, the executive flatly refused. And, although the party would not go so far as to allow Wadsworth to hold a joint meeting with Wilson, MacDonald was instructed to tell Wadsworth of this decision in a letter written in a 'friendly and appreciative spirit'.[2]

The two most significant results in the January election were in Holmfirth and Morley, where the miners had the opportunity of choosing between Liberal and Labour candidates. In Holmfirth Pickles could muster only 1,643 votes (as against 6,339 for his Liberal opponent), and it was thought that a good deal of his support had come from the textile workers in the constituency, who were said to be more collectivist in their outlook than the miners.[3] As there were about 3,000 miners in the division well under half of them must have voted for Pickles. And in Morley (where there were about 5,000 miner voters) Herbert Smith, though President of the Y.M.A., could attract only just over 2,000 votes, and by no means all of them would have come from the miners. On this showing, well over half the Yorkshire miners were not yet prepared to support straight Labour candidates in opposition to Liberals, even when, as in Morley, the Labour candidate was one of their own union leaders.

As a result of Smith's unhappy experience in Morley, the Y.M.A. decided to review its electoral policy, and early in 1910 the miners were asked if they wanted the union to contest any further constituencies. The outcome of this ballot, announced in April, was a further set-back to the hopes of Labour supporters: by 28,952 votes to 27,019 the

---

[1] *LPEC*, 2 Dec. 1909, 17 Dec. 1909.   [2] Ibid., 30 Dec. 1909.
[3] *The Times*, 17 June 1912.

Yorkshire miners voted against any additional candidatures.[1] When Keir Hardie spoke at the annual demonstration in June he told the miners that their decision was a disgrace and they ought to be ashamed of it.[2] But it made no difference, and at the second general election of 1910 in December the Y.M.A. merely defended its two seats in Normanton and Hallamshire, and in Hallamshire Wadsworth made no attempt to dispense with the help of his Liberal friends. There can be no doubt that the I.L.P. was far more influential here in Yorkshire than, for example, in Derbyshire or Nottinghamshire; but it had been slow to make an impact on the union, and what momentum it had built up was badly checked by the special circumstances of the 1910 elections.

Yet the I.L.P. was nothing if not resilient and before long the Socialists in the Y.M.A. were reasserting themselves. In June 1911 the union undertook to organize a series of educational meetings, after which there was to be another ballot on the question of further candidatures; the obvious implication of this was that the Y.M.A. was going to try to persuade its members to reverse their earlier verdict. And in the summer of 1912 a by-election in the Holmfirth division provided the occasion for a final and explicit break with the Liberals. When the sitting Liberal announced that he intended to retire, the council of the Y.M.A. voted by an overwhelming majority to put up a miners' candidate, and eventually their choice fell on William Lunn, an avowed Socialist, a member of the I.L.P. since 1893, and one of the hardy pioneers who had supported Pete Curran at the notorious Barnsley by-election in 1897.[3]

The Holmfirth Liberals, apparently still under the impression that the Y.M.A. would co-operate with them,

---

[1] *YMA*, 11 Apr. 1910.

[2] *YMA*, June 1910. In February 1910 the Y.M.A. had also let slip the chance of contesting the Rotherham seat when it fell vacant. The Liberal candidate was J. A. Pease, the former Chief Whip, who had lost his seat at Saffron Walden in the general election in January. The miners' decision not to oppose him led to a good deal of dark talk about an 'arrangement'. See *Rotherham Express*, 24 Sept. 1910.

[3] See Lawson, op. cit., p. 74; and the *Labour Leader*, 12 Apr. 1912, 13 June 1912. According to Beatrice Webb, Lunn was, 'unlike most miners' representatives, sympathetic to and experienced in Labour politics unconnected with mining'. *Diaries, 1912–1914*, 1952 (10 Feb. 1919).

invited the miners to place the name of their nominee on the short-list from which the Liberal Association would choose its next candidate, arguing that since nine-tenths of the Liberal Association's members were working men, the miners' choice would stand at least as good a chance of selection as anyone else. Here was a critical test of the Y.M.A.'s loyalty to the Labour Party, and the Lib-Lab element in the union's executive fought hard to preserve the alliance with the Liberals. But in the end the Y.M.A. curtly informed the Holmfirth Liberal Association that the miners had already chosen their candidate and that it was no business of the Liberals to say whether or not he was suitable. The Liberals thereupon adopted Sidney Arnold and the rupture was complete.[1]

Holmfirth was certainly not a mining constituency in the sense that some of the other Yorkshire county divisions like Osgoldcross, Barnsley, Doncaster, and Rotherham were. The miners were concentrated on the Barnsley side of the constituency and according to contemporary estimates numbered no more than about 3,200 voters, or roughly a quarter of the electorate. At first sight therefore the Y.M.A.'s keen interest in the seat is somewhat odd. But the fact was that there were over 4,000 textile workers in the constituency, and the union may well have been pinning its hopes upon them as much as on the miners, who were said to be far from unanimous in their support for a Labour candidate. Indeed, it soon became clear that a high proportion of the local miners were not prepared to desert their traditional radicalism even out of loyalty to one of their own checkweighmen. Over half of Arnold's nomination papers were signed by miners, and when Arthur Peters, the Labour Party's

---

[1] See *The Times*, 17 June 1912, *Leeds Mercury*, 19 June 1912, *Barnsley Chronicle*, 8 June 1912. It is true, of course, that the Y.M.A. had already found itself in conflict with the Liberals once over the Morley seat in January 1910. Nevertheless, until the Holmfirth by-election, there was no overt and unmistakable repudiation of the long-established electoral pact. As late as April 1912 J. Compton-Rickett, the Liberal Member for Osgoldcross, referring to a rumour that a Labour candidate might be run against him at the next election, pointed out that a number of Labour Members in neighbouring divisions held their seats with Liberal support, and remarked that 'any interference with the general arrangements in this part of Yorkshire might have other results which he could not control'. *Wakefield Express*, 4 Apr. 1912.

national agent, visited the constituency he noted that
'contrary to the usual situation, the rank and file were not
ahead of their leaders, who with one exception were helping
Lunn'.[1] Considering that no organizational or propaganda
work had been done in the constituency since Pickles had
fought the seat in January 1910, and considering that
Arnold had held forty meetings before Lunn even opened his
short pre-election campaign,[2] the Labour Party did as well as
could be expected, doubling its previous vote. If the Holmfirth
by-election had revealed how much remained to be done before
Labour won over the mining vote in its entirety, it had at least
finally severed the Y.M.A. from the Yorkshire Liberals.

There was, of course, a certain amount of disappointment
at the Holmfirth result. But the movement for more parliamentary representation was now in full swing again,— so
much so that at the end of 1913 the Y.M.A. branches voted
to contest an extra seven seats at the next general election. The
pot was now well and truly on the boil again, and in January
1914 it was decided that the union would fight Doncaster,
Rotherham, Wakefield, Morley, Osgoldcross, Holmfirth,
and Barnsley, and that the candidates were to be S. Roebuck,
W. Lunn, J. Guest, I. Burns, E. Hough, T. W. Grundy,
and J. Potts.[3] Under the constitution of the Labour Party
candidates could be selected only at properly convened
meetings of all trade union and Socialist organizations
within each division. Strictly speaking, therefore, the Y.M.A.
could not simply nominate the Labour candidate; it could
only provide a panel from which the final choice could be
made. In practice the numerical strength of the miners in
the mining seats could almost always ensure that the miners'
man was selected, and in any case, provided that the miners'
nominee was prepared to run as a straight Labour candidate,
the other Labour organizations within a constituency were
usually glad enough to be able to draw upon the political
fund of the M.F.G.B. to meet the election expenses.

The Y.M.A.'s decision to make itself responsible for a
total of no less than nine candidates represented such a
sweeping challenge to the Liberals that some of the more

[1] *Labour Leader*, 27 June 1912.
[2] *Leeds Mercury*, 6 June 1912.   [3] *YMA*, 12 Jan. 1914.

sceptical members of the I.L.P. could scarcely bring themselves to believe that the union was not involved in some
devious and discreditable plot with the Liberals designed to
hoodwink the Socialists. According to one of them, Y.M.A.
candidates were to be placed in the field as a 'notice to
trespassers'. Once a miners' nominee had been adopted no
other candidate could be considered; on the eve of the election, so the argument ran, these Y.M.A. candidates would
be withdrawn, but not until it was too late for any other
candidates to come forward.[1] The theory of a Machiavellian
union installing candidates who were never intended to go to
the poll but were there simply to frustrate the Socialists was
certainly ingenious, and, whilst there is nothing to show that it
was based on anything more than imagination, it was an interesting indication of the residuum of suspicion and resentment that remained in the minds of Socialists who for years
had struggled against the Lib-Lab policies of the miners.

In spite of suspicions like these, there was a quick response
to the Y.M.A.'s initiative from the local L.R.C.s in the
Yorkshire mining seats. In January 1914 the Holmfirth
Labour Party invited Lunn to contest the seat again; in
March Roebuck was asked by the local trade unionists to
fight Doncaster at the next election; in April Grundy was
adopted by the Rotherham trade unionists; and in May the
Osgoldcross Labour Party adopted John Potts. When the
M.F.G.B. ruled that it could finance only ten further candidates over the whole country, and Yorkshire's allocation
was cut to two extra seats, the Y.M.A. decided in June 1914
that it would concentrate on Holmfirth and Doncaster, the
former because it had already been fought once before, and
the latter because the mining vote there was growing faster
than anywhere else in the country.[2] Enthusiasm for more
candidatures was running so high that immediately after this
decision the Barnsley Labour Party adopted John Potts, even
though it was made quite clear that there was no money to
be had from the miners to finance him.

---

[1] J. L. Jeffs, letter to the *Rotherham Express*, 14 Feb. 1914.
[2] By 1910 no fewer than 14 new collieries were being developed in the Doncaster
area. *Rotherham Express*, 2 July 1910. In 1906 the miners constituted about 30 per
cent of the electorate; by 1914 they made up nearly 50 per cent.

Thus, by the summer of 1914, the Y.M.A. had undertaken to fight Normanton, Hallamshire, Holmfirth, and
Doncaster, whilst two other seats, Osgoldcross and Barnsley,
were to be contested by miners with the moral though not
the financial backing of the Y.M.A.[1] In August 1914 the
union decided to set up central committees in every constituency which it had decided to contest or which it might in
the future contest, and at the same time a full-time agent was
to be appointed for the Normanton, Hallamshire, Holmfirth,
and Doncaster divisions.[2] Everything now pointed to a head-
on collision between the Y.M.A. and the Liberals. In 1909
this was a prospect that had proved altogether too much for
the union; but by 1914 it was far too deeply and thoroughly
committed to avoid going through with its challenge to the
Liberals in their recognized strongholds. For their part the
Liberals too were in a belligerent mood, and, indeed, now
that the agreeable John Wadsworth was to stand down, they
were thinking seriously of trying to regain Hallamshire from
the miners. Although the chances are that thousands of
Yorkshire miners would still have been voting Liberal had a
general election taken place in 1914 or 1915 there was no
longer any doubt that the union and the Liberal Party were
on opposite sides.

(ii) SOUTH WALES

The South Wales coalfield has long been associated with a
fiery and militant brand of Socialism. Yet the I.L.P. was
slow to make its influence felt among the South Wales
miners, and before 1914 the Labour Party's progress here
was just as halting and uncertain as in Yorkshire. For almost
twenty years after the general election of 1885 the Lib-Lab
W. Abraham (Mabon) was the sole representative of the
South Wales miners in Parliament, and there is nothing to
suggest that they were seriously dissatisfied with the Liberal
M.P.s who sat for the Welsh mining constituencies. Until

---

[1] In June 1914 it was announced that John Wadsworth would not be contesting
Hallamshire at the next election. His place was to be taken by T. W. Grundy, who
withdrew from Rotherham, where by this time he had been adopted by the local
L.R.C.

[2] *YMA*, 4 Aug. 1914.

the turn of the century the stuff of politics was still the
grievances of nonconformity and of Welsh nationalism, and
the Liberal Party was still the vehicle of protest, uniting all
classes in opposition to the established church and the
English gentry.[1] So long as there was industrial peace in the
coalfield, and so long as the chapel retained its grip upon
the miners, there was no room for a new party preaching the
doctrine of working-class solidarity.

Even had the South Wales miners cherished political
ambitions of their own in the latter part of the nineteenth
century, the structure of trade unionism in the coalfield
before the formation of the South Wales Miners' Federation
in 1898 would have made it difficult for them to secure
parliamentary representation on any scale. Until 1898 they
were organized in a number of small and autonomous
district associations, each with its membership confined to
one particular area or valley, and, at a time when communications between valleys were poor, there was little sense of
common interest and little prospect of concerted action. Few
of these district associations possessed either the leaders of
sufficient calibre or the numerical strength necessary to
persuade or compel a local Liberal Association to accept
their nominee. Only the Cambrian Miners' Association in the
Rhondda had both an outstanding personality, in the shape
of Mabon, and a large membership concentrated in one
parliamentary division, and even they had been first required
to demonstrate their power by defeating a Liberal coal-
owner in 1885 before the Liberals would consent to combine
with the miners to form a Liberal and Labour Association
in the constituency. At the same time, lack of unity robbed
the South Wales miners of the bargaining power that they
might otherwise have been able to exploit in their dealings
with the Liberals. In Durham and Yorkshire, it will be
remembered, the county unions had been able to secure a
clear run for their candidates by offering their support for
Liberal candidates in other mining constituencies in the area.
It was under arrangements of this kind that John Wilson and
Ben Pickard won and held Mid Durham and Normanton.

[1] See Sir Reginald Coupland, *Welsh and Scottish Nationalism*, 1954, pp. 216 et
seq.

But until the end of the century there was no union covering the whole of the South Wales coalfield, and consequently it was never possible to induce the Liberals to support one particular nominee, because it was never possible to offer or threaten to withhold the miners' backing for Liberal candidates fighting mining seats elsewhere. The formation of the S.W.M.F. not only marked the end of a period of industrial harmony in the coalfield, it also provided the miners with the organization through which they could channel their newly awakened political aspirations.[1]

The reasons for the sudden change that occurred in the mood of the miners at the turn of the century have already been discussed in Chapter IV. Now the latent conflict of interest between capital and labour was out in the open: the origins of the notorious Taff Vale dispute were in the very heart of the coalfield, and the S.W.M.F. itself was soon locked in battle with the owners over the 'stop-day' cases. In the circumstances it was natural enough that when the M.F.G.B. adopted its scheme for more parliamentary representation in 1902 the proposals were taken up enthusiastically in South Wales. Mabon himself welcomed the possibility of more Labour men in the House of Commons, though he probably envisaged more Lib-Labs like himself. When the S.W.M.F. decided to support the scheme, he commented that some fifty Members could be returned to 'advocate the policy of the Federation on the floor of the House', and rejoiced that they would have 'no more Home Secretaries turning a deaf ear to the legislative requirements of the miners, [whereas] if this course were not pursued, mining legislation apparently would be coming to a standstill'.[2] At the annual conference in 1903 the S.W.M.F. decided to schedule no less than eleven seats—Rhondda, Gower, South Glamorgan, East Glamorgan, Mid Glamorgan, the two

---

[1] The 1898 lock-out, besides producing the S.W.M.F., also had more direct political consequences: the I.L.P. movement in general and Keir Hardie in particular seized the opportunity to gain a foothold in the coalfield. Nevertheless, many of the I.L.P. branches which sprang up in the Rhondda and Aberdare districts at this time were probably short-lived, and Hardie's election for Merthyr Tydfil in 1900 owed as much to the hostility of the miners to the Boer War as to his socialism. See H. Pelling, *The Origins of the Labour Party*, 1954, pp. 192 and 225.

[2] Quoted in E. W. Evans, op. cit., pp. 74–5.

Merthyr Borough seats, East Carmarthenshire, North Monmouthshire, South Monmouthshire, and West Monmouthshire—for miners' candidates in the future, though it had already been made clear that the union did not necessarily intend to contest these seats so long as the sitting Members continued to behave in a way that satisfied the miners.[1]

But, if Liberal M.P.s had little reason to fear that the union would try to turn them out, it was clearly the policy of the S.W.M.F. gradually to fill these seats when a suitable opportunity arose, and this, of course, was not a prospect that appealed to local Liberal Associations in South Wales. In 1903, when William Brace, the Vice-President of the S.W.M.F., was nominated for South Glamorgan (which was actually held by a Conservative at the time), it was only after considerable pressure from Herbert Gladstone, the Chief Liberal Whip, that the Liberal Association agreed to back the miners' man. And in the following year, when Sir William Harcourt, the Liberal Member for West Monmouthshire, decided to retire, it was only with the greatest reluctance that the local Liberals adopted Tom Richards, the Secretary of the S.W.M.F., even though Richards assured them that he accepted the programme of the Liberal Party and would take the Liberal whip. Although in the end Richards was elected easily enough, and joined Mabon at Westminster, the grudging attitude of the Liberals was naturally exploited to the full by Socialist propagandists. The moral to be drawn from the episode was that the working class could hope for nothing from the Liberal Party. Vernon Hartshorn's description of the selection procedure underlined the lesson:

A conference is convened of workers in the constituency at which Richards is unanimously selected as Labour candidate. The Liberals scour the country in search of a candidate to oppose him. All who are approached realize the utter hopelessness of the task and decline with thanks. There is but one possible candidate—Mr. Richards. He appears before the Liberal Five Hundred. He makes it abundantly clear that he is not connected with either of the great political organizations which are working for a stalwart Labour Party in the House of Commons. . . . He knew the Liberal programme and enthusiastically

[1] *The Times*, 29 Jan. 1902.

supported every item of it. He would willingly accept the Liberal
Whip. The whole position of the Labour Party is surrendered, and
Richards comes out as a fully-fledged Liberal candidate; and with what
result? Of the Liberal Five Hundred 62 voted for his adoption and 51
against, and the 51 declared that they are not licked yet.[1]

When the general election of 1906 came there was more
trouble with the Liberals, this time in the Gower division,
which the miners had decided to contest in 1903. Only about
a fifth of the electors were miners, but besides the miners
there was a large and well-organized body of tin-plate
workers in the constituency, who had unsuccessfully run
John Hodge as an L.R.C. candidate at the general election
of 1900. Prominent among the Liberal candidate's supporters in that election was John Williams, the local miners'
agent.[2] When Gower became one of the S.W.M.F.'s
scheduled seats, Williams himself was adopted as the next
Labour candidate; but, despite the help he had previously
given them, the Liberals decided to bring forward a man of
their own against him, on the grounds that he had refused to
submit himself to the Liberal Association for selection.

As the Liberals decided to support the S.W.M.F.'s other
three candidates, Mabon, Brace, and Richards, Gower saw
the only open fight between the Liberals and the miners at
the general election of 1906. But it must already have been
perfectly clear to anyone who could read the writing on the
wall that in the long run a much more widespread conflict
was inevitable. For the present the S.W.M.F.'s policy was
merely to contest Liberal seats as they fell vacant; and up to
this point its nominees had been older men with Liberal
leanings. Seeing that even this moderate and unprovocative
line had brought difficulties in South Glamorgan, West
Monmouthshire, and Gower, it may well have been dawn-
ing upon the miners that middle-class Liberal Associations,
often dominated by local employers, were in no mood to
adopt working-class trade unionists, even when they were
sound Liberals and were prepared to stand as Lib-Labs of
the traditional type. But there was nothing sacrosanct about
the union's policy of leaving sitting Liberals unmolested, and

[1] *South Wales Gazette*, 11 Sept. 1904.
[2] John Hodge, *Workman's Cottage to Windsor Castle*, 1931, pp. 140 et seq.

by now there were signs that some of the more adventurous
spirits among the miners were anxious to fight any seat that
looked promising, no matter who held it. Furthermore, the
odds were that future S.W.M.F. nominees would not be
agreeable Lib-Labs like Mabon, Brace, and Richards, but
younger men like Vernon Hartshorn and C. B. Stanton, who
would certainly insist on running as straight Labour candidates.

In fact there were very nearly two other clashes between
the miners and the Liberals at the election of 1906. Although
barely a tenth of the electors were miners at this stage,
Breconshire had been added to the S.W.M.F.'s list of
scheduled constituencies by 1905. A month before the
general election, without a word of warning, the local
Liberal Association announced that their sitting Member
was retiring and that they had adopted another candidate in
his place. The Breconshire miners were so indignant at this
piece of sharp practice that they came close to putting up
a candidate of their own, and only the hasty intervention
of the S.W.M.F. executive dissuaded them.[1] The Mid
Glamorgan miners were also pressing strongly for a Labour
candidate to oppose the Liberal S. T. Evans, and again it
was the executive that intervened to bring the movement to
a stop, though not before the Mid Glamorgan miners had
made it quite clear that the S.W.M.F.'s policy of letting
sleeping Liberals lie no longer commanded universal support
among the rank and file.[2]

It was widely suspected that the executive's caution was
in part dictated by concern for William Brace's exposed
position in South Glamorgan. When the S.W.M.F. originally undertook to fight the full quota of eleven seats that it
was allowed under the terms of the M.F.G.B. scheme, it
automatically committed itself to contesting some constituencies where the miners were not numerous enough on
their own to exercise a decisive influence over the result. On
the basis of the M.F.G.B. scheme of one candidate for every
10,000 union members, the S.W.M.F. was indeed entitled
to eleven seats; but of course the union's membership was

---

[1] *South Wales Gazette*, 22 Dec. 1905 and 12 Jan. 1906.
[2] *Western Mail*, 30 Dec. 1905.

not evenly spread over all eleven parliamentary constituencies, and, whilst some divisions like the Rhondda and West Monmouthshire contained far more than 10,000 miners, others on the S.W.M.F. list, like Gower, South Glamorgan, South Monmouthshire, Breconshire, and East Carmarthenshire, contained far fewer. This was a matter of some importance in South Glamorgan, where William Brace, unable to rely on the solid support of a substantial mining vote, had no hope of winning the seat without the help of the Liberals. And the Liberals were said to have made it quite clear to the S.W.M.F. executive that if there were a miners' candidate in Breconshire, Brace could expect no help from them in South Glamorgan.[1]

Relations between the S.W.M.F. and the Liberals were put under a further strain in the summer of 1906 when the M.F.G.B.'s ballot on the question of affiliation to the Labour Party was held. The issue immediately split the S.W.M.F. executive, with the Socialists urging that the men should be advised to vote in favour of joining the Labour Party, and the Lib-Labs naturally objecting to this proposal. When a vote was taken there were nine in favour of giving an official lead and nine against, whereupon Mabon as chairman refused to give his casting vote and the motion was lost.[2] Whilst in many of the English coalfields the 1906 ballot passed almost unnoticed and attracted little interest or publicity, in South Wales it stirred up enormous interest. Mass meetings were held in every valley and district, and Socialists among the miners' leaders, ignoring their executive's decision, vigorously spelt out the case for affiliation; most of the Lib-Labs, on the other hand, kept silent. The outcome was a clear majority for affiliation, with 41,843 votes in favour and 31,527 against.

If the Lib-Labs were now on the defensive, they were still well enough entrenched in the executive to head off any direct electoral challenge to the Liberals. Under the leadership of Vernon Hartshorn a particularly strong socialist faction had developed among the miners of Mid Glamorgan, and, after their unsuccessful attempt to run a candidate against S. T. Evans in 1906, they had formed a divisional

<hr>

[1] Ibid., 1 Jan. 1906.   [2] *South Wales Gazette*, 17 Aug. 1906.

L.R.C. in conjunction with the other trade unions, trade councils, and I.L.P. branches in the constituency. As there were to be no less than three by-elections in this division in the next few years, besides the two general elections of 1910, Mid Glamorgan came to be the main bone of contention between the Socialists and the Lib-Labs in the S.W.M.F. The first passage of arms occurred in the autumn of 1906, when S. T. Evans was compelled to seek re-election to the House of Commons on his promotion to the Recordership of Swansea. A meeting of lodge delegates was at once called and by a large majority the miners voted in favour of running a Labour candidate. A deputation from Mid Glamorgan then met the S.W.M.F. executive, which flatly rejected their request for a candidate by seventeen votes to four.[1] The Lib-Labs certainly did not control the executive to this extent, but they no doubt made the most of the argument that it would be unwise to try to exploit the technical resignation of a Member who had previously been considered 'acceptable' by the miners, and they probably convinced the more moderate Labour supporters that a churlish attempt to unseat a well-known M.P. on the occasion of his promotion might place a Labour candidate at an initial disadvantage.

However, Mid Glamorgan did serve to draw attention to the inadequacy of the union's electoral preparations. The S.W.M.F. still held only four of the twelve seats to which it was now entitled under the M.F.G.B. scheme; there were no candidates in readiness to contest any other mining seats that might fall vacant, and nothing had been done by way of propaganda or organizational work in the more obviously promising constituencies. The first move to remedy these shortcomings was made at the end of 1906, when the S.W.M.F. instructed its members in Breconshire, East and Mid Glamorgan, North and South Monmouthshire, East Carmarthenshire, and Merthyr Boroughs to select their candidates.[2] As a result, in 1907 Hartshorn was chosen for Mid Glamorgan and Evan Thomas for East Glamorgan, Alfred Onions the Treasurer of the S.W.M.F. was selected for South Monmouthshire in 1908, and in 1909 David

[1] *Mid-Glamorgan Herald*, 6 Oct. 1906.
[2] *Aberdare Leader*, 29 Dec. 1906.

Morgan was chosen for East Carmarthenshire. And in January 1908 the union appointed three paid agents to be responsible for registration work in the mining constituencies.[1]

Soon afterwards another by-election became necessary in Mid Glamorgan, this time because S. T. Evans had been appointed Solicitor-General. Once more a deputation from the local miners urged the executive of the S.W.M.F. to put up Vernon Hartshorn under the M.F.G.B. scheme, and once again the executive turned down their request on the grounds that 'exceptional circumstances' had brought about the vacancy. On this occasion, however, the executive added that the union would be prepared to run a candidate, provided the local miners wanted one, in any of the South Wales mining seats where a vacancy occurred as a result of the permanent removal of the sitting Member from the House or, and this was the important undertaking, in the event of a general election.[2] On the face of things this seemed to represent an important change of policy. It was certainly interpreted as such by the *Labour Leader*, which happily declared that all the sitting Liberal Members in South Wales would be left undisturbed only until the next general election, and hailed the executive's decision as a great step forward. Hartshorn himself, confident that he would soon be fighting Mid Glamorgan, launched a vigorous propaganda campaign and as late as October 1909 he was telling the Rhondda I.L.P. that he had high hopes of winning the seat. The general election of January 1910 was to show that he was sadly mistaken.

In the meantime the second M.F.G.B. ballot on affiliation to the Labour Party was held in May 1908, and this time, on a very high poll, the South Wales miners voted even more decisively in favour of joining the Labour Party. The result was, for affiliation 74,675, against 44,616. When the M.F.G.B. as a whole became affiliated to the Labour Party early in 1909 it became necessary for all future S.W.M.F. candidates to sign the party constitution and conduct their election campaigns independently of the Liberals. This

[1] *SWMF*, 10 Jan. 1908.
[2] *Glamorgan Free Press*, 7 Feb. 1908; *SWMF*, 3 Feb. 1908.

meant that at the next general election Mabon, Brace, Richards, and Williams would have to stand as straight Labour candidates. In addition, by this time three more constituencies, East Glamorgan, Mid Glamorgan, and East Carmarthenshire, had also chosen candidates, and in line with the decision reached at the time of the by-election in Mid Glamorgan in 1908 the S.W.M.F. was bound to sanction these contests. So it was that when the executive met on 15 November 1909 it was boldly announced that no less than seven Labour candidates would be sponsored at the coming election. Since the sitting Liberals in the three new constituencies had given no sign that they intended to stand down, the scene appeared to be set for a full-scale clash with the Liberals. As in Yorkshire, however, the collision never took place, because just before the election the S.W.M.F. hastily abandoned all three of its extra candidatures.

The South Wales miners were open to much the same line of reasoning as their colleagues in Yorkshire. This was no time to split the progressive vote with the fate of the 'people's budget' at stake. Since the Labour Party was unquestionably the third party, surely it should wait for a more propitious moment to make its bid for increased parliamentary representation? And, to reinforce the appeal to reason, there were hints that there might be reprisals if the S.W.M.F. persisted in its policy of attacking sitting Liberals. There were reports, for example, that the Liberals were thinking seriously of opposing John Williams in Gower, and it was made clear that the decision would depend largely upon whether the miners ran a candidate in Mid Glamorgan.[1] And, as usual, there was the even more vulnerable position of William Brace in South Glamorgan to be considered.

When the S.W.M.F. executive met again on 6 December 1909 there had clearly been some powerful second thoughts. The miners' candidate for East Carmarthenshire was withdrawn without explanation. As it happened, the man originally selected by the local miners for East Glamorgan had died and there was no candidate ready. The executive decided to hold a ballot of the East Glamorgan miners asking them if they were still in favour of contesting the seat,

[1] *The Times*, 6 Dec. 1909.

with the wording on the ballot-paper being framed in such a way as to invite the answer 'no', which was the answer duly given by the lodges.[1] But, as in the past, it was the Mid Glamorgan division that caused most difficulty. To all appearances this was one seat that the S.W.M.F. was firmly committed to fighting; indeed, by this time Hartshorn's candidature had already been endorsed by the M.F.G.B. Yet at the executive meeting Mabon opened the proceedings by declaring that 'he would not appear on the platform of any man who tried to oust from his seat such an old and tried friend as Sir S. T. Evans, who had also at all times proved himself to be a true friend of Labour.' Brace was equally emphatic in speaking against Hartshorn's candidature, pointing out that if the S.W.M.F. countenanced a contest in Mid Glamorgan his own position in South Glamorgan would be prejudiced and that many of his present Liberal supporters would abstain. Other members of the executive, like Tom Richards and Alfred Onions, grudgingly conceded that if Hartshorn insisted on standing they would support him, but they also made it clear that in their opinion this was not the right time for a battle with the Liberal Party. Avowed socialists like C. B. Stanton, James Winstone, and George Barker took the line that the seat should be contested regardless of the consequences. After two hours of heated argument, in the course of which Hartshorn offered, in the event of his being successful in Mid Glamorgan, to resign his seat there in favour of Brace, if the latter were beaten in South Glamorgan, it was finally decided that the candidature should be dropped and that the Mid Glamorgan miners should be asked to accept this verdict. Hartshorn himself was bitterly disappointed; as a local political correspondent put it, his parliamentary ambitions had been ruthlessly sacrificed so that the Welsh miners' M.P.s could hang on to the Liberal vote in their own constituencies.[2] The manœuvre could not have been more successful. In South Glamorgan the Liberal Five Hundred unanimously agreed to work and vote for Brace in his capacity as the Progressive candidate; in Gower the Liberal Association promptly shelved its plans for

---

[1] *Western Mail*, 6 Dec. 1909; *SWMF*, 3 Jan. 1910.
[2] *Western Mail*, 7 Dec. 1909.

running a candidate against Williams; in West Monmouthshire Tom Richards attributed his huge majority to 'the
absolute unanimity of all the Progressive organizations in the
Division'. And in the Rhondda Mabon continued to enjoy
the support of the Liberals, including his old friend S. T.
Evans.

This spirit of harmony and understanding, so much in
evidence in January 1910, suddenly came to a dramatic end.
Only three months after the general election the Progressive
alliance was decisively and irretrievably split, and once again
it was Mid Glamorgan that lay at the centre of the storm.
In March 1910 there was yet another by-election in Mid
Glamorgan, this time because Sir S. T. Evans had been
appointed President of the Divorce Court. Unlike his previous promotions this one required him to resign his seat in
the House of Commons, and now that there was no question
of opposing the sitting Member even the Lib-Labs on the
S.W.M.F. executive, including Mabon, considered that
Hartshorn had a rightful claim to the seat. In their naïvety
they appeared to be under the impression that the union's
forbearance in the past would be justly rewarded; in their
view the Liberals ought now to stand aside and give the
miners' candidate a straight fight against the Conservative.
In due course it became clear that, whilst Liberal Party
headquarters shared their feelings, the local Liberal Association saw the situation in a very different light. Even had the
Mid Glamorgan Liberals been willing to accept a working-
class trade unionist, and no Liberal Association in the South
Wales coalfield had willingly done so yet, and even had they
been ready to support a prominent socialist, which they
certainly were not, the affiliation of the M.F.G.B. to the
Labour Party at the beginning of 1909 made anything that
had happened in the past totally irrelevant as far as they were
concerned. As the Mid Glamorgan Liberals were well aware,
now that the miners had become part of the Labour Party
they would have no say in the selection of Hartshorn as
candidate, and he would be in no way responsible to them
after he was elected. To stand aside now would mean the end
of the Liberal Association in the constituency, and they
knew it.

Finding a Liberal willing to contest the seat proved to be difficult, for behind the scenes the Chief Liberal Whip was busy trying to dissuade potential candidates from opposing the miners' nominee. Naturally, it was not long before the Mid Glamorgan Liberals had wind of this, and when eventually they found a candidate in F. W. Gibbins, a local tinplate manufacturer, they let Elibank know how they felt in forthright terms, making public a telegram to him protesting at what they called his 'cruel betrayal of Liberalism and Welsh Nationalism'. To Elibank in London the position looked rather different. He knew that the South Wales miners expected the reversion of Mid Glamorgan when it fell vacant, and if there were a feud over this seat he was worried about the consequences in the rest of the area.[1] Furthermore, the intransigence of the Mid Glamorgan Liberals could serve only to strengthen the hand of the I.L.P. faction in the S.W.M.F. and to make it impossible for the union to co-operate with the Liberals in the future. An old Lib-Lab like Mabon could see this only too clearly and he did his best to persuade the Liberals to withdraw their candidate. As he pointed out in the columns of the *South Wales Daily News*, the miners had foregone the chance of fighting Mid Glamorgan several times in the past:

Each time the Federation refrained the miners' leaders were eulogised by the Liberals and at the same time incurred the odium of our men for so doing. Is all this to go for nothing now? But the most important phase of all in respect of the political future of Wales, after the present contest in Mid Glamorgan between the Liberal nominee and the nominee of the Miners' Federation is over,—whether Mr. Gibbins wins or not—will be the relationship left. There is no man living sanguine enough to hope that the Miners' Executive, if it desired to do so, would be allowed to continue its former policy towards Liberalism and Welsh Nationalism.[2]

Yet even though the leaders of the S.W.M.F. were at last united in their opposition to the Liberals, as the result of the by-election was to show, thousands of the rank and file were sticking to their traditional allegiance. There were probably about 11,000 miner voters in the constituency: Hartshorn's

[1] *South Wales Daily News*, 14 Mar. 1910; 15 Mar. 1910. *Mid-Glamorgan Herald*, 19 Mar. 1910.   [2] *South Wales Daily News*, 22 Mar. 1910.

total vote was only 6,210, and much of his support undoubtedly came from railwaymen, steel-workers, and
dockers. Gibbins, with nearly 9,000 votes, was an easy
winner, and in their jubilation the Mid Glamorgan Liberals
at once dispatched another telegram to the Chief Whip,
informing him that 'The Master of Elibank is not master of
Mid Glamorgan.'

From now onwards there was no question of compromise
between the miners and the Liberals, and at the December
election of 1910 the S.W.M.F. took the bull by the horns,
and, besides defending the four seats it already held, decided
to fight both Mid Glamorgan and East Glamorgan. The
Liberal Member for East Glamorgan, Sir Alfred Thomas,
was not seeking re-election, and the Liberals had replaced
him with Clem Edwards, a formidable candidate because of
his long and friendly association with the trade union movement.[1] Interestingly enough, Edwards had been one of the
Liberals who had declined to stand against Hartshorn in
Mid Glamorgan in March; by now he evidently felt that the
damage had been done and that there was no longer any
point in trying to avert a quarrel between the Liberals and
the miners. The miners adopted the militant Socialist
C. B. Stanton. Despite the attempts of Keir Hardie and
others to exploit a great deal of local bitterness at the Liberal
Government's use of troops and police to quell the Rhondda
riots, it is clear that Edwards did at least as well among the
miners as his Labour opponent. As there were about 13,000
miners on the electoral register, even on the unlikely
assumption that all of Stanton's 4,675 votes were cast by
miners, there was no escaping the conclusion that the
Liberals, with a total of over 9,000 votes, still commanded
a healthy following in the mining communities of East
Glamorgan. In Mid Glamorgan, Vernon Hartshorn resumed
his long and unsuccessful quest for the seat, and, though he
managed to reduce the margin of defeat, he was still 1,500
votes behind the Liberal.

[1] Edwards had begun his working life as a farm labourer, studied law, and been
called to the Bar in 1889. He had been associated with Ben Tillett at the time of the
dockers' strike in 1889, was the author of a standard work on railway nationaliza-
tion, and had helped in the agitation for an eight-hours bill in the mining industry.
See John Saville, 'Unions and Free Labour' in *Essays in Labour History*, p. 324.

In face of these challenges, the Liberals reacted quite mildly in the rest of the coalfield. Tom Richards and Mabon had such enormous majorities in West Monmouthshire and the Rhondda that there probably seemed little point in opposing them. More surprisingly, Brace in South Glamorgan and Keir Hardie in Merthyr Boroughs also escaped any Liberal opposition, though Hardie was always saying that he would welcome a trial of strength between two Liberals and two Labour candidates in Merthyr. The one sitting S.W.M.F. Member who did find himself with a Liberal opponent was John Williams in Gower. The Gower Liberal Association had never liked Williams, and now that it was clear that there was to be no give and take in South Wales, it felt itself no longer under any restraint. There was some difficulty in finding a candidate, and in the end they adopted a Young Liberal named W. F. Phillips, who was present at the selection meeting in Swansea only by complete chance. The prospect of Liberal opposition threw Williams into a great deal of unnecessary alarm, and to the annoyance of the local Socialists he issued a statement praising the good works of Lloyd George and claiming that he was 'no enemy of really true Liberalism'.[1] In the event he was returned with a much larger majority over the Liberals than in 1906.

It was at about this time that a new movement, far more militant and revolutionary than the Labour Party, began to gain ground in the South Wales coalfield. Early in 1909 a group of young miners very much under the influence of Tom Mann, returned from Ruskin College, Oxford, and set up the South Wales wing of the Plebs League. The object of the League was to spread independent working-class education, with the theory of the class war as the underlying principle of instruction. Very soon it had branched out into industrial activities too, in the shape of an organization named the Unofficial Reform Committee, which set itself the task of reorganizing and reorienting the S.W.M.F. It was not long before the Syndicalists, as they came to be called, were in the thick of the bitter and prolonged strike in the Rhondda in 1910, urging the men to fight to the last for a

[1] *South Wales Daily News*, 29 Nov. 1910.

minimum wage.[1] The Syndicalists' programme for the coal industry was set out in the celebrated pamphlet *The Miners' Next Step*, published at Tonypandy in 1912. In essence the plan was to achieve workers' control over the industry through direct industrial action—the strike, working to rule, and going slow. The tactics were to agitate for a minimum wage and a reduction in hours, and to press these demands so far that in the end the employers would be deprived of the whole of their profit and would be only too willing to surrender the industry to the workers. Many of the Syndicalists rejected political action altogether: as they pointed out, it had taken twenty-five years to secure the Eight Hours Act and it might take as long again to get a minimum wage if they relied on parliamentary activity.[2] In any case, for the Syndicalists a minimum wage was only a step on a long road, and not an end in itself.

As it was then organized and led, the M.F.G.B. was totally incapable of carrying out the ruthless programme that the Syndicalists were intent upon. Its leadership, they claimed, was far too timid and cautious and this was partly because it had become entangled in politics. When trade union officials were elected to Parliament, the argument ran, they tended to grow apart from the rank and file, to become gentlemen, and to lose their zest for industrial battles. The remedy lay in the complete reorganization of the Federation. Under the model rules as proposed in *The Miners' Next Step*, the Federation was to have a Central Executive Committee, on which no agent or permanent official would be eligible to sit. Any agent who was elected to Parliament would be required to give up his trade union position and duties. No M.P. was to be eligible to seek or retain a seat on his local or the national executive; any M.P. should at once vacate his seat in Parliament if a ballot of his union's membership so decided; and, on all proposed Labour legislation, miners' M.P.s would vote in accordance with instructions they received from their unions. In other words, M.P.s sponsored

[1] Lewis, op. cit., p. 173; *Plebs*, no. 1; *The Rhondda Socialist*, Feb. 1912.

[2] *The Industrial Syndicalist*, 11 Feb. 1911. Not all the Syndicalists, however, believed that political action should be abandoned altogether. One sentence in *The Miners' Next Step* read: 'Political action must go on side by side with industrial action.'

by the miners were to be little more than trade union delegates at Westminster. Under these conditions the more
ambitious and able of the miners' leaders were not likely to
seek election to Parliament, especially since they would have
to give up their positions of authority in the union, and at the
same time would hold their parliamentary seats only at the
pleasure of the union's membership.

When the first great venture in direct action, the national
strike for a minimum wage in 1912, ended in partial failure,
the wrath of the Syndicalists was vented upon the union
leaders, who had failed to pursue the aggressive policy that
was necessary. Even Hartshorn, a revolutionary Socialist in
the eyes of the Liberals, was condemned out of hand, for so
quickly was opinion moving leftward among some sections
of the miners that the extremist of yesterday had become the
selfish reactionary of today.[1] The Syndicalists had a colour-
ful line in invective at their command, and they were prepared to use it on the S.W.M.F. leaders in full measure.
Writing under the pseudonym 'Syndic' in April 1912,
W. F. Hay launched into a typical attack:

A bitter day of reckoning is coming for those who, like Hartshorn,
Brace, Richards, Onions etc have seized upon, misled, and betrayed
the most important industrial movement of modern times. Chief
among these traitors, occupying this despicable pre-eminence stands
Vernon Hartshorn. Puffed into rapid and undeserved eminence,
trading on the ideas and efforts of abler men, he stands today a leading
figure in the coalfield. . . . A politician by temperament, and a dema-
gogue by training, he seeks the wider area of Parliamentary life to
gratify his personal ambition, and it is to secure this prize that he has
assisted in the base intrigue that has caused our defeat.[2]

It is hard to tell how large a following the Syndicalists had,
or how influential they were inside the S.W.M.F. In 1911
four of them, Noah Ablett, John Hopla, Noah Rees, and
Tom Smith, were all elected to the S.W.M.F. executive;
Hopla was also the chairman of the Glamorgan Working
Men's Committee, representing men from two collieries

---

[1] Arthur Horner, for example, who was much influenced by the Syndicalist
Noah Ablett, refers to Hartshorn as 'one of the right-wing miners' leaders'. See
Incorrigible Rebel, 1960, p. 42.
[2] *The Rhondda Socialist*, Apr. 1912.

employing over 4,000 miners, and Noah Rees was chairman of the Cambrian Colliery workmen. And in addition to the headquarters of the movement in Tonypandy there were half a dozen other branches, mainly in the Rhondda.[1] In the end, of course, the grand design of the Syndicalists came to nothing. But in the short run their attacks on the miners' leaders, both as trade union officials and as politicians, can have done little to enhance the popularity or prestige of the Labour Party.

Between the second election of 1910 and the early part of 1913 there was hardly any political activity on the part of the South Wales miners. Like a number of other miners' unions the S.W.M.F. had been served with an injunction restraining it from using its funds for political purposes, and, although it raised a voluntary levy which was reasonably successful, there was little money available by the end of 1912. The East Carmarthenshire seat fell vacant in the summer of 1912, but the S.W.M.F. had no stomach for a fight and the opportunity of winning another seat passed by. And in December 1912 financial stringency compelled the union to dismantle part of its electoral machinery and lay off its three registration agents.

In the summer of 1913, as in most of the other major coalfields, there were moves afoot for a new political offensive at the next general election. William Brace had by this time decided that no Labour candidate could hope to hold South Glamorgan, and had announced that he for one was not prepared to stand there again. But in August it was announced that the S.W.M.F. would contest Gower, Mid Glamorgan, East Glamorgan, Merthyr Boroughs, Rhondda, and North, South, and West Monmouthshire.[2] At the outbreak of war in 1914 the final selection of candidates had not been made, but it was reasonably certain that Hartshorn would again fight Mid Glamorgan, that Brace and David Watts Morgan would replace Tom Richards in West Monmouthshire and Mabon in the Rhondda, and that Alfred Onions, James Winstone, and John Williams would be the S.W.M.F.'s

[1] For Syndicalist activity and influence, see Ness Edwards, *History of the South Wales Miners' Federation*, 1938, p. 66 et seq.; Lewis, op. cit., p. 176; *The Times*, 28 Feb. 1912. [2] *SWMF*, 9 Aug. 1913.

candidates in East Glamorgan, North Monmouthshire, and Gower respectively. The Liberals for their part were said to be ready to challenge the miners in Gower and West Monmouthshire.[1] In other words, there were to be at least five clashes between the S.W.M.F. and the Liberals, and indeed, in North Monmouthshire it was to be Winstone, the Vice-President of the union, against the Liberal Home Secretary, Reginald McKenna. The breach between the old allies was now complete and final.

[1] *The Times*, 15 Apr. 1914.

APPENDIX

(i) *The mining vote* c. *1910*

	Constituency	Electorate	Estimated no. of miner votes	Miners as per cent of total vote
Yorkshire	Normanton	16,466	8,070	49
	Barnsley	20,861	9,800	46
	Osgoldcross	18,286	7,740	42
	Rotherham	20,487	8,180	39
	Doncaster	21,511	8,130	37
	Hallamshire	19,935	6,670	33
	Morley	15,823	5,030	31
	Holmfirth	12,788	3,550	27
	Barkston Ash	10,871	2,170	19
	Borough constituencies calculated from 1911 census:			
	Pontefract	3,792	1,000	26
	Wakefield	6,557	1,240	18
	Attercliffe	16,575	2,330	14
South Wales	Rhondda	17,760	13,590	76
	West Monmouthshire	20,399	13,350	65
	Mid Glamorgan	20,017	11,230	56
	East Glamorgan	23,979	12,980	54
	Merthyr Tydfil	23,219	10,020	43
	North Monmouth-shire	15,711	5,710	36
	Gower	14,712	3,870	26
	South Monmouth-shire	19,134	4,220	22
	South Glamorgan	22,953	4,420	19
	East Carmarthenshire	12,268	2,090	17
	Breconshire	13,432	1,400	10
North Wales	East Denbighshire	11,911	5,340	44
	Flintshire	12,774	1,720	13
Gloucestershire	Forest of Dean	10,881	3,020	27
Somersetshire	Frome	13,168	1,760	13

(ii) *Election results, 1906–14: miners' candidates are in italic*

	1906	1910 (January)	1910 (December)
Yorkshire			
Normanton	*F. Hall* (L-L)	*F. Hall* (Lab) E. Bartlett (U)	*F. Hall* (Lab) 9,172 3,540
Barnsley	J. Walton (L)	J. Walton (L) A. W. Groser (U)	Sir J. Walton (L) 12,425 5,053
Osgoldcross	J. C. Rickett (L) 8,482 G. Wheler (U) 4,358	J. C. Rickett (L) G. Hargreaves (U) 9,517 4,840	Sir J. C. Rickett (L) 8,518 M. Campbell Johnstone (U) 4,347
Rotherham	W. H. Holland (L)	W. H. Holland (L) 12,225 J. H. Dransfield (C) 4,667 By-election, 1910: J. A. Pease (L)	J. A. Pease (L) 9,385 J. H. Dransfield (U) 4,511
Doncaster	C. N. Nicholson (L) 9,315 Sir F. W. Fison (C) 5,646	C. N. Nicholson (L) 10,654 C. W. Whitworth (U) 7,085	C. N. Nicholson (L) 9,240 C. W. Whitworth (U) 6,696
Hallamshire	*J. Wadsworth* (L-L) 8,375 F. Kelley (C) 6,807	*J. Wadsworth* (Lab) 10,193 S. Timmis (U) 6,185	*J. Wadsworth* (Lab) 8,708 D. T. Smith (U) 5,837
Morley	A. E. Hutton (L)	G. A. France (L) 8,026 J. S. Charlesworth (U) 3,395 *H. Smith* (Lab) 2,191	G. A. France (L)

(ii) Election results, 1906–14: miners' candidates are in italic (cont.)

	1906	1910 (January)	1910 (December)
Yorkshire (cont.)			
Holmfirth	H. J. Wilson (L) 6,850 S. G. Jebb (C) 2,677	H. J. Wilson (L) 6,339 R. Ellis (U) 3,043 *W. Pickles (Lab)* 1,643 By-election, 1912: S. Arnold (L) 4,749 R. Ellis (U) 3,379 *W. Lunn (Lab)* 3,195	H. J. Wilson (L)
Barkston Ash	G. R. Lane-Fox (C) 4,894 J. O. Andrews (L) 4,246	G. R. Lane-Fox (U) 5,299 F. Horne (L) 4,546	G. R. Lane-Fox (U) 5,066 F. Horne (L) 4,372
Pontefract	T. W. Nussey (L) 1,837 C. Yate (C) 1,030	Sir T. W. Nussey (L) 1,924 J. R. Shaw (C) 1,515	F. H. Booth (L) 1,679 J. R. Shaw (U) 1,627
Wakefield	E. A. Brotherton (C) 2,285 *S. Coit (Lab)* 2,068 *T. Snape (L)* 1,247	E. A. Brotherton (C) 3,121 *S. Coit (Lab)* 2,602	A. H. Marshall (L) 2,837 E. A. Brotherton (U) 2,651
Attercliffe	*J. B. Langley (L)* 6,523 A. Wilson (C) 5,736	*J. Pointer (Lab)* 7,755 S. K. Farlow (U) 6,079 By-election, 1909: *J. Pointer (Lab)* 3,531 S. K. Farlow (C) 3,380 R. C. Lambert (L) 3,175 A. M. Wilson (C) 2,803	*J. Pointer (Lab)* 6,532 S. Walker (U) 5,354
South Wales			
Rhondda	*W. Abraham (L-L)*	*W. Abraham (Lab)* 12,436 H. Lloyd (U) 3,471	*W. Abraham (Lab)* 9,073 H. Lloyd (U) 3,701

	1906	1910 (January)	1910 (December)
West Monmouthshire	*T. Richards* (L-L)	*T. Richards* (Lab) 13,295 J. Cameron (U) 3,045	*T. Richards* (Lab)
Mid Glamorgan	*S. T. Evans* (L)	Sir *S. T. Evans* (L) 13,175 G. H. Williams (U) 3,382 By-election, 1906: S. T. Evans (L) 1908: S. T. Evans (L) 1910: *F. W. Gibbins* (L) 8,920 *V. Hartshorn* (Lab) 6,210	*J. H. Edwards* (L) 7,624 *V. Hartshorn* (Lab) 6,102
East Glamorgan	Sir *A. Thomas* (L)	Sir *A. Thomas* (L) 14,721 F. H. Gaskell (U) 5,727	*A. C. Edwards* (L) 9,088 F. H. Gaskell (U) 5,603 C. B. Stanton (Lab) 4,675
Merthyr Tydfil (two Members)	*D. A. Thomas* (L) 13,971 *J. K. Hardie* (Lab) 10,187 H. Radcliffe (L) 7,776	*E. Jones* (L) 15,448 *J. K. Hardie* (Lab) 13,841 A. C. Fox-Davies (U) 4,756 W. P. Morgan (Ind. L) 3,639	*E. Jones* (L) 12,258 *J. K. Hardie* (Lab) 11,507 H. Watts (U) 5,277
North Monmouthshire	*R. McKenna* (L) 7,730 Sir C. Campbell (C) 3,155	*R. McKenna* (L) 8,596 E. G. Carmichael (U) 4,335	*R. McKenna* (L) 7,722 D. E. Williams (U) 4,586
Gower	*J. Williams* (L-L) 4,841 *T. J. Williams* (L) 4,542 E. Helme (C) 1,939	*J. Williams* (Lab) 9,312 P. Simner (U) 2,532	*J. Williams* (Lab) 5,480 W. F. Phillips (L) 4,527
South Glamorgan	*W. Brace* (L-L) 10,514 W. H. Wyndham-Quin (C) 6,096	*W. Brace* (Lab) 11,612 L. Morgan (U) 7,411	*W. Brace* (Lab) 10,190 L. Morgan (U) 7,252

(ii) Election results, 1906–14: miners' candidates are in italic (cont.)

	1906	1910 (January)	1910 (December)
South Wales (cont.)			
East Carmarthen-shire	A. Thomas (L)	A. Thomas (L) 7,619 M. Peel (U) 2,451 By-election, 1912: J. T. Jones (L) 6,082 M. Peel (U) 3,354 J. H. Williams (Lab) 1,089	A. Thomas (L) 5,825 M. Peel (U) 2,315 J. H. Williams (Lab) 1,176
Breconshire	S. Robinson (L) 5,776 R. C. Devereux (C) 3,499	S. Robinson (L) 6,335 R. C. Devereux (C) 3,865	S. Robinson (L) 5,511 C. Lloyd (U) 3,631
South Monmouthshire	I. C. Herbert (L) 7,503 C. C. Morgan (C) 6,216	I. C. Herbert (L) 9,738 L. Forestier-Walker (U) 6,910	Sir I. Herbert (L) 8,597 L. Forestier-Walker (U) 6,656
North Wales			
East Denbighshire	S. Moss (L)	E. G. Hemmerde (L) 6,865 D. Rhys (U) 3,321 By-election, 1906: E. G. Hemmerde (L) 5,917 A. S. G. Boscawen (C) 3,126 1909: E. G. Hemmerde (L) 6,265 Sir E. E. Cunliffe (LU) 3,544	E. T. John (L) 6,449 A. Hood (U) 3,186
Flintshire	J. H. Lewis (L) 6,294 H. Edwards (C) 3,572	J. H. Lewis 6,610 H. R. Howard (C) 4454	J. H. Lewis (L)

	1906	1910 (January)	1910 (December)
Gloucestershire			
Forest of Dean	Sir C. Dilke (L)	Sir C. Dilke (L) 6,141 / J. H. Renton (U) 3,279 By-election, 1911: H. Webb (L) 6,174 / D. H. Kyd (U) 3,106 1912: H. Webb (L)	Sir C. Dilke (L) 5,544 / D. H. Kyd (U) 2,820
Somersetshire			
Frome	J. E. Barlow (L) 6,297 / C. T. Foxcroft (C) 4,552	Sir J. E. Barlow (L) 6,248 / C. T. Foxcroft (U) 5,469	Sir J. E. Barlow (L) 5,944 / C. T. Foxcroft (U) 5,366

VII

THE LAGGARDS

(i) DERBYSHIRE AND NOTTINGHAMSHIRE

THERE were few mining districts where the Labour Party made slower progress or encountered more opposition than Derbyshire and Nottinghamshire. Here in the east Midlands the miners' unions had become so enmeshed with the Liberal Party in the latter part of the nineteenth century that in 1907 one of the leading newspapers in the area thought it astonishing that anyone could be so ill informed as to think that they were in any sense separate for political purposes. 'As a matter of fact', it declared, 'they are part and parcel of it. Look at our Liberal central councils—a large proportion of the Liberal representatives sent from different polling districts are miners. They don't cease to be miners because they are Liberals, and they are no worse Liberals because they are miners.'[1] True, the early socialists and other 'Labourist' advocates of independent political action had faced a similar problem when they arrived on the scene in most of the other major coalfields; but, whereas in Durham, Northumberland, Yorkshire, and South Wales they had ousted the Lib-Labs and gained control over the miners' unions long before the outbreak of war, in Derbyshire it was not until 1914 that the union reluctantly broke with the Liberals and ran a parliamentary candidate on independent Labour lines. The candidate, it should be said, was no young firebrand from the rising new generation of socialists, but the seventy-year-old President of the Association and a life-long Liberal. And in Nottinghamshire the pre-war era closed with the expulsion of the union's General Secretary and one M.P. from

[1] *Derbyshire Courier*, 5 Jan. 1907. There were, of course, *some* Conservative miners in Derbyshire, as there were in all of these predominantly Liberal coalfields. In 1890 an Ilkeston Conservative Miners' Association was formed: but it never had more than 183 members, and by 1901 it had faded away altogether. See Williams, op. cit., pp. 491–2.

the Labour Party for repeatedly and unrepentantly violating
the party constitution.[1] The reasons for the strength and
persistence of the Liberal tradition in the east Midlands
have already been discussed in Chapter IV. Prosperity,
industrial harmony, company paternalism, and the willing-
ness of the Liberals to meet the miners' claims for parliamentary representation, together with the presence of such
powerful Lib-Labs as James Haslam and W. E. Harvey in
Derbyshire and J. G. Hancock in Nottinghamshire, all
combined to make this an unpromising area for Socialist
infiltration, and by 1910 there were no more than about
twenty I.L.P. branches in the colliery districts of the two
counties, and some of these were very small.

Surprisingly enough, the long period of close and friendly
co-operation between the Derbyshire miners and the Liberals
had begun with an open fight. At the general election of
1885, five years after its formation, the Derbyshire Miners'
Association had insisted on putting up its General Secretary,
James Haslam, for the newly created Chesterfield division.
The Liberals refused to allow him a clear run, and he finished
last in the ensuing three-cornered contest. Before the next
election in the following year Haslam and T. Bayley, the
Liberal nominee, agreed that both should submit their
names to the local Liberal Association, on the understanding
that they would both accept its verdict as to which of them
should stand in the Liberal interest.[2] The choice fell on
Bayley, and for the next twenty years he had the loyal
support of Haslam and the Derbyshire miners, as, indeed,
did the Liberal Members for North-East Derbyshire,
Ilkeston, and Mid Derbyshire, the three other mining
constituencies in north Derbyshire.[3] In Nottinghamshire,
too, the miners' union was wholeheartedly committed to the
Liberal Party. At the general election of 1900 the Nottinghamshire Miners' Association had called upon its members
to support the Liberal candidates in Mansfield, Rushcliffe,
and West Nottingham; and before the election of 1906, on
the suggestion of J. G. Hancock, the union not only

---

[1] See p. 155.   [2] See Williams, op. cit., pp. 488–91.
[3] The miners resident in the South Derbyshire constituency were members of a
separate and much smaller union.

endorsed all the Liberals standing for mining seats, but also sent out an official request that the lodges should act as canvassing organizations on their behalf.[1] In effect, the N.M.A. had become part of the Liberal Party's election machinery.

This affection for the Liberal Party did not make the Derbyshire and Nottinghamshire miners any less anxious to secure parliamentary representation on their own account, and immediately after the M.F.G.B. scheme was adopted in 1902 both unions let it be known that they intended to run candidates if and when suitable mining seats fell vacant. The D.M.A. was lucky, because in December 1905 the Liberal Member for Chesterfield announced that ill health would prevent him from standing at the next election. The Chesterfield Liberal Association, without argument or haggling, promptly adopted Haslam as its candidate. It was true that in 1900 the Liberal majority had dropped danger-ously low, and some of the Liberals may have calculated that a miner's candidate had the best chance of polling the full weight of the mining vote. Haslam, moreover, was no pit-man straight from the coal-face; by now he was a respect-able middle-class worthy, a perfectly sound Liberal, and he was to be paid for by the miners. Still, the Derbyshire Liberals were displaying considerably more political acumen than their counterparts in Durham, Yorkshire, and South Wales, where the refusal of local Liberal Associations to make concessions of this kind was helping to drive the miners into the arms of the Labour Party. The Nottingham-shire miners were not so fortunate, because none of the seats that they had scheduled—Mansfield, Rushcliffe, and West Nottingham—became available, and, of course, there was no question of opposing a sitting Liberal.

At this stage there was little Socialist activity in the coal-field, and it came as no surprise when both the Derbyshire and Nottinghamshire miners voted heavily against joining the Labour Party in 1906. In Derbyshire the result was, for affiliation 1,789 and against 11,257; in Nottinghamshire the figures were, for joining the Labour Party 1,806, against 11,292. Both unions issued official statements advising

[1] *Mansfield Chronicle,* 12 Jan. 1906.

their members to reject affiliation, and in Derbyshire the leadership went out of its way to attack what were called 'L.R.C. emissaries' who had come into the county, though in actual fact it was not the policy of the Labour Party to try to influence the miners in these ballots. Indeed, the cordial alliance between the Liberals and the D.M.A. was further reinforced when another Derbyshire mining seat became vacant early in 1907 on the death of T. D. Bolton, the Member for North-East Derbyshire. Far from resisting a second miners' M.P., it seems that a group of influential Liberals in the area, probably with the encouragement of the Whips' office, took the initiative and put themselves out to make sure that the candidature went to W. E. Harvey.[1] What opposition there was to this idea came from disgruntled miners who took the view that the place for union officials was in the coalfield and not at Westminster. Among those who campaigned for Harvey were Enoch Edwards, Sir Walter Foster (the Liberal M.P. for Ilkeston), Richard Bell, Charles Fenwick, and William Brace, whilst the chairman of his election committee was Sir Arthur Markham, the Liberal M.P. for Mansfield and one of the biggest coal-owners in the Midlands. It was a perfect example of the old-style Lib-Lab arrangement, which was appropriate enough, seeing that this was the last seat to be fought under the M.F.G.B.'s scheme before the Federation became part of the Labour Party.

Although Derbyshire and Nottinghamshire again voted decisively against joining the Labour Party in 1908, Derbyshire by 16,519 votes to 5,811 and Nottinghamshire by 6,877 votes to 3,705, both districts were, of course, carried into the Labour Party along with all the other miners' unions at the beginning of 1909. From now onwards, in accordance with the Chester resolution,[2] all M.F.G.B. candidates were required to sign the party constitution and operate independently of the Liberals. Unfortunately it was in Derbyshire, the least suitable of all the mining districts, that the new partnership between the Federation and the Labour Party came into play for the

---

[1] *Sheffield Daily Independent*, 2 Jan. 1907.
[2] See p. 34.

first time at a by-election in Mid Derbyshire in the summer of 1909. Mid Derbyshire, with a mining vote comprising nearly 50 per cent of the electorate, was one of the safest Liberal seats in the east Midlands. Certainly the Labour Party had never shown any interest in it, and as late as October 1908 the national executive had told the local railwaymen that the constituency was far too ill organized to warrant a Labour candidate in the foreseeable future.[1] In 1906, however, the Liberals had promised the Derbyshire miners that when the sitting Member, Sir Alfred Jacoby, died or retired, the seat would be theirs. At that time only one of the D.M.A.'s officials, James Haslam, was in Parliament; in the meantime W. E. Harvey had also been elected, and though the leading Liberals in the coalfield were apparently quite willing to see a third Derbyshire miner at Westminster, the union now had no one of sufficient calibre to bring forward. The Nottinghamshire Miner's Association, on the other hand, still had no representative in Parliament, because none of the Nottinghamshire mining seats had yet become available. When the Derbyshire miners' officials and the local Liberal leaders put their heads together the obvious move seemed to be to offer the seat to J. G. Hancock, who had been the N.M.A.'s parliamentary nominee since 1904.[2] As it happened, Mid Derbyshire was a particularly suitable seat for Hancock, because by an historical accident about 4,000 of the miners resident in the constituency were members of the N.M.A. and not the D.M.A. Hancock was willing, the Nottinghamshire miners approved of the proposal, and the Chief Liberal Whip gave his blessing. The Mid Derbyshire Liberal Association, however, realizing that a somewhat strange situation was beginning to develop, and uneasy about Hancock's future status, decided to interview him before making up its mind.

The Labour Party was also worried about Hancock's position, and Ramsay MacDonald was soon in touch with the M.F.G.B. inquiring whether its nominee was going to stand as a straight Labour candidate as the Chester resolution required. When the Federation's executive considered the question it had before it a letter from Hancock which seemed to dispose of any doubts on this score: he had met the members of the I.L.P. in the constituency, he had told them that he was going to sign the constitution, and they were perfectly satisfied with his attitude. Given these assurances, the M.F.G.B. endorsed Hancock's candidature, and a few days later, on receipt of a signed copy of the constitution, the national executive of the Labour Party adopted him as a Labour candidate—the first miner to stand as an official Labour candidate after the M.F.G.B.'s affiliation—and delegated Keir Hardie, Will Crooks, and Arthur Henderson to help him at the by-election.[1] Having thus squared the Labour side, Hancock turned his attention to the Liberals, and at his meeting with the Mid Derbyshire Association assured them that, though unavoidably he was a Labour candidate, his personal views were those of a progressive Liberal.[2] They, too, were convinced, and Hancock had now brought off a remarkable trick: he had been officially adopted by both the Liberal and Labour Parties.

As soon as the campaign started it became apparent that so far as Hancock was concerned the Labour Party might not have existed. He continued to employ the Liberal election agent, most of his helpers were Liberals, and when Keir Hardie arrived in Mid Derbyshire he was treated as an embarrassing and unwelcome interloper. Hancock himself was apologetic about his connection with the Labour Party —'circumstances over which he had no control obliged him, if he stood at all, to stand as a Labour candidate', he said; in any case, he claimed, there was a good understanding between the Liberal and Labour Parties, and this contest, he hoped, would be the forerunner of many others like it, a comment that must have horrified Keir Hardie and everyone else engaged in the grim struggle to establish an independent identity for the Labour Party. He certainly gave the Liberals no cause for complaint, and telegrams of support were received from Asquith and Lloyd George, whilst Sir Arthur Markham happily described Hancock as 'a straightforward, simple-minded [sic] Liberal and as good

---

[1] *LPEC*, 24 June, 7 July 1909; *MFGB*, 29 June 1909.
[2] *Belper News*, 2 July 1909.

as any that sat in the House of Commons'.[1] For the Labour
Party there was some consolation in seeing Liberal votes
and the Liberal election machinery carrying a 'Labour'
candidate into Parliament, and short of plunging into a
violent controversy with the M.F.G.B. there was nothing
that could be done for the time being. But within a year or
two events were to show that Hancock was to be one of those
nominal Labour M.P.s who were a great deal more trouble
than they were worth.

Towards the end of 1909 all the M.F.G.B.'s sitting
Members had to decide whether or not they were going to
sign the constitution. There were few Lib-Labs less in
sympathy with the Labour Party and its objectives than
Haslam and Harvey; but unlike John Wilson, Charles
Fenwick, and Thomas Burt in the North-East, who stuck
to their principles and damned the consequences, the two
Derbyshire leaders evidently concluded that signing was
the better part of valour—thereby assuring themselves of
their election expenses and parliamentary salaries. At the
same time, they were anxious not to offend their Liberal
friends, and both of them did their best to avoid referring
to the Labour Party; but for persistent questioning from a
handful of Conservatives and Socialists few of the electors
would have realized that they had any connection with it at
all. Haslam was particularly evasive. In December 1909 he
was saying that he had not yet signed the constitution and
might not do so, and a few days later he irritably told an
election meeting that 'those who were with him knew where
he stood, and those who were not with him had no right to
know and were not going to know'. At no point in the
campaign did he acknowledge that he had become a member
of the Labour Party, and when some Conservatives mis-
chievously began to put it about that he had gone over to
the Socialists, he was understandably enraged—not that this
accusation carried much conviction, for as a local newspaper
commented, 'Mr. Haslam has been actively supported by
all the substantial old-fashioned Liberals who are large
employers of Labour, and to whom out-and-out revolutionary

---

[1] For accounts of the Mid Derbyshire by-election, see *Labour Leader*, 23 July
1909, *Sheffield Daily Independent*, 12 July 1909, and *Belper News*, 9 July 1909.

Socialism is as detestable as it is to the smuggest Tory
reactionary in Chesterfield.'[1] Industrial relations in Derbyshire had always been exceptionally good: even so, Labour
supporters up and down the country may well have reflected
that it was an odd species of Labour candidate who enjoyed
the whole-hearted backing of all the major employers in his
constituency. In North-East Derbyshire Harvey was equally
off-hand about his obligations to the Labour Party, and like
Haslam usually managed to side-step awkward questions
about his political allegiance. For candidates who were
relying on Liberal votes and a Liberal organization theirs
was a prudent enough line to take; but naturally it was soon
to lead them into a number of brushes with the Labour
Party.

At the next general election in December 1910 Haslam
and Harvey had every intention of repeating the tactics that
had served them so well in January. This time, however, the
local Socialists, by now in open rebellion against their
'Labour' M.P.s, succeeded in making a nuisance of themselves. At a meeting of the Derbyshire Socialist League,
consisting of representatives from the I.L.P. branches in the
county, a resolution was carried condemning Haslam and
Harvey and calling upon trade unionists in Chesterfield and
North-East Derbyshire to withhold their support. The
resolution came to the notice of the Conservative candidate
for North-East Derbyshire, and very soon the entire district
was flooded with handbills declaring that the Labour Party
had disowned Haslam and Harvey.[2] Greatly disconcerted,
the Liberal election agent for the two constituencies, S. E.
Short, urgently wired Ramsay MacDonald in London,
pleading with him to come to Derbyshire to refute this
allegation and to speak in support of Haslam.[3] Considering

---

[1] *Sheffield Daily Independent,* 20 Jan. 1910.
[2] *Derbyshire Courier,* 10 Dec. 1910.
[3] S. E. Short to MacDonald, *LPLF,* 9 Dec. 1910. Short's various activities were
in themselves an interesting commentary on the ties between the miners, the Liberals,
and the colliery companies in Derbyshire. Apart from being the Liberal agent in
NE. Derbyshire and Chesterfield, he was also the auditor and occasional financial
adviser to the D.M.A. and chairman of the Eckington coal company, J. and G.
Wells Ltd. The D.M.A.'s chief legal adviser, it should be added, was Sir William
Clegg, a well-known Sheffield businessman and chairman of the Hallamshire
Liberal Association.

that Haslam and Harvey were unwilling to admit that they
were members of the Labour Party (Harvey was not even
describing himself as a Labour candidate, employing instead
the label 'Progressive and Free Trade'), and seeing that they
rarely troubled to conceal their contempt and dislike for the
party, perhaps even MacDonald smiled at the sheer effront-
ery of these Derbyshire Lib-Labs. They certainly had no
intention of changing their ways, for, as Haslam put it, with
a touch of unconscious irony: 'it is only by the help of
Liberal votes that Harvey and I, and men of our character
can get into Parliament at all. Why should we flout them?
I am not prepared to flout them.'[1]

The N.M.A. was hardly affected at all by the affiliation
of the M.F.G.B. to the Labour Party. J. G. Hancock, of
course, was defending his seat in Mid Derbyshire and he
ignored the constitution just as thoroughly in 1910 as he had
at the by-election in 1909. None of the seats which the
N.M.A. had designs upon fell vacant, and there was no
question of challenging sitting Liberals. The Nottinghamshire miners, indeed, were caught up in the traditional
Liberal-versus-Conservative battle even more than most of
the others, for Lloyd George's budget was a particularly
contentious issue here. Nottinghamshire was a county of
great estates, and in fact no less than five members of the
House of Lords—the Dukes of Portland, Newcastle, and
Rutland, Earl Manvers, and Lord Saville—had their
country seats in the 'Dukeries', a large part of which fell
within the Bassetlaw division. The discovery of coal beneath
their lands had brought them enormous fortunes from
mineral royalties and way-leave payments, and naturally
Lloyd George's proposals to tax this income aroused their
wrath. It so happened that one of Lloyd George's advisers
in framing the royalty and way-leave clauses in his budget
had been Sir Arthur Markham, the Member for Mansfield.[2]
Markham himself was a capitalist and a coal-producer, not
a landowner; and like the miners he employed, he deeply
resented the unearned and untaxed income that his enter-
prise put into the pockets of the noble lords. The Duke of
Devonshire alone, he claimed, drew £8,000 a year in royalties

[1] *Derbyshire Courier*, 3 Dec. 1910.   [2] *Mansfield Chronicle*, 21 Jan. 1910.

from his company. For their part, the landed nobility were infuriated at finding one of the architects of their discomfiture on their own doorstep, and in an atmosphere like this, with traditional loyalties and antagonisms taking on a fresh lease of life, it was the merits of the budget and the arrogance of the peers that primarily interested the Nottinghamshire miners, not Socialism and the case for independent Labour representation.

Throughout 1910 and for a year or two afterwards the three miners' M.P.s in Derbyshire continued to defy the Labour Party with impunity. But there were limits to what the local Socialists would tolerate and to what the Labour Party could countenance, and the first to feel the disciplinary squeeze upon him was J. G. Hancock in the summer of 1912. By this time the Mid Derbyshire Labour Party had reached the end of its patience with Hancock and was determined to thrash things out with him once and for all. Their sense of exasperation and frustration comes out in a letter from the secretary of the local party to Arthur Henderson, explaining the situation:

As you are aware, our M.P.—J. G. Hancock—has all along had the support of the Liberal Party in this division. The secretary of the Liberal Party is his Agent, and the sub-agents are all Liberals. For nearly three years we have been trying to appoint a Labour Agent, but he has always put it off with various excuses—'it will alienate a large number of voters etc.' Those have been his reasons, but we think the true explanation is that he is a milk and water Lib-Lab man. However, there are now persistent rumours that the Liberals will contest this seat at the next election. I think it is a certainty. That being so, we are determined to strengthen our position: to this end we held a meeting of delegates last evening and with Hancock discussed the question of appointing a Labour Agent. I must confess I did not get much help or sympathy from Hancock. He raised all kinds of objections: the Agent's salary, the cost of contesting an election, and a host of other expenses. We pointed out that these expenses had been met on previous occasions, and that financial support could be again obtained from the same sources. Hancock replied that his Agent—Mr. Cash—had never been paid a penny for his services; this seems a lot to swallow, seeing that Cash is a lawyer. The sub-agents, he paid out of his own pocket at the rate of £50 per annum. This appeared to land us at a dead end, till one of the delegates obtained from Hancock a half promise that he would, in the event of our deciding to appoint a Labour Agent, divert this £50 and allow it to be used for the purpose of providing a salary for a Labour Agent.[1]

The very next day Hancock thought better of even this modest commitment, and informed the Mid Derbyshire Labour Party that after discussing the position with his union he would have to withdraw what he had said about giving financial help. If the £50 for the sub-agents had really come out of his own pocket it was, of course, no business of the N.M.A.s if he chose to make it over to the Labour Party. What seems more likely is that this money was being provided by the N.M.A. itself, a conclusion that evidently occurred to the Labour Party national executive when these exchanges came to its notice, for soon afterwards it was asking the M.F.G.B. whether the Federation itself or any of its district organizations were still contributing directly or indirectly to the funds of the Liberal Party in the constituencies held by miners' Members.[2]

Hancock's position on the fence was now becoming increasingly precarious. The local Labour Party had never had any confidence in him; now the Mid Derbyshire Liberals were beginning to grow restive too. He was being criticized for not attending Liberal meetings more frequently, and there was talk of running a Liberal candidate against him at the next election. The dissatisfaction of the Liberals evidently frightened Hancock more than the anger of the Socialists, for he hurriedly attended a meeting at Alfreton, attacked 'extreme' Labour men, and promised that in future he would make a point of being at functions organized by the Liberal Association. For the Mid Derbyshire Labour Party this was the last straw, and Hancock was told that unless he made it plain where he stood, and broke with the Liberals, they would feel compelled to ask the national executive to take action against him. If there was one thing above all else that Hancock was anxious to

[1] F. Burton to Henderson, *LPLF*, 25 July 1912.

[2] *LPEC*, 31 July 1912. A resolution passed by the council of the N.M.A. on 4 Dec. 1909 throws some doubt on Hancock's truthfulness: 'That a grant of £120 for the Parliamentary agent, and £50 for the sub-agents be made out of the Parliamentary fund.'

avoid it was an unambiguous statement about where he
stood, and when a friendly admonition from the M.F.G.B.
failed to persuade him to mend his ways, the Labour Party
was at last obliged to intervene.

There was no question of expelling him from the party
without a thorough inquiry, and in October 1912 the
national executive decided to call a conference in Mid
Derbyshire at which delegates from the local party and
representatives from the M.F.G.B. and the national executive would try to clear up the difficulties that had arisen.
From the start Hancock was reluctant to participate and by
a variety of stratagems he managed to delay the conference
until April 1913. When the meeting eventually did take
place the two M.F.G.B. representatives, Robert Smillie and
William Straker, were presented with the familiar catalogue
of complaints, and in their report to the Federation they
made it clear that the only political organization behind
Hancock was the Mid Derbyshire Liberal Association, and
that the D.M.A. and N.M.A. lodges in the division were
determined to go on working with the Liberals. The fact
that they were part of the M.F.G.B., which was affiliated to
the Labour Party, did not seem to disturb them in the least.[1]
Hancock himself, with the full support of his union, decided
to ignore the Labour Party, and throughout 1913 and 1914,
despite repeated warnings from the M.F.G.B., he refused to
co-operate with the local Labour Party. Finally, when he
failed to appear before the Federation's executive in October
1914 to explain his conduct, the M.F.G.B. disowned him
altogether.[2] Mid Derbyshire therefore ceased to be a Labour
seat, and in the circumstances it need hardly be added that
the N.M.A. had no plans for running another 'Labour'
candidate at the next general election.

Whilst this running fight between Hancock and the
Federation was in progress, a far more serious crisis had
developed over the Chesterfield seat. James Haslam was by
now an old man of nearly seventy, and because he had been
originally elected as a Lib-Lab and was understandably set
in his ways, the Labour Party had been inclined to allow
him a certain amount of latitude so as to avoid worsening its

[1] *MFGB*, 23 Apr. 1913.   [2] Ibid. 10 Nov. 1914.

already strained relations with the D.M.A. But it was
certainly not prepared to see another Lib-Lab in his place,
and when it was announced in April 1913 that Haslam
would not be contesting the Chesterfield seat again, the
Labour Party immediately began to take a keen interest in
this constituency. For a start, the national executive was
determined that Labour candidates in mining divisions
should be selected in accordance with the rules of the party:
that is to say, candidates were to be chosen at properly
convened conferences of all the Labour and Socialist
organizations in these constituencies, and were not to be
simply nominated by the miners' unions regardless of everyone else. Consequently, though the D.M.A. had already
chosen Barnet Kenyon (its Assistant Secretary) as Haslam's
successor, in June Arthur Peters travelled to Chesterfield
and insisted that Kenyon should be formally adopted as the
Labour candidate at a joint meeting of delegates from the
D.M.A. and the Chesterfield Trades Council. Kenyon had
no objection to this procedure, and since in the meantime
his candidature had been endorsed by the M.F.G.B., everything seemed to be going smoothly on the Labour side.

By this time, however, Kenyon had discovered that the
Chesterfield Liberals were not prepared to support him (and,
indeed, might even put up a candidate of their own) unless
he agreed to address their annual general meeting every
year. Seeing nothing amiss in this arrangement he wrote to
Arthur Henderson (who had replaced Ramsay MacDonald
as Secretary of the Labour Party) telling him that he proposed to accept the Liberals' terms because in a three-
cornered contest the seat might well go to the Conservatives.[1]

So far as the Labour Party was concerned, an undertaking of this kind was unthinkable, and when the national
executive met on 17 June it was decided that Kenyon must
be left in no doubt that he could not appear before the
Chesterfield Liberal Association once a year, or at all.[2]
Kenyon evidently chose to ignore this injunction, for within
the week the executive of the Chesterfield Liberal Association had agreed to recommend the full Liberal council to

[1] B. Kenyon to Henderson, *LPLF*, 9 June 1913.
[2] *LPEC*, 17 June 1913.

give him their backing. His next move was to address
the joint conference of the D.M.A. lodges and the
Trades Council, and, after he had assured the meeting
that if elected he would support the programme of the
Labour Party, a resolution pledging support for him was
carried almost unanimously. From there he went back to
face the Liberal council, where he succeeded in convincing the assembled Liberals that at heart he was really one
of them.[1]

Only the endorsement of the Labour Party was now
required, and since he happened to be in London, Kenyon
was invited to meet the executive on 15 July. In the course
of his interview he admitted that he had already attended
one Liberal gathering, and he also gave the executive to
understand that if there were a by-election in the near
future, S. E. Short, the Secretary and Treasurer of the
Chesterfield Liberal Association, would be his agent. This
was a disquieting prospect, and the next day Henderson and
Clynes met the M.F.G.B. executive, which also happened
to be sitting in London at the same time. Henderson told
them that the Labour Party was anxious that the campaign
should not begin in an atmosphere of suspicion, and was
especially concerned that Kenyon should not place himself
under any obligation to the Liberal Party. They therefore
intended to send a member of the national executive to
discuss the situation with the D.M.A., and they hoped that
the M.F.G.B. would do likewise.[2] The Federation agreed,
and on 1 August Henderson himself, with John Robertson
of the Scottish miners, arrived in Chesterfield. After
questioning Kenyon they understood him to have promised
to 'accept, sign and observe the constitution in its entirety'.
Henderson and Robertson concluded that Kenyon's attitude
justified them in asking the Labour Party and the M.F.G.B.
to take him at his word, and, since Haslam had died during
the previous week and speed was now of some importance,
Kenyon was told of their decision without more ado. Before
leaving Chesterfield, Henderson telephoned Jim Middleton,
his Assistant Secretary, telling him to let the other members

---

[1] *Derbyshire Courier*, 19 July 1913, 9 Aug. 1913.
[2] *LPEC*, 15 July 1913; *MFGB*, 16 July 1913.

of the national executive know that he, Henderson, was satisfied that they could safely endorse Kenyon. When the replies came back, however, it was clear that the national executive was by no means unanimous: eight were in favour of taking a chance on Kenyon, five were against, and Ramsay MacDonald was doubtful. In the circumstances the emergency committee decided that the question should be left over to the next meeting of the full executive on 12 August.[1]

Meanwhile, in Chesterfield Kenyon had opened his campaign. Knowing that he had made a favourable impression on Arthur Henderson, and confident that the endorsement of the Labour Party would be forthcoming, he now concentrated on reassuring the Liberals. If the Liberals had adopted someone else, he claimed, the D.M.A. would have supported this other nominee; his signature on the Labour Party constitution, he implied, meant only that he would not be bound to vote with the Liberals in the House on labour issues; and in his election address he styled himself the 'Progressive and Labour candidate'.[2] At a later stage the officials of the D.M.A. were to allege that Kenyon had taken up with the Liberals only because he received no help from the Labour Party in the first week of the by-election. In fact he was angling for Liberal support from the very outset.

So it was that when the Labour Party national executive met on 12 August it had before it a sizeable collection of press reports establishing beyond doubt that Kenyon was conducting his campaign on totally unacceptable lines. Arthur Henderson, who was away at a trade union conference in Scotland, was still not prepared to change his mind, and wrote to the executive urging them not to repudiate Kenyon. He conceded that the miners had caused enough trouble already, and that Kenyon had made a bad beginning; but to abandon him, he wrote, would 'risk the loss of a seat to the Party and would probably be much misunderstood by many of our Trade-Union supporters throughout the country'.[3] This plea had no effect on the executive,

---

[1] Henderson to Middleton, *LPLF*, 9 Aug. 1913; *LPEC*, 8 Aug. 1913.
[2] *Derbyshire Courier*, 9 Aug. 1913.
[3] Henderson to Middleton, *LPLF*, 9 Aug. 1913.

which unanimously refused to endorse Kenyon and carried a resolution asking all members of the executive and the Parliamentary Party to stay out of the Chesterfield constituency.

The next step was to persuade the M.F.G.B. to accept the party's verdict. The Federation had already endorsed Kenyon, and now it was being asked to disown a well-known and respected union official who enjoyed the full support and confidence of his own district. This was a crucial test of the Labour Party's authority over one of its most powerful affiliated organizations, an organization, moreover, which had never in the past shown itself to be particularly co-operative or compliant. To make matters even more difficult and embarrassing, the Labour Party's decision reached the Federation just after it had heard a favourable report on Kenyon's candidature from Robertson. There is no record of what was said at this important executive meeting, but in the end a resolution repudiating Kenyon was carried against a more moderate one calling for a meeting with the Labour Party executive to try to patch up the situation.[1]

Along with the news that the Labour Party was not, after all, going to endorse him, Kenyon received a weighty letter of condemnation from Ramsay MacDonald, accusing him of going back on his promises:

I think it is far better under such circumstances if you want to be a Liberal candidate to say so quite honestly. If you are to run as a Labour candidate you must accept certain responsibilities. To try to do both is wrong morally, and if acquiesced in would make the continued existence of the Party impossible. I was asked, for instance, to speak with Mr. Ure [the Liberal Advocate] on your behalf. Such a suggestion was so absurd that I wondered if we really had been in existence for the last thirteen years. It is quite true, as you say, that you talked the matter over with Mr. Henderson, and that he, on receiving certain explanations and pledges from you, agreed to advise the Executive to endorse your candidature. But unless the papers are lying very much more than usual, you have not carried out your pledges. . . .[2]

The Labour Party's decision came as a complete surprise in Chesterfield, and both the Derbyshire miners and, oddly

[1] *MFGB*, 7 Oct. 1913.   [2] *Derbyshire Courier*, 16 Aug. 1913.

enough, the Chesterfield Liberals reacted angrily. The most urgent problem confronting Kenyon was to find the funds for his campaign, since nothing could now be expected from the M.F.G.B. or the Labour Party. Eventually, the D.M.A. had to approach Sir Arthur Markham, who agreed to guarantee Kenyon's bank loan of £1,700.[1] All the Derbyshire miners' leaders resolved to ignore the Labour Party and to stand by Kenyon, who was presented as a political martyr, bravely defying 'the dictation of the Socialist junta in London'.[2] The result of the by-election, a comfortable majority of over 2,000 for Kenyon, was widely hailed as a blow to the prestige of Ramsay MacDonald and the Socialist element within the Labour movement. Other observers saw in the successful defiance of Kenyon and the D.M.A. a victory for the miners over the Labour Party. *The Times* commented: 'The miners have thrown back the Labour Party's repudiation of their candidate in its face. All parties agree in attributing the size of Kenyon's majority to the interference of the Labour Party Executive....' And the *Daily Express* dwelt upon the possible consequences of the episode:

Even more serious than the loss of the seat to the Labour Party is the loss of prestige and the split between the Labour Party and the rank and file of the miners. MacDonald's belated attempt—by repudiating Kenyon—to show that the Labour Party in the House of Commons is independent of the Radicals has been treated with contempt, and the miners have proved that they are prepared to break with the Labour Party rather than be dragooned by a mock heroic caucus. Other mining areas are likely to follow Chesterfield's lead.[3]

The 'Kenyon affair' was indeed to be an episode of some significance in the early history of the Labour Party. But the appearances of August 1913 were deceptive; the battle of wills had only just started, and it was to end six months later not in the secession of the miners but in the complete surrender of the D.M.A.

[1] The D.M.A. itself was in no position to help Kenyon. In July 1910 a miner named Joseph Fisher had obtained an injunction against the union restraining it from using its funds for political purposes. Subsequently the D.M.A. had tried a system of voluntary contributions, but this had met with little success. *Derbyshire Courier*, 16 July, 10 Sept. 1910. And see Williams, op. cit., p. 502.

[2] *Derbyshire Courier*, 16 Aug. 1913.

[3] Quotations from the *Belper News*, 29 Aug. 1913.

The D.M.A., insisting that it was more sinned against than sinning, decided in its indignation to carry the fight against the Labour Party to the M.F.G.B. annual conference in October 1913. There its delegates argued that Kenyon had been treated unfairly and unjustifiably both by the Labour Party and by the Federation, a charge which naturally stung some members of the M.F.G.B. executive to hit back at the D.M.A. Herbert Smith, for example, thought it incredible that Kenyon's election agent should be the secretary of a local colliery company, and Thomas Greenall noted that W. E. Harvey had described Kenyon's election as a victory for Liberalism. What sort of effect, he wanted to know, was a remark like that calculated to have on hitherto Conservative miners in Lancashire? If this was to be the attitude of the D.M.A., he declared, the sooner it left the M.F.G.B. the better. Robert Smillie stressed that the Derbyshire miners, and others too, must learn that the Labour Party was absolutely independent of all other parties. Possibly Kenyon had fallen into the wrong hands, but they had to recognize that the M.F.G.B. was becoming 'a standing disgrace' to the Labour Party—'not a week passed', he said, 'but complaints were made to the Labour Party about some miners' Member'. At the end of the debate the conference approved the executive's repudiation of Kenyon but called for a joint meeting of the executives of the Labour Party and the Federation to discuss the possibility of admitting Kenyon to the party.[1]

The Derbyshire miners remained as intransigent as ever and when the D.M.A. council met in December 1913 it was not prepared to yield an inch. Unless Kenyon was adopted as a Labour Member, and his election expenses paid by the M.F.G.B., the union threatened to organize a ballot of its members to see if they wished to sever their connection with the Federation. And until the issue was settled the D.M.A. decided to defer payment of the political levy.[2] The Derbyshire miners' tactics were to play upon the Federation's fear of disunity in its own ranks in the hope that the M.F.G.B. would try to persuade the Labour Party

[1] *MFGB*, 7 Oct. 1913; *The Times*, 9 Oct. 1913.
[2] *DMA*, 29 Dec. 1913.

to accept Kenyon; and as time went by there were signs that these methods might produce results. In January 1914, for example, Thomas Ashton was saying that several members of the Federation executive believed that Kenyon ought to be taken back into the fold; in his opinion 'whatever Kenyon did at the time of the Chesterfield by-election should be forgotten and buried'.[1] When the M.F.G.B. executive met in January 1914 to interview Kenyon this was a view that was evidently gaining ground. If Kenyon would sign the constitution, take the Labour whip, and help in establishing Labour election machinery in Chesterfield, the Federation agreed that a fresh approach should be made to the Labour Party. Somewhat reluctantly Kenyon accepted these conditions, but there still remained a difficulty over his promise to address the local Liberal Association once a year. In the end he promised to ask the Liberals to release him from this obligation; if they agreed the Federation would then ask the Labour Party to endorse him.[2]

When Kenyon returned to Chesterfield he soon discovered that the Liberals were not prepared to play; and, considering that he had been elected with Liberal votes, with the help of the Liberal organization, and with his election expenses guaranteed by a leading Liberal in the district, their attitude was not altogether unreasonable. In their view they were entitled at the very least to insist that Kenyon should be answerable to them once a year for his activities in Parliament.[3] As soon as it was clear how the land lay, Kenyon rapidly changed tack, and announced that he could not sign the constitution after all unless he were allowed the same latitude that Haslam had enjoyed. In taking this stand he had the full support of the D.M.A. council, which if anything seemed to be growing even more aggressive, for at its meeting on 2 February it decided to press for changes in the party constitution with the object of reducing the number of representatives from the Socialist societies on the national executive and of allowing parliamentary candidates to accept help from outside the Labour Party.[4]

A few days later, to general astonishment, the D.M.A.

[1] *Derbyshire Courier*, 3 Jan. 1914.   [2] *MFGB*, 14 Jan. 1914.
[3] *Mansfield Chronicle*, 9 Apr. 1914.   [4] *DMA*, 2 Feb. 1914.

suddenly capitulated. On 4 February Frank Hall, the Association's General Secretary, argued the Derbyshire miners'
case for the last time at a meeting of the M.F.G.B. executive.
By now the Federation had lost patience with Kenyon and
his vacillations, and the executive decided that in view of his
latest statement it could not possibly ask the Labour Party
to endorse him.[1] Hall evidently sensed that they had reached
the end of the road and that nothing was to be gained from
applying further pressure on the M.F.G.B., for on his return
from London he immediately called together the D.M.A.
council and told it that the Federation was adamant and that
the battle was lost. The council thereupon ruled that
Kenyon must break with the Liberals. Kenyon seemed to
acquiesce, and after the meeting Hall wrote to Arthur
Henderson and in effect offered his union's surrender:
Kenyon, he said, had agreed to set aside his personal feelings
and objections to the Labour Party constitution so as to
work for the unity of the D.M.A. and the Federation. He
was now ready to sign the constitution 'unconditionally'.[2]
On 9 February Hall and Kenyon travelled to London to
meet the emergency committee of the national executive,
where Kenyon repeated these assurances. Satisfied that at
last he meant what he said, the emergency committee
recommended the Parliamentary Labour Party, which
happened to be holding its annual meeting on the same day,
to accept Kenyon as a new Member, which it agreed to do
by thirty-one votes to five.[3]

Overnight Kenyon had become a Labour M.P. Taken
aback by this unexpected transformation, the Chesterfield
Liberals naturally wanted to know why, after all its earlier
bluster, the D.M.A. had given way so abjectly. Somewhat
lamely, Frank Hall explained that had Kenyon not been
adopted by the Labour Party the D.M.A. would have been
obliged to find his election and registration expenses whilst
at the same time continuing to contribute to the M.F.G.B.
political fund. If they voted to withdraw from the political
fund then they would be required to meet W. E. Harvey's

[1] MFGB, 4 Feb. 1914.
[2] DMA, 7 Feb. 1914; Labour Leader, 19 Feb. 1914.
[3] LPEC, 9 Feb. 1914; Derbyshire Courier, 14 Feb. 1914.

expenses, as well as those of Kenyon, out of their own resources; and, in any case, manœuvres of this kind would mean constant strife within the union and ill feeling between the D.M.A. and the M.F.G.B. In the circumstances they felt that they had no alternative but to give in.[1] Nobody said it, but the implication was obvious: the D.M.A.'s bluff had been called.

There was still one more twist to the Kenyon story. On 18 February, after further reflection, he announced that he was withdrawing from the Labour Party. Kenyon was certainly a difficult man to pin down, because he now claimed that, although he had accepted the constitution unconditionally, he had always been under the impression that he would be treated in the same way as James Haslam, who had been permitted to address his supporters from both Labour and Liberal platforms. To his surprise, he was not, after all, to be allowed this privilege. This, of course, was patent nonsense, and the real reason for this final change of heart was explained in a letter to Frank Hall. As a result of conversations with a few fellow spirits like John Wilson, Charles Fenwick, Albert Stanley, William Johnson, and John Ward, all elderly Lib-Labs, he had come to the conclusion that there was no future for the Labour Party and that the sooner he cut loose from it the better. Sir Arthur Markham and other influential Liberals had made it clear that the Chesterfield seat would always be at the disposal of the Derbyshire miners, and Kenyon hinted that Hall would be the obvious successor to himself. Frank Hall was not impressed: the battle was over and he knew it. He wrote back to Kenyon and told him that in future he would be on his own.[2]

The Labour Party had asserted its authority over the D.M.A. only just in time, for in April 1914 W. E. Harvey died and the North-East Derbyshire seat fell vacant. The full significance of the Kenyon affair had not yet been grasped in Derbyshire, and for a while it was believed that any D.M.A. candidate was bound to be acceptable to the

[1] *Derbyshire Courier*, 14 Feb. 1914.

[2] Correspondence between Kenyon and Hall, made available by Dr. J. E. Williams of the University of Leeds.

Liberals; the suggestion that the Liberals might oppose the miners' nominee was dismissed as absurd.[1] At the end of April the D.M.A. executive recommended that North-East Derbyshire should be contested and that the candidate should be either Frank Hall or James Martin, the President of the union. When the miners' council met on 4 May it had before it a letter from Sir Arthur Markham making it clear that if the D.M.A. settled for a Lib-Lab candidate the North-East Derbyshire Liberal Association, on the authority of the Chief Whip, would give him their full support and would pay his election expenses; on the other hand, if the miners ran a straight Labour candidate, who refused to appear on Liberal platforms, the Liberals would put up a man of their own. It was an offer that must have tempted many of the staunch Liberals on the council; but after the Kenyon imbroglio another Lib-Lab candidature was out of the question. The only point at issue was whether they were to let the seat go by default or contest it on independent Labour lines. There was a general feeling that after the deaths of Haslam and Harvey the union could not afford to lose the services of Hall in Derbyshire, and so the lodges were asked if they wanted James Martin to fight the by-election.[2]

The following afternoon a hurried lodge vote was held and the result was a majority in favour of fighting. The Liberals complained, with some justification, that the vote was even more unrepresentative than usual, because so many men were working the afternoon shift when the lodge meetings were held; at one of the largest collieries only sixteen men were said to have voted out of several thousand lodge members. Nevertheless, the die was cast, and the next day a deputation from the D.M.A., led by Frank Lee, the union's Assistant Secretary, met the executive of the North-East Derbyshire Liberal Association to try to persuade them not to oppose Martin. Lee did his best to soothe the Liberals. He himself, he said, had been a Liberal sub-agent for more years than he cared to count, and his own sympathies were very largely Liberal; the Derbyshire miners intended to try to 'broaden' the Labour Party constitution;

[1] *Derby Daily Telegraph*, 5 May 1914.   [2] *DMA*, 4 May 1914.

Martin was certainly not a Socialist—nor, indeed, were any of the Derbyshire miners Socialists, except in the sense that the Liberals too were Socialists—and he was certainly the right man to unite the progressive forces. The effect of all this was somewhat marred when Lee was forced to admit that, whilst Martin would not be able to speak from Liberal platforms, Liberals would be welcome if they wanted to help him, an admission that was apparently greeted with some derision.[1] Seeing no reason why they should tolerate a candidate who might be a Liberal in spirit but over whom they would have no control, the Liberals adopted J. P. Houfton, the managing director of a local colliery company.[2]

On the same day Martin and Hall were in London to discuss the situation with the M.F.G.B. executive. Hall assured the Federation that there would be no repetition of the Kenyon affair and that there would be no co-operation with the Liberals. In his view it was unlikely that the Liberals would fight the seat anyway, since a Liberal candidature would require the approval of the North-East Derbyshire Liberal council, and out of the 200 members of this body 150 were miners, who could be relied upon to veto any move to run a candidate against one of their own officials. Martin himself then delivered a forceful speech promising to stick to the letter of the constitution and to do his utmost to build up his own Labour organization.[3] The D.M.A. on display for the M.F.G.B.'s benefit was certainly

[1] Shorthand transcript made available by Dr. J. E. Williams. For a Liberal view, see Violet Markham, op. cit., p. 19: 'We thought it unfair and ungenerous that Labour should proceed to bite the Liberal hands that had fed it, and many of our Lib-Lab. friends were unhappy and embarrassed by the part they were forced to play. But looking back, I can appreciate the political wisdom of this action. The astute leaders of the Labour Party realised the importance of freeing themselves from entangling alliances of any kind. It was essential to the emergence of a full-blooded Socialist philosophy that all compromises should be eliminated and the vat stand on its own bottom.'

[2] Having decided to fight the miners in a mining constituency, the Liberals could hardly have chosen a better man. Houfton was the son of a working collier, and had risen from office-boy to general manager. He had lived in the constituency all his life and in the past had been prominent among W. E. Harvey's supporters. His firm—the Bolsover Colliery Company—justifiably enjoyed a high reputation for enlightened paternalism.

[3] *MFGB*, 6 May 1914.

a very different organization from the union that was being described to the North-East Derbyshire Liberals on the same afternoon.

For their part, the Liberals were puzzled and angry. 'Why couldn't they send us another Barnet Kenyon?', Houfton plaintively inquired. Realizing that the seat might now go to the Conservatives on a minority vote, the miners and the Liberals turned fiercely on each other. There were ill-tempered wrangles about their relative contributions to the upkeep of the constituency in the previous five years, and about the money that the D.M.A. allegedly owed the Liberal election agent.[1] At one point in these heated exchanges Frank Hall vowed that in future the D.M.A. would run a candidate in every mining division in the county, a threat that may have been taken seriously at the Liberal Party headquarters in London, where the contest was said to be considered 'ill advised and inopportune'.[2] To the Liberal Party managers it probably did seem foolish to antagonize a hitherto friendly trade union; but, as Houfton pointed out, if the North-East Derbyshire Liberal Association had not fought on this occasion it could have closed its doors for good. As polling-day came nearer it was plain that Martin could not hope to win. None of the miners who had been previously employed as Liberal sub-agents went over to Labour, and Martin's most enthusiastic supporters were to be found not among his fellow miners, but among the local railwaymen. In the end, and largely as a result of the split between the D.M.A. and the Liberals, North-East Derbyshire returned a Conservative Member for the first time in its history; Martin finished well behind the Liberal and probably won just under half the mining vote. But the North-East Derbyshire by-election was important not so much because it exposed the undeniable weakness of the Labour Party amongst the Derbyshire miners but because it severed the D.M.A. from the Liberals. The break was a long time coming in Derbyshire; but when it did it was acrimonious, noisy, and final.

1 *Derbyshire Courier*, 16 May 1914; *Sheffield Daily Independent*, 12 May 1914.
2 *The Times*, 13 May 1914.

(ii) STAFFORDSHIRE AND WARWICKSHIRE

In Staffordshire and Warwickshire,[1] as in the east Midlands, Lib-Lab politics persisted and flourished well into the twentieth century, though the miners' unions and the Liberals were never so close here as in Derbyshire and Nottinghamshire. The North Staffordshire Miners' Federation had first shown an interest in parliamentary representation in 1892, when it nominated Enoch Edwards, its General Secretary, for the Newcastle under Lyme seat; the local Liberal Association, however, refused to support Edwards, and so as to avoid a three-cornered contest that might help the Conservatives he dutifully withdrew. Eight years later the miners managed to persuade the Hanley Liberals to adopt Edwards, though like all the Liberals in the five north Staffordshire seats he was beaten in the 'khaki' election of 1900. When the M.F.G.B. scheme for fighting more seats came into operation in 1902 the N.S.M.F. decided that it would definitely fight Hanley again at the next election.[2]

The situation was complicated by a Liberal revival and the formation in 1902 of the North Staffordshire Liberal Federation. The moving spirit behind this new organization was Sir Alfred Billson, an energetic character who made such a favourable impression on the demoralized Liberals that very soon both Hanley and Stoke-on-Trent Liberal Associations were talking of him as a possible candidate. Unfortunately John Ward of the navvies' union had already been provisionally adopted, albeit reluctantly, by the Liberals in Stoke, and in Hanley, of course, the miners were determined to run Enoch Edwards again. At first the Liberals tried to induce Edwards to move to North-West Staffordshire, where, as they pointed out, there were far more miners than in Hanley; but, on the grounds that the

---

[1] The miners in these two counties formed part of the Midland Miners' Federation. In 1910 the constituent unions of this Federation were: the North Staffordshire Miners' Federation (8,143 members), the Warwickshire Miners' Association (11,000 members), the Cannock Chase Miners (9,400 members), the Shropshire Miners (2,300 members), the South Staffordshire and East Worcestershire Miners (1,595 members), and the Old Hill and Highley Miners (1,116 members).

[2] *NSMF*, 29 Dec. 1902.

borough constituency was cheaper and easier to work, Edwards refused to budge. Eventually it was agreed that Billson should fight North-West Staffordshire and that the Liberals would give their full support to the two trade union candidates, Ward in Stoke and Edwards in Hanley, on the condition that the local Labour organizations did all they could to help the Liberals in the three remaining north Staffordshire seats, Newcastle under Lyme, Leek, and North-West Staffordshire.[1] Thus, at the general election of 1906, Edwards's candidature in Hanley formed part of a Liberal-trade union pact of the kind that had been worked out twenty years earlier in Durham and Yorkshire. The arrangements worked smoothly and effectively and all five seats were regained from the Conservatives.

The miners gained a second seat in the summer of 1907 when a vacancy occurred in North-West Staffordshire on the death of Sir Alfred Billson. Enoch Edwards made it plain that the miners were going to fight this seat whether the Liberals liked it or not; in fact he claimed that it was only lack of funds that had prevented them from doing so years earlier. Now, with the M.F.G.B. scheme in force, they had the money, and in Albert Stanley, a Cannock Chase miners' agent, they had the ideal candidate.[2] As it happened there was no resistance from the Liberals, and in any case they had little cause for complaint, because Stanley was a well-known Liberal (as far back as 1894 he had been one of the founder-members of the Midland Liberal Federation), and during the election campaign he made so much of his hostility towards Socialism that the local I.L.P. branches refused to have anything to do with him.

Like all the other M.F.G.B. Members, Edwards and Stanley were required to stand as straight Labour candidates at the two general elections of 1910, and as in many of the other coalfields their new labels made no difference at all. In fact the local newspapers, quite understandably, continued to describe them as Lib-Labs. Edwards was adopted at a joint meeting of the Hanley Trades Council and Hanley Liberal Association, and as late as November 1910 the

[1] *Staffordshire Sentinel*, 1 Jan. 1906; 16 Jan. 1906; 4 July 1912.
[2] Ibid., 17 July 1907.

N.S.M.F. was still officially advising its members to support the Liberal candidates in Newcastle under Lyme and Leek.[1]

In Warwickshire there had been a similar pattern of events. The Warwickshire Miners' Association had first ventured into politics in 1892, when its General Secretary, William Johnson, unsuccessfully stood for Tamworth. In 1900 he contested the far more suitable Nuneaton division, but was beaten by the sitting Conservative. For social rather than political reasons (for he was a perfectly orthodox Liberal) the Nuneaton Liberals had never really approved of Johnson.[2] But as the miners were prepared to pay his expenses, and since Nuneaton was, after all, a Conservative and not a Liberal seat at the time, they agreed to support him again in 1906. This time he was returned with a comfortable majority and continued to sit as a Lib-Lab for the next four years. He signed the Labour Party constitution in 1909, though as he remarked, with rather more frankness than some of the other Lib-Labs—'It wouldn't matter to him and his colleagues whether he signed or not.' In both general elections in 1910 his agent and election machinery were provided by the Nuneaton Liberals, and he contrived to go right through both campaigns without mentioning the Labour Party at all. Ironically, Nuneaton was one of the seats singled out by the Midland Liberal Federation before the December election as being in special danger; a large number of extra sub-agents were drafted into the constituency, and when Johnson managed to hold the seat the Midland Liberals congratulated themselves on 'a most notable victory'.[3]

Although Enoch Edwards and Albert Stanley were never as bitterly hostile towards the Labour Party as some of the miners' leaders in Derbyshire and Nottinghamshire, in the years immediately after affiliation neither of them made a serious effort to develop separate Labour organizations in their constituencies. Ramsay MacDonald tried repeatedly to persuade Edwards that he must establish his own election machine in Hanley, but Edwards was convinced that on his

---

[1] *NSMF*, 28 Nov. 1910.   [2] *Midland Counties Tribune*, 12 Jan. 1906.

[3] *Midland Liberal Federation Minutes*, 19 Jan. 1911. After 1910 Johnson flatly refused to break with the local Liberal Party, and after a series of skirmishes with the Nuneaton L.R.C. he was eventually disowned by the M.F.G.B. in March 1914 and ceased to be a Labour M.P. *MFGB*, 17 Mar. 1914.

death or retirement the Liberals would accept another
Labour man in his place. In his view it was unthinkable that
they would turn their organization against a Labour candidate: as MacDonald sorrowfully noted, 'I seemed to be
casting doubt on the honesty of men who were his friends,
and he resented it.' It was on these optimistic assumptions
that the Midland Miners' Federation continued to make an
annual grant of £200 towards the upkeep of the constituency,
and this money, of course, was put at the disposal of the
local Liberal officials.[1]

In June 1912 Edwards died, and Hanley at once became
the centre of a violent dispute between the Labour Party and
the Liberals. Both parties saw that this was something of a
test case, for Hanley was one of those mining seats where
the Member had been originally elected as a Lib-Lab, but,
technically at least, had become a Labour M.P. on signing
the constitution in 1909. When the seat fell vacant it was
the right of succession that was at stake. The Liberals
claimed that Edwards had been elected with Liberal votes
and with the help of the Liberal organization, and, harking
back to the pact made in 1903, protested that they had
agreed to support two Labour candidates in north Staffordshire on condition that the Liberals had first claim on the
other three seats; but since Stanley had been elected for
North-West Staffordshire in 1907 these proportions had
been reversed. On the other side, the Labour Party would
have none of these arguments. As Ramsay MacDonald
pointed out, the L.R.C. had never been a party to the 1903
agreement, and in any case the Labour Party did not count
Stoke as one of its seats, because John Ward had refused to
join the party. Furthermore, the money for the previous
three elections had been found by the miners, who had also
contributed regularly to the registration expenses.[2] The fact
was that the Labour Party could not allow Hanley to revert
to the Liberals, for if this precedent were established, the

---

[1] *Labour Leader*, 18 July 1912. *Midland Liberal Federation Minutes*, 26 Oct.
1910; 27 Nov. 1911. An instalment was paid over to the Liberals shortly before
Edwards's death. As a result, when the Liberal and Labour Parties found themselves in opposition at the subsequent by-election, the miners' money was used
against their own candidate.

[2] *Staffordshire Sentinel*, 6 July 1912; *The Times*, 5 July 1912.

party stood gradually to lose a number of other seats as the miners' Members died or retired. Consequently there was a good deal of alarm in the national executive when the news reached London that the Hanley Liberal and Labour Association had been in action and seemed willing to adopt R. L. Outhwaite, a Liberal land-reformer and single-taxer. Worried that the seat might be surrendered without a fight, MacDonald warned the Trades Council not to endorse Outhwaite and urged them to ask the North Staffordshire miners to nominate a candidate. At the same time, Arthur Henderson, Stephen Walsh, and Arthur Peters were dispatched to Hanley to take charge of this dangerous situation. The Liberals, as MacDonald had foreseen, were not prepared to support another miner, and on 2 July 1912 they formally adopted Outhwaite. Two days later it was announced that the Labour candidate was to be Samuel Finney, the President of the N.S.M.F.

With the Hanley by-election of July 1912, Lib-Lab politics in the west Midlands came to an end in a welter of bitter recrimination. Labour supporters everywhere rounded angrily on the Liberals, and at one time it was being seriously suggested that all the Labour M.P.s should leave Westminster (where the Liberal Government needed their votes) and make their way to Hanley to help Finney.[1] As it was, most of the party leaders, including Keir Hardie, MacDonald, Henderson, Snowden, and Will Crooks, did campaign for Finney, and even Albert Stanley turned on the Liberals, professing complete indifference to the views of his own Liberal supporters in North-West Staffordshire. Outhwaite was a forceful and energetic character, and, concentrating entirely upon the issue of land reform, he was soon outshining his pedestrian Labour opponent. The situation was not without irony, for until his adoption as the Labour candidate Finney had always been known for his moderate Liberal views, and not surprisingly, confronted with a Liberal opponent far more radical than himself, was completely out of his depth. And by contrast with his predecessor, the bluff and genial Enoch Edwards, Finney was something of a religious zealot and by all accounts a

---

[1] *The Times*, 3 July 1912.

totally uninspiring candidate.[1] The result was a victory for Outhwaite, with the Conservative second and Finney a very poor third.

The Liberals were naturally exultant that their candidate had so easily outscored the Labour man in a so-called Labour seat. Yet already a certain prescient apprehension was creeping in, for as the Secretary of the Midland Liberal Federation wrote, 'while it was a pleasing thing to win Hanley and thus strengthen the position of the Chief Whip in dealing with Labour, it must be confessed that a series of such struggles would be fraught with the utmost danger to Progressive politics'. With little or no organization and a weak candidate Labour had still won enough support to bring the Liberal majority over the Conservatives perilously low, and far from being disheartened by their heavy defeat, all the indications were that the miners, in their anger at the behaviour of the Liberals, were determined to fight again and do better on the next occasion. In August 1912 the N.S.M.F. abruptly cut its financial ties with the local Liberal Party and resolved to set up a separate Labour organization in Hanley.[2] There were so many extraneous considerations distorting the simple Labour-versus-Liberal issue in Hanley that the outcome of the by-election was hardly a fair guide to Labour's support among the north Staffordshire miners at this stage. But, as a landmark in the relationship between the Liberals on the one side and the Labour Party and the miners on the other, it was of some significance; if, like several other by-elections in the years 1910 to 1914, it showed how far the Labour Party still had to go in the coalfields, it nevertheless did the party a considerable service in widening the breach between the Liberals and the M.F.G.B.

---

[1] For accounts of this by-election, see J. C. Wedgwood, *Memoirs of a Fighting Life*, 1940, p. 83; *Midland Liberal Federation Minutes*, 31 July 1912; *Staffordshire Sentinel*, July 1912.

[2] *NSMF*, 19 Aug. 1912. It was this by-election that led the M.F.G.B. to look again at its rule permitting a miner to stand for Parliament only in his own district. For financial and tactical reasons the Labour Party had been willing to see Hanley contested by a miner; but, as the M.F.G.B. rules then stood, the choice was restricted to the best man the Midland Miners' Federation could provide. In October 1912 the M.F.G.B. promised the Labour Party that this rule would be changed. *MFGB*, 1 Oct. 1912.

APPENDIX

(i) *The mining vote* c. *1910*

	Constituency	Electorate	Estimated no. of miner voters	Miners as per cent of total vote
Derbyshire	Chesterfield	16,248	6,870	42
	Mid Derbyshire	13,660	5,670	41
	NE. Derbyshire	17,701	5,820	32
	Ilkeston	19,467	6,060	31
	South Derbyshire	17,368	1,860	10
Nottinghamshire	Mansfield	21,075	9,470	44
	Rushcliffe	19,640	3,690	18
	Bassetlaw	12,012	2,080	17
	Borough seat calculated from 1911 census:			
	Nottingham West	17,624	2,370	13
Staffordshire	NW. Staffordshire	16,498	5,480	33
	Hanley	16,543	2,330	14
	Stoke-on-Trent	15,079	2,190	14
	Newcastle under Lyme	10,512	1,530	14
	West Staffordshire	12,197	3,740	30
	Lichfield	10,703	2,850	26
Warwickshire	Nuneaton	17,451	4,830	27
	Tamworth	18,228	2,300	12
Leicestershire	Bosworth	13,681	4,330	31

(ii) *Election results, 1906–14: miners' candidates are in italic*

	1906	1910 (January)	1910 (December)
Derbyshire			
Chesterfield	*J. Haslam* (L-L) 7,254 G. Locker-Lampson (C) 5,590	*J. Haslam* (Lab) 8,234 G. Radford (U) 5,693	*J. Haslam* (Lab) 7,283 G. Radford (U) 5,055
	By-election, 1913: *B. Kenyon* (L-L) 7,725 E. Christie (U) 5,539 J. Scurr (Soc) 583		
Mid Derbyshire	Sir J. A. Jacoby (L) 7,065 S. Cresswell (C) 3,475	*J. G. Hancock* (Lab) 7,557 F. Francis (U) 4,268	*J. G. Hancock* (Lab) 6,557 Sir D. Rhys (U) 4,287
	By-election, 1909: *J. G. Hancock* (Lab) 6,735 S. Cresswell (U) 4,392		
NE. Derbyshire	T. D. Bolton (L) 7,665 J. Court (C) 5,896	*W. E. Harvey* (Lab) 8,715 J. Court (C) 6,411	*W. E. Harvey* (Lab) 7,838 J. Court (U) 6,088
	By-election, 1907: *W. E. Harvey* (L-L) 6,644 J. Court (U) 5,915 1914: H. Bowden (U) 6,469 J. P. Houfton (L) 6,155 *J. Martin* (Lab) 3,669		
Ilkeston	Sir W. Foster (L) 9,655 L. Tipper (C) 5,358	Sir W. Foster (L) 10,632 F. Morrow (U) 6,432	J. E. B. Seely (L) 9,990 M. Freeman (U) 5,946
	By-election, 1910: J. E. B. Seely (L) 10,204 H. F. Wright (U) 6,871 1912: J. E. B. Seely (L) 9,049 M. Freeman (U) 7,838		

(ii) *Election results, 1906–14: miners' candidates are in italic (cont.)*

	1906	1910 (January)	1910 (December)
Derbyshire (cont.)			
South Derbyshire	H. Raphael (L) 7,961 J. Gretton (C) 6,468	H. Raphael (L) 8,259 J. Marsden-Smedley (U) 7,473	H. Raphael (L) 7,744 J. Marsden-Smedley (U) 7,373
Nottinghamshire			
Mansfield	A. B. Markham (L)	A. B. Markham (L) 12,622 J. G. Campbell (U) 4,382	A. B. Markham (L) 11,383 F. Cockerill (U) 4,200
Rushcliffe	J. E. Ellis (L) 9,094 H. F. Wyatt (LU) 5,460	J. E. Ellis (L) 9,942 C. Disraeli (U) 7,098	Lief Jones (L) 9,186 C. Disraeli (U) 6,580
Bassetlaw	F. H. Newnes (L) 5,365 Sir F. Milner (C) 4,834	W. E. Hume-Williams (U) 5,631 F. H. Newnes (L) 5,290	W. E. Hume-Williams (U) 5,436 W. Stopford-Brooke (L) 5,221
Nottingham West	J. H. Yoxall (L) 8,107 W. L. Rowley (LU) 5,262	J. H. Yoxall (L) 8,955 H. Lygon (U) 6,652	Sir J. H. Yoxall (L) 8,141 B. S. Wright (U) 5,949
Staffordshire			
NW. Staffordshire	Sir A. Billson (L) 7,667 Sir J. Heath (C) 5,557	*A. Stanley* (Lab) 8,566 G. Nugent (U) 5,754	*A. Stanley* (Lab.) 8,125 L. de Gruyther (U) 4,940
	By-election, 1907:	*A. Stanley* (L-L) 7,396 T. Twyford (C) 5,047	
Hanley	*E. Edwards* (L-L) 9,183 A. H. Heath (C) 4,287	*E. Edwards* (Lab) 9,199 G. H. Rittner (U) 5,202	*E. Edwards* (Lab) 8,343 G. H. Rittner (U) 4,658
	By-election, 1912:	R. L. Outhwaite (L) 6,647 G. H. Rittner (U) 5,993 *S. Finney* (Lab) 1,694	

	1906	1910 (January)	1910 (December)
Stoke-on-Trent	J. Ward (L-L) 7,660	J. Ward (L-L) 7,688	J. Ward (L-L) 7,049
	D. H. Coghill (C) 4,288	D. H. Kyd (U) 5,697	S. J. Thomas (U) 5,062
Newcastle under Lyme	J. C. Wedgwood (L) 5,155	J. C. Wedgwood (L) 5,653	J. C. Wedgwood (L) 5,280
	Sir A. S. Haslam (U) 2,948	E. S. Grogan (U) 4,245	E. S. Grogan (U) 4,086
West Staffordshire	H. D. McLaren (L) 5,586	G. A. Lloyd (U) 5,892	G. A. Lloyd (U) 5,602
	Sir A. Henderson (LU) 4,708	H. D. McLaren (L) 5,327	W. Meakin (L) 5,123
Lichfield	T. C. T. Warner (L) 5,421	T. C. T. Warner (L) 5,220	Sir T. C. T. Warner (L) 5,058
	R. V. Grosvenor (LU) 2,991	G. Coates (C) 4,353	A. Chetwynd (U) 4,213
Warwickshire			
Nuneaton	*W. Johnson* (L-L) 7,677	*W. Johnson* (Lab) 8,154	*W. Johnson* (Lab) 8,199
	F. A. N. Newdigate (C) 5,849	H. Maddocks (U) 7,893	H. Maddocks (U) 7,501
Tamworth	P. A. Muntz (C) 7,561	F. A. N. Newdigate (C) 10,313	F. A. N. Newdigate (U)
	J. S. Leary (L) 4,842	C. H. Brampton (L) 4,799	
	By-election, 1909: F. A. N. Newdigate (U)		
Leicestershire			
Bosworth	Sir C. B. McLaren (L) 7,678	Sir C. B. McLaren (L) 7,709	H. D. McLaren (L) 7,500
	A. Stoneham (LU) 3,627	Sir Keith Fraser (U) 4,427	Count Garowski (U) 4,120

N

VIII

THE ROAD TO THE LEFT

ONCE we know the end of the story there is always a danger of looking back and forcing events into a deterministic scheme of our own making; knowing as we do what did happen after 1918 it is difficult to exclude altogether a note of inevitability from a description of the political changes that were taking place in the coalfields in the decade or so before the First World War. In 1900 the Labour Representation Committee was still an untried instrument, shunned and distrusted by most of the miners' unions. The Social-Democratic Federation and the Independent Labour Party had made scant impression on the mining communities. Most of the miners and their union leaders were firmly committed to the Liberal Party, and what little they knew of Socialism and its concomitant idea of independent parliamentary representation for the working class they heartily disliked. By 1914 the situation had been transformed. The Miners' Federation of Great Britain was part of the Labour Party, its executive was controlled by Labour supporters, as were the executives of all the major district unions; and, although thousands of miners could not yet be relied upon to vote Labour at parliamentary elections, Labour candidates in mining constituencies could at least be sure of a respectable poll. Ten years after the end of the war the process was complete and the loyalty of the miners was almost beyond question. They had become the Praetorian guard of an explicitly socialist Labour Party. Had there been no war in 1914, and had the Liberal Party not torn itself apart, events might conceivably have taken a different course. But history is full of accidents, and the facts are that the Labour Party did survive and it did prosper; and if the evidence from the coalfields is any indication of what was happening elsewhere, it owed its resilience as much to the strength of the roots put down before 1914 as to good fortune.

All trade unionists (and, indeed, the working class as a whole) were exposed to much the same set of industrial and social stimuli before 1914, and all of them, some faster and some slower, tended to react in much the same way. There was no question of individual trade unions and different occupational groups going over to Labour each for their own separate and particular reasons; the growth of the Labour Party was not just the aggregate of its progress within entirely unconnected sections of the community, and it would be patently misleading to try to describe it in these terms. Yet the miners were something of a special case, because in many respects they did live in an isolated world of their own and they did present Labour propagandists with special problems. It was not just a matter of writing a fresh gospel on a blank page; more often the task was to persuade the miners and their leaders to abandon a well-established faith in favour of a new creed that deliberately and unequivocally set out to undermine and destroy their cherished Liberalism. Nor was it all a question of high principles. An effective political machine bestows status and advantage upon those that it supports and promotes, and most of the older leaders had a vested and vital interest in preserving the Lib-Lab organizations that dominated so many of the mining constituencies. We know now that time was on Labour's side. The older men died, or were pushed aside by the new generation of miners' leaders, and as often as not when a union threw over a long-accepted policy of co-operation with the Liberals it was a change of personnel at the top rather than a change of heart that accounts for the break. Similarly, by no means all of the miners who voted for Labour and against Liberal (or for that matter Conservative) candidates in the years between 1900 and 1914 were converts; many of them were no doubt young men, with no previous attachment to any other party, coming on to the electoral register and voting for the first time. Even so, political loyalties are transmitted strongly from one generation to another, and in the mining towns and villages to capture the sons was an undertaking scarcely less formidable than winning over the fathers.

The political persuaders of sixty years ago had no means

of reaching millions of voters in an instant over the whole country. Naturally in due course the constituencies responded to great events at the centre; but before the days of mass communication political propaganda was inevitably much more of a local responsibility, and this was particularly true for a new party which as yet possessed few leaders with national reputations. So far as the Labour Party was concerned the laborious job of spreading the word among the miners rested mainly with the network of I.L.P. branches and with individual Socialists. Those who advocate change and innovation are always given a readier hearing when they preach against a background of discontent, and, although conditions varied a great deal from one mining district to another, there were ample grounds for dissatisfaction in most of the coalfields, and the early propagandists for Labour found opportunities enough for exploiting it.

It was nothing new for bad times to follow the good in the coal industry. The miners were used to that. But between 1900 and 1914 wage fluctuations fell into a pattern that was particularly calculated to produce a smouldering sense of injustice and anxiety. From 1897 to 1900 wages had risen steeply; but after reaching a peak in 1900 they fell sharply in the next five years, and, though there was something of a recovery between 1905 and 1907, the upswing was cut short in 1907 long before wages had reached their level of 1900. Thereafter they fell again, and it was not until 1911, when they were still 11 per cent below the peak of 1900, that another gradual rise began. All of this coincided with a steady and perceptible rise in the cost of living between 1900 and 1913. Higher prices affected everyone; but, largely because of the drop in their money wages between 1907 and 1911, by the outbreak of the war the position of the miners in relation to other groups of workers had noticeably worsened. By 1913 wage-rates in coal had barely climbed back to their 1900 level; in textiles they were 13 per cent above the 1900 figure.[1]

---

[1] J. H. Clapham, *An Economic History of Modern Britain*, Book 4, 1951, pp. 466–8. Labour propagandists naturally attributed low wages to the rapacity of the owners, allegedly bent upon expropriating far too large a share of the industry's earnings for themselves. See, for example, T. Richardson and J. Walbank, *Profits and Wages in the British Coal Trade, 1890–1910*, 1911, in which the authors argue

In 1900 there were 624,000 men employed underground in the pits; in 1910 the figure was 828,000, and by 1913 it had reached 910,000. Other things being equal, in an industry that was expanding as rapidly as this, earnings might have been expected to rise if only to attract the extra labour required. Unfortunately coal was beset by all the difficulties that typically confront a labour-intensive industry; it was also unlucky enough to be saddled with a management for the most part conservative in outlook and highly suspicious of technical innovation. So it was that output could be increased only by taking on more men; but at the same time, as the easier seams were progressively exhausted, productivity fell as total production went up.[1] The figures tell their own story. In 1881 382,000 miners were each producing an average of 403 tons of coal a year; by 1901 the labour force had grown to 644,000, but output per man was down to an average of 340 tons. And by 1911 877,000 men were averaging only 309 tons a year each. Put in another way, by 1911 36 per cent. more miners were being employed to produce 19 per cent. more coal, and marginal costs were rising rapidly.[2] Furthermore, from the 1890s onwards a number of extra financial burdens were laid on the owners: the Coal Mines Act (1896), the Workmen's Compensation Act (1897), the export duty on coal (1901), and a new set of Home Office safety regulations (1902)[3] all

that in the previous thirteen years dividends had increased by five times as much as wages; and C. B. Stanton, *Maxims for Miners*, 1914, for a comprehensive list of colliery company profits for the year 1912.

[1] Rowe, op. cit., pp. 13–14; and A. J. Taylor, 'Labour Productivity and Technological Innovation in the British Coal Industry, 1850–1914', *Econ. Hist. Review*, vol. xiv, 1961.   [2] Clapham, op. cit., p. 63.

[3] Clegg, Fox, and Thompson, op. cit., p. 337. Not that the owners were given much credit for spending more money on safety precautions. Socialists argued that higher output was often put before men's lives, and, although the accident rate in the mines was gradually being reduced, a series of major disasters occurred between 1906 and 1914. Some of the worst accidents were at the Maypole pit in Lancashire in 1908 (75 deaths); West Stanley, County Durham, in 1909 (168 deaths); Whitehaven, Cumberland, in 1910 (136 deaths); the Hulton pit in Lancashire in 1910 (344 deaths); Cadeby, Yorkshire, in 1912 (88 deaths); and Senghennyd, South Wales, in 1913 (439 deaths). Dozens of miners were killed every year in less spectacular accidents, of course. It was not always the owners and management who were to blame; but this did not affect the Socialist argument that safety regulations would be properly enforced only when the mines were nationalized and the profit motive eliminated.

helped to push up costs of production at a time when the price that coal would fetch was actually falling.[1] In the circumstances the owners and their agents naturally tried to hold down costs, and in the search for economies they naturally turned their attention to wages, by far the biggest single item in their expenditure. It was hardly surprising that industrial relations deteriorated, and, as it happened, matters were made even worse by a new development within the industry. Coal was never subject to the same degree of concentration as occurred in some other industries (even as late as 1925 there were still 1,400 colliery undertakings owning 2,500 mines);[2] but the growth of giant syndicates and amalgamations like the Joicey and Horden companies in Durham, Pease Partners in Yorkshire, and the Cambrian Combine in South Wales undoubtedly had the effect of driving masters and men further apart, because in the eyes of the miners these massive new combines were impersonal, ruthless, and remote by comparison with the smaller firms they replaced.

The political consequences of industrial strife were all to the disadvantage of the Liberals. For a party that claimed to represent the interests of the working class (and especially of the miners) it was embarrassing enough that so many prominent coal-owners were also well-known Liberal M.P.s; it was certainly not easy to pass off D. A. Thomas (the Chairman of the Cambrian Combine and until 1910 the Member for Merthyr Tydfil) as the miners' friend when he was locked in a life-and-death struggle with his employees in the Rhondda. Even in the 1910 Parliament there were still at least eleven mining constituencies represented by Liberal coal-owners; what sense did it make, asked the Socialists, to send your industrial enemies to Westminster to protect your political interests? It was hard to find a convincing answer.[3]

---

[1] Clapham, op. cit., p. 467.   [2] Ibid., p. 263.

[3] An article in *The Rhondda Socialist* (13 Mar. 1913) provides a typical example of this kind of argument. Entitled 'To a Liberal workman' it went on: 'How is the Liberal Party made up in the House of Commons? It is made up of hundreds of capitalists—merchants and manufacturers, cotton and woollen lords, mining shareholders and railway directors. When Labour questions are to the front the Liberal employer is as hostile to the workers as the Tory. Have you forgotten which of the

Yet, important though this background of industrial unrest was, it does not by itself fully account for the shift to the left amongst the miners before the First World War, nor does it explain why some coalfields moved much faster than others. In fact, when the pattern of industrial unrest is compared with the incidence of political militancy, there are enough divergencies to suggest that the former by no means offers a complete explanation of the latter.

There is no entirely satisfactory yardstick for measuring a phenomenon like industrial unrest; but 'propensity to strike', as reflected in the proportion of the labour force involved in disputes, does provide an index that is useful enough for purposes of comparison. Table 10 lists the major mining districts on the basis of a simple ratio between the number of men employed and the number engaged in strikes in the period 1906 to 1913.[1]

TABLE 10

Area	Men involved in disputes	Divided by no. of men employed (1910)
Wales and Monmouthshire	488,000	2·14
Durham, Northumberland, Cumberland	278,000	1·25
Midlands	133,000	0·73
Yorkshire	101,000	0·68
Lancashire and Cheshire	51,000	0·51
Scotland	45,000	0·32

masters took the lead against the miners who were fighting for a fair wage: was it not Mr. D. A. Thomas, of South Wales, who is not only a Liberal, but sat as a Liberal for Merthyr Tydfil and Cardiff.

In the London Dock Strike which of the masters was most firm in refusing to meet the men, in trying to break the strike by famine? Was it not Lord Devonport, a Liberal. . . . It is rich men of the type of Thomas and Devonport who pay money into the secret funds of the Liberal Party. It is rich men who control its policy when an industrial issue is being discussed. . . . In the main the Tory Party stands for the landed interests; in the main the Liberal Party stands for the capitalist interests; the Socialist movement stands wholly for the workers' interests.'

1 *Reports on Strikes and Lock-outs* (Labour Department of the Board of Trade). Some of the figures given in these reports relate to inconveniently wide areas. Those available for the Midlands, for example, refer to all the mining counties in the area; other evidence suggests that Derbyshire and Nottinghamshire may have been rather less, and the rest of the coalfield rather more, strike-prone than this table indicates.

As a supplementary indicator, Table 11 grades the coalfields in order of their apparent enthusiasm for the minimum wage strike in 1912.

TABLE 11

District	For the strike	Against	Ratio
Yorkshire	63,736	10,477	6·3
Cumberland	4,918	813	6·3
South Wales	103,526	18,419	5·6
Scotland	60,611	12,035	5·0
Midland Federation	26,069	5,275	4·9
North Wales	7,327	1,566	4·6
Lancashire	50,517	11,393	4·4
Nottinghamshire	17,086	5,386	3·1
Northumberland	22,595	7,557	2·9
Derbyshire	17,999	6,186	2·6
Durham	57,490	28,504	2·0

It would obviously be foolish to read too much into these two sets of figures. Table 10, for example, probably exaggerates the militancy of the North-East because of one major dispute, the strike over the introduction of the Eight Hours Act in 1910, which alone involved no less than 115,000 Durham and Northumberland miners in the early part of that year. Table 11, on the other hand, may well under-emphasize the militancy of this area; having been on strike for three months in 1910, the miners were probably less enthusiastic than they might otherwise have been for another stoppage in 1912.[1] Nevertheless there are some conclusions that can be drawn from these statistics without straining them too far. South Wales was clearly in a class of its own for militancy. But on the evidence of Table 10 Lancashire, Yorkshire, and Scotland were no more militant than the Midlands and the North-East; and, although Yorkshire comes out at the head of the list in Table 11, Lancashire and Scotland still do not emerge as startlingly turbulent, especially when it is remembered that there was

[1] For a comparative study that emphasizes the industrial quiescence of the North-East by comparison with South Wales, see K. G. J. C. Knowles, *Strikes—a study in industrial conflict. With special reference to British experience between 1911 and 1947*, 1952, pp. 186–93.

probably a special reason for the very low ratio in the North-East in 1912.

Political militancy is also a difficult phenomenon to measure satisfactorily, and here there is even less quantifiable evidence. The district ballots on the issue of joining the Labour Party in 1908 do provide some guide, and Table 12 sets out the ratio of union members favouring to those opposing affiliation in 1908.

TABLE 12

Lancashire and Cheshire	2·20	South Derbyshire	0·61
Cumberland	1·85	Midland Federation	0·54
South Wales	1·67	Nottinghamshire	0·50
Somerset	1·59	North Wales	0·41
Yorkshire	1·58	Derbyshire	0·35
Northumberland	1·40	Leicestershire	0·29
Scotland	1·24		

A second yardstick is the number of genuinely independent Labour candidates sponsored by each district between 1906 and 1914, although these figures are slightly misleading because they take no account of the number of seats that might reasonably have been contested had the union been so minded. For what they are worth, the figures are: Scotland thirteen, Lancashire nine, Durham six, South Wales six, Yorkshire two, Cumberland two, and Derbyshire and North Staffordshire one each. The only other indicator of any use for comparative purposes is the date at which each of the district unions unmistakeably committed itself to independent political action irrespective of the wishes of the other parties. The Scottish miners, of course, always had pursued a militantly independent line of their own, from the time of Keir Hardie's contest in Mid Lanark in 1888 onwards; the Lancashire miners decided to run only independent Labour candidates in 1900; Durham and Cumberland broke with the Liberals in 1909; South Wales did the same in 1910; Yorkshire and North Staffordshire came into conflict with the Liberals in 1912; and in Derbyshire the break finally came in 1914. It would plainly be absurd to try to draw fine distinctions on the basis of this information. But except for the rather low position of Scotland in Table 12 all the signs are in broad agreement and they suggest that Labour had made most headway in Lancashire, Scotland, the North-East, and Cumberland, that it was faring nearly but not quite as well in South Wales and Yorkshire, and that everywhere else it was making much slower progress or had made hardly any impact at all.

Fragmentary though the evidence may be, there is enough of it to demonstrate that something more than the presence of industrial unrest is required in order to explain the varying degrees of success enjoyed by the Labour Party in each of the coalfields. Lancashire, Scotland, and Durham were clearly nowhere near as militant, in the industrial sense, as South Wales; yet the indications are that Labour's performance in the three former districts was markedly superior. And, whilst on the evidence of Table 10 some of the Midland coalfields were every bit as strike-prone as Yorkshire, Lancashire, and Scotland, it was, of course, in these Midland districts that the Labour Party was at its weakest. Nor does prosperity, or its absence, square exactly with political militancy, though in this respect there is a somewhat closer association. It is true that some of Labour's best areas, Lancashire, Scotland, and Cumberland, for example, were amongst the poorest districts, and some of its worst areas, Derbyshire and Nottinghamshire for example, were amongst the richest; but North Wales and Cannock Chase were also impoverished coalfields, and they were certainly no hotbeds of Socialism. Yorkshire was the richest coalfield of all, yet by 1914 Labour had unquestionably made more progress here than in some of the rather less prosperous Midland districts.[1]

None of this, it should be emphasized, is to deny that mounting industrial unrest and dissatisfaction were important in helping to shift all the miners to the left. But at the same time it is clear enough that there must have been other important elements in the situation, and only by reverting to some of the more narrowly political considerations discussed in Chapter IV is it possible to account for the wide range of political militancy encountered in the

[1] For miners' earnings in 1914, see Table 9, p. 55.

coalfields in the decade before 1914. Take Lancashire, for example. It may well be that the statistical evidence in Tables 10 and 11 rather underestimates the extent of the miners' dissatisfaction; perhaps they were too poor and too insecure to strike frequently and stay out for lengthy periods. But, even if it is conceded that there are times when figures do not tell the whole story, it would still be necessary to look for other reasons for Labour's success among the Lancashire miners; in this case it seems that events took the course they did mainly because the miners were uncharacteristically divided between the Liberal and Conservative Parties and the new Labour Party provided the obvious channel for the union's political ambitions. In the North-East it was the increasingly anachronistic attitude of the union's Lib-Lab leaders on industrial issues that presented the I.L.P. with its opportunity. In Durham, Scotland, South Wales, and Yorkshire the unwillingness of local Liberal Associations to co-operate in meeting the miners' demands for more parliamentary representation inevitably played into the hands of the Labour Party. In the Midlands, on the other hand, the miners had little reason for complaint on this score. Again, Labour's progress was naturally governed to some extent by the strength of the existing ties between the miners and the Liberals in any particular area. In South Wales, for example, the Liberal Party had always been more than just a political organization; in the nine-teenth century it had been the vehicle for the religious and nationalist aspirations of the Welsh people. Loyalty to the Liberals went very deep among the Welsh miners, and, for all the undoubted industrial unrest in the coalfield, a new political party, breaking fresh ground, could not help but find the going hard.

One final question remains for discussion: how much support did Labour have amongst the miners over the country as a whole? This is not an easy question to answer, because at first sight some of the evidence is puzzling and conflicting. Between 1906 and 1914 the M.F.G.B. held three ballots that provided its members with the opportunity of making it clear what their attitude was towards the Labour Party. In 1906, on a 57 per cent poll, the Federation rejected affiliation to the Labour Party by 101,714 votes to 92,222; two years later, on a 69 per cent poll, 213,137 miners voted in favour of joining the party and 168,446 voted against. There was a third political ballot in 1913 (as required by the 1913 Trade Union Act), and this time the miners were asked whether or not they were in favour of setting up and contributing to a political fund; the result showed that 261,463 approved and 194,800 were against.

It is true that the 1908 ballot tells us nothing about the views of tens of thousands of M.F.G.B. members who did not trouble to vote; nor is it any guide to the opinions of those miners who were not members of their district unions. But it must be remembered that, had Durham not been debarred from voting for legal reasons, the total number of miners voting would have been much larger, and so, in all probability, would the majority in favour of affiliation.[1] There is certainly no reason to suppose that, of those who for one reason or another did not vote, the vast majority were hostile to the Labour Party. Because it came at the very end of the period under examination the 1913 ballot was probably the most significant, and whilst the majority was not overwhelming the outcome can hardly be regarded as a disappointing set-back for Labour.[2] No doubt some of the miners who voted for a political fund were not Labour supporters at all; possibly some Liberals and Conservatives agreed, as a matter of principle, that their union should have the right to use its money as it pleased, and voted accordingly. But it would be surprising if there were many in this category, for it must have been generally assumed that if a fund were established it would be used to further the interests of the Labour Party; and it must have been equally apparent that if Labour made more headway in the coalfields it was the Liberal Party that chiefly stood to lose. Moreover, not all the miners who voted against the fund were necessarily irreconcilable opponents of the Labour Party: apart from Liberals and Conservatives the minority

---

[1] See p. 73.

[2] For an interpretation of this kind, see J. H. Stewart Reid, *The Origins of the British Labour Party*, 1955, p. 170, where the majority is wrongly given as 45,000, perhaps in confusion with the 1908 ballot.

would certainly have included miners who were disillusioned
with politics generally, those who simply objected to paying
another shilling a year to their union, and even Syndicalists,
for whom the Labour Party was too tame. Leaving aside
the 1906 result, which was soon reversed, it would seem
from these ballots that a clear majority of the miners were in
sympathy with the Labour Party and its objects.

By contrast, the performance of Labour candidates at
parliamentary elections in mining constituencies presents a
very different picture. Generally speaking, if a Liberal
candidate was also in the field it was rare for the Labour man,
even if he himself was a miner or miners' official, to poll as
much as half of the mining vote in the constituency. In
Bishop Auckland, North-West Durham, Houghton-le-
Spring, Mid Glamorgan, East Glamorgan, Leigh, Morley,
Holmfirth, North-East Derbyshire, Hanley, North-East
Lanarkshire, Mid Lanarkshire, and Midlothian, Labour
candidates either took a smaller share of the miners' vote
than their Liberal opponents or at best managed to break
even. This was only to be expected in districts like Derbyshire and Staffordshire which had voted decisively against
affiliation in 1908. But in South Wales, Yorkshire, and
Scotland (all coalfields where sizeable majorities in favour
of joining the Labour Party were recorded in 1908), and in
Durham too for that matter, Labour's inability to outscore
the Liberals is on the face of things rather surprising.

There are a number of possible explanations. To begin
with, there is the possibility that some of the miners who
voted for affiliation in 1908 and for a political fund in 1913
nevertheless continued to vote Liberal rather than Labour at
parliamentary elections. It was not exactly the logical thing
to do; but political inertia is always a force to be reckoned
with, and, once established, party loyalty tends to persist,
sometimes for years after it has ceased to be consistent with
the rest of an individual's attitudes and beliefs. In a general
way a miner might wish the Labour Party well and believe
that the Miners' Federation ought to be part of it; he could
still choose to vote Liberal in his own constituency, especially
if he were persuaded that the bigger the Labour vote the
more chance there was of a Conservative victory. Secondly,

the poor record of so many Labour candidates in mining seats may be in part attributable to sheer lack of preparation. In the years 1906 to 1914 these constituencies more often than not were being fought for the first time; electoral organizations were usually improvised at short notice, and only rarely had there been any preliminary propaganda campaign. There were only a few mining constituencies where Labour did contest the seat more than once against the Liberals during this period, but where there was a second contest under comparable circumstances in the same division, as at Mid Glamorgan and Bishop Auckland in December 1910 and Holmfirth in 1912, Labour gained appreciably in relation to the Liberals on the second occasion.[1] And thirdly, the miners who took part in trade union ballots were not precisely the same body of men as voted in parliamentary elections. In a union ballot all paid-up members were entitled to vote: the parliamentary franchise on the other hand was based mainly on householder qualifications, and since a year's residence in the same constituency was also required, the more mobile younger men were almost certainly penalized. Consequently the age group from which Labour could hope to draw most support tended to be under-represented on the electoral register, whilst a considerably higher proportion of the older and more settled men, among whom loyalty to the Liberal Party was strongest, were enfranchised. The likelihood is that many a Labour supporter never cast a vote at a parliamentary election before 1914.[2]

[1] It must be admitted that this was not always the case in Scotland. Labour improved its position in West Fife, but lost ground in relation to the Liberals in NE. Lanarkshire, Mid Lanarkshire, and North Ayrshire.

[2] J. J. Lawson, for example, though an intensely active man in public life, did not vote until he was nearly 30, see J. J. Lawson, *A Man's Life*, 1932, p. 175. According to a contemporary estimate there were almost 12 million adult males in the United Kingdom in 1910. Of these a little over 2 million did not qualify for the vote because they were paupers, foreigners, domestic servants, and removals. There were a further 2 million adult males without the vote, and many of these, it was thought, were lodgers and other young men who for a variety of reasons were not placed on the electoral register until a number of years after they had reached the age of 21. See S. Rosenbaum, 'The General Election of January 1910 and the bearing of the results on some problems of representation', *Journal of the Royal Statistical Society*, vol. lxxiii, May 1910; E. Halevy, *History of the English People in the Nineteenth Century*, vol. vi, 1961 edition, pp. 442–4; and Neal Blewett, op. cit.

There is no denying that on the eve of the First World War the Labour Party's future was still uncertain, and it is true that in terms of electoral support its progress in the coalfields had been slow and often punctuated with disappointments. But even allowing for wisdom after the event it is hard to avoid the impression that Labour had come to stay, and that although it faced a long haul, its prospects both in the short run and beyond were set reasonably fair. The next generation of miners' leaders were committed to Labour almost to a man, and with the mere passage of time more and more of the unenfranchised young men of yesterday would have found their way on to the register to swell the Labour vote. Even in the immediate future the outlook was quite promising. The revival of interest in politics amongst the miners in 1913 and 1914 has already been described; had there been a general election in 1915 the ground would have been far better prepared than on previous occasions. From 1885 onwards the mining vote had provided the Liberal Party with many of its safest seats. In about 1906 a perceptible change began to come over the coalfields, and by 1929 the Liberals had been thoroughly routed in the colliery districts. The old Liberal strongholds had become the new citadels of Labour: by then the transformation was complete.

APPENDIX A

Explanatory note on the technique employed to calculate the strength and distribution of the mining vote

FOR the purposes of this book, the expression 'mining seat' has been used to describe those constituencies where on the best available estimates the miners formed 10 per cent and upwards of the electorate. This Appendix explains how the size of the mining vote was calculated for those parliamentary constituencies which because of their geographical position within the major coalfields qualified for possible classification as mining seats. It was necessary to devise a technique that could be applied systematically because, although contemporary estimates do occasionally come to light, they are scattered in place and time, and many of them seem to be based on nothing more than inspired guesswork. It is true that occupational analyses are obtainable from the 1901 and 1911 census figures; but unfortunately, except in the case of a handful of counties, county boroughs, and boroughs, the boundaries of census units do not coincide with those of parliamentary constituencies.

The initial assumption that had to be made was that the number of miners resident in a constituency was roughly equal to the number employed there. This is not an unreasonable premise, for the general tendency certainly was for miners to live fairly close to their place of work; indeed, the greater part of the labour force for many pits was supplied from an associated colliery village. If there was any reason to suppose that the number of miners resident and the number employed in a constituency were not approximately equal, appropriate adjustments were made. In this Appendix the calculations made in connection with the Durham constituency of Houghton-le-Spring have been used throughout for purposes of illustration. With a few exceptions that are mentioned later, exactly the same procedure was used for all the other mining constituencies.

The first step was to locate and identify all the collieries of any size that lay within the constituency: this was done with the help of the second edition of the Ordnance Survey six-inches-to-one-mile map. The number of men employed at each of these collieries for the year 1909 was extracted from an annual Home Office publication of this period entitled the *List of Mines*. (See Table 13.)

The figures given in the *List of Mines*, however, refer to men over the age of 16: clearly men between the ages of 16 and

21 must be excluded from this total, for they were not even potential voters. An examination of the occupational section of the 1911 census, which breaks down each occupation into age-groups, suggests that about 15 per cent of the labour force in the coal-mining industry was aged between 16 and 21. The total number of miners employed in each constituency was therefore reduced by 15 per cent in order to arrive at the approximate number of adults, the potential voters. On this basis the 21,250 miners in Houghton-le-Spring becomes 18,060 adult miners.

TABLE 13

Houghton-le-Spring: men employed, 1909

Colliery	
Ryhope	2,365
Silksworth	2,145
Seaham	2,905
Murton	3,030
Hetton	940
Hetton Hazard	695
Lumley 6th	735
Lumley 3rd	555
Hetton Eppleton	1,085
Houghton	1,885
Bourn Moor	1,245
Newbottle	1,505
Herrington	965
Hylton	1,195
Total:	21,250

By no means all of these adult miners were on the electoral register. In Houghton-le-Spring, as in many other mining constituencies, the adult miners alone, quite apart from anyone else, easily outnumber the total electorate. The next problem was to estimate roughly what *proportion* of these adult miners had the vote. Two methods were used to establish a percentage of enfranchised miners, and both led to broadly similar conclusions.

(i) For each parliamentary constituency the 1901 and 1911 censuses give the total male population and the size of the electorate. Using the census figures which break down the population of the country as a whole into age-groups the proportion of the total male population aged over 21 was calculated: in 1901 and 1911 the figures were 55 per cent and 57 per cent respectively. Since there is no reason to think that the percentages for the mining areas were very different from those of the country as a whole, the number of adult males in the mining constituencies was calculated on the assumption 55 per cent and 57 per cent of the male population in each of these constituencies was aged over 21 in 1901 and 1911. With the number of adult males now estimated, and the size of the electorate available from the census, it was possible to calculate what proportion of the adult male population in each constituency was enfranchised. The relevant figures for the Houghton-le-Spring division are set out below in Table 14.

TABLE 14

Date	Total population	Total males	Estimated number of adult males	Electorate	% of adult males enfranchised
1901	80,382	41,311	22,720	14,446	63
1911	99,774	50,999	29,070	18,004	61

The 'percentage of adult males enfranchised' refers, of course, to *all* adult males in the constituency, and not to miners alone. But, since in Houghton-le-Spring, and in many of the other constituencies under consideration, the miners formed a high proportion of the total male population, it seems likely that the percentage of all adult males on the register would reflect, fairly closely, the figure for miners. Most of these percentages indicating the enfranchised proportion of the male population in mining constituencies fell within the 55 per cent to 65 per cent range, though there were a few seats where the figures were markedly higher or lower. At this point, however, two qualifications must be made. Firstly, the proportion of any working-class occupational group, like the miners, on the electoral register would probably have been rather lower than the enfranchised proportion of the *total* adult population. And, secondly, official returns showing the size of the electorate in each constituency really enumerate not the number of individual electors but the number of votes that could be cast. In many of the county divisions the electorate contained a number of 'outvoters', individuals resident in nearby borough constituencies but entitled to cast a vote in specified county divisions by virtue of property qualifications. When this factor is taken into account it seems reasonable, as well as convenient, to settle for 55 per cent, the figure at the lower end of the range, as the proportion of adult miners with the vote. Where there were strong reasons for supposing that a higher or lower figure would be more appropriate in particular constituencies, the necessary adjustments were made.

(ii) The second method used to estimate the likely percentage of miners on the electoral register was based upon figures drawn from a sample of Durham and Northumberland polling-districts. At election times local newspapers customarily published lists showing the number of registered electors in each of the polling-districts in the constituencies within their area of coverage. In Durham and Northumberland these polling-districts were often colliery villages. Where both the colliery and its associated village appear from the contemporary ordnance survey map to have been isolated from other collieries and villages it seems probable that most of the workers at the pit would have been resident in the nearby village (and polling-district) and that most of the voters in the village would have been miners employed at the local pit. On the basis of their topographical suitability a number of these polling-districts were selected, and the electorate in each of them expressed as a percentage of the adult labour force at the associated colliery. (See Table 15.)

TABLE 15

Constituency	Colliery and polling-district	Adult miners	Electorate	Miners as % of electorate
Durham				
Jarrow (1906)	Boldon	1,060	658	62
Houghton-le-Spring (1906)	Ryhope	1,655	871	52
	Murton	2,445	1,261	51
	Silksworth	1,820	1,041	57
Chester-le-Street (1906)	Usworth	1,095	754	68
	Waldridge	425	279	65
	Victoria Garesfield	455	246	53
SE. Durham (1913)	Shotton	1,550	1,075	69
	Horden	2,260	1,144	50
	Thornley	1,465	618	42
	South Hetton	1,005	526	52
				Average 56
Northumberland				
Morpeth (1906)	Cambois	830	503	60
	West Sleekburn	605	291	48
	Bebside	625	314	50
Wansbeck (1906)	Broomhill	1,225	841	68
	Pegswood	645	450	69
	Seghill	720	375	52
	Ashington	2,703	1,259	46
	North Seaton	805	393	48
				Average 55

Taking them together, methods (i) and (ii) do suggest that a figure of 55 per cent is not likely to be wildly astray.

Working on the reasonable hypothesis that 55 per cent of the miners had the vote in 1910, and given the number of adult miners employed (and, it is assumed, resident) in each constituency, the next step was to calculate the actual number of miners with the vote in all the constituencies under examination. From there it was a straightforward matter to calculate what proportion the enfranchised miners formed of the total electorate. (See Table 16.)

TABLE 16

Houghton-le-Spring (1910)

Electorate	Estimated no. of miner voters	Miners as % of total electorate
17,504	9,935	56

The technique described above has been applied to most of the constituencies that were examined. It is based on the assumption that the number of miners employed in a constituency was roughly equal to the number living there. Naturally some miners would have crossed constituency boundaries in travelling from home to work, but there is usually no reason to think that large numbers were involved, and in any case, since men probably crossed boundaries in both directions, the net gain or loss for any parliamentary division is not likely to have been substantial. There were, however, a few occasions when some modification of the basic technique seemed desirable. By using the Ordnance Survey six-inch map it was possible to pinpoint all the larger collieries with complete accuracy, and sometimes it was clear that an important colliery was situated on one side of a divisional boundary whilst the town or village from which most of its workers would have come lay on the other. In cases like this it seemed sensible to assign the pit total to that constituency in which the adjoining town or village was situated. To give one example: in South Wales some of the important Mardy and Ferndale pits lay in East Glamorgan; but, since there was no adjacent built-up area of any consequence in East Glamorgan, the chances are that most of the men employed at these collieries lived in the nearby towns of Mardy and Ferndale, which were situated in the Rhondda division. In calculating the number of men working in these two constituencies, these pit totals were therefore allocated to the Rhondda. Modifications of this kind were not often warranted. A second type of adjustment to the basic technique was sometimes necessary in dealing with certain borough constituencies. It is probable that many of the men working at pits close to boroughs like Gateshead, Sunderland, South Shields, Nottingham, and Wigan would have lived within these boroughs even though their colliery was situated in the adjoining county constituency. Fortunately the 1911 census does provide the number of miners living in these and other county boroughs, and, after making the necessary subtractions from the totals for the relevant county divisions, these census figures have been used to estimate the strength of the mining vote in most of the parliamentary boroughs that have been classified as mining seats.

The results of all these calculations are set out in the appendices to Chapters V, VI, and VII. Given the acknowledged limitations of the technique it would obviously be absurd to claim complete accuracy for the percentage figures displayed in those appendices. Were there any infallible way of discovering the truth it would be surprising to learn that the miners really did constitute exactly 56 per cent of the electorate in Houghton-le-Spring in 1910: but there is every reason to believe that just over half the electors in this constituency were miners.

APPENDIX B

Electoral history of the mining constituencies, 1885–1914

County	Constituency	Mining Vote (1910)	Electoral History								By-elections
			1885	1886	1892	1895	1900	1906	1910	1910	
ENGLAND AND WALES											
Glamorgan	Rhondda	over 70%	L-L	L-L	L-L	L-L	L-L	L-L	Lab	Lab	
Monmouthshire	West Monmouthshire	over 60%	L	L	L	L	L	L-L	Lab	Lab	1904: L-L
Northumberland	Wansbeck	,,	L-L	L-L	L-L	L-L	L-L	L-L	L-L	L-L	
Durham	NW. Durham	,,	L-L	L	L	L	L	L	L	L	1914: L
	Mid Durham	,,	L-L	L-L	L-L	L-L	L-L	L-L	L-L	L-L	1890: L-L
	Houghton-le-Spring	over 50%	C	C	L	L	L	L	L	L	1913: L
	Chester-le-Street	,,	L	L	L	L	L	Lab	Lab	Lab	
Glamorgan	Mid Glamorgan	,,	L	L	L	L	L	L	L	L	1890: L, 1900: L 1908: L, 1910: L
	East Glamorgan	,,	L	L	L	L	L	L	L	L	
Lancashire	Leigh	,,	L	L	L	L	L	L	L	L	
	Wigan	,,	C	C	C	C	C	Lab	L	C	
Northumberland	Morpeth	over 40%	L-L	L-L	L-L	L-L	L-L	L-L	L-L	L-L	
Yorkshire	Normanton	,,	L-L	L-L	L-L	L-L	L-L	L-L	Lab	Lab	1904: L-L 1905: L-L
	Barnsley	,,	L	L	L	L	L	L	L	L	1889: L 1897: L
	Osgoldcross	,,	L	L	L	L	L	L	L	L	
Derbyshire	Mid Derbyshire	,,	L	L	L	L	L	L	Lab	Lab	1909: Lab
	Chesterfield	,,	L	LU	L	L	L-L	L-L	Lab	Lab	1913: L-L
Nottinghamshire	Mansfield	,,	L	L	L	L	L	L	L	L	
Denbighshire	East Denbighshire	,,	L	L	L	L	L	L	L	L	

County	Constituency	Mining Vote (1910)	1885	1886	1892	1895	1900	1906	1910	1910	By-elections
Glamorgan	Merthyr Tydfil (2 Members)	over 40%	L	L	L	L	L	L	L	L	
			L	L	L	L	Lab	Lab	Lab	Lab	
Lancashire	Newton	"	C	C	C	C	C	Lab	Lab	C	1889 : C
Cumberland	Whitehaven	over 30%	C	C	L	C	C	L	C	Lab	1891 : C
Durham	Bishop Auckland	"	L	L	L	L	L	L	L	L	
	Barnard Castle	"	L	L	L	L	L	Lab	Lab	Lab	1903 : Lab / 1898 : L
	SE. Durham	"	L	LU	L	LU	LU	LU	L	L	
Yorkshire	Doncaster	"	L	L	L	C	C	L	L	L	1888 : LU / 1892 : L / 1899 : L
	Rotherham	"	L	L	L	L	L	L	L	L	
	Hallamshire	"	L	L	L	L	L	L-L	Lab	Lab	
	Morley	"	L	L	L	L	L	L	L	L	
Derbyshire	NE. Derbyshire	"	L	L	L	L	L	L	Lab	Lab	1907 : L-L / 1914 : C
	Ilkeston	"	L	L	L	L	L	L	L	L	1887 : L / 1910 : L
Monmouthshire	North Monmouthshire	"	L	L	L	L	L	L	L	L	
Leicestershire	Bosworth	"	L	L	L	L	L	L	L	L	
Staffordshire	NW. Staffordshire	"	C	C	C	C	C	L	Lab	Lab	1907 : L-L / 1898 : LU
	West Staffordshire	"	L	LU	LU	LU	LU	L	C	C	
Northumberland	Tyneside	over 20%	L	L	L	L	L	L	L	L	1907 : Lab
Durham	Jarrow	"	L	L	L	L	L	L	L	L	
Yorkshire	Holmfirth	"	L	L	L	L	L	L	L	L	1912 : L
	Pontefract	"	C	C	C	C	L	L	L	L	1893 : L
Lancashire	St. Helens	"	C	C	C	C	C	Lab	Lab	C	
	Ince	"	C	L-L	C	C	C	Lab	Lab	Lab	
Monmouthshire	South Monmouthshire	"	C	C	C	C	L	L	L	L	

Electoral history of the mining constituencies, 1885–1914 (cont.)

County	Constituency	Mining Vote (1910)	1885	1886	1892	1895	1900	1906	1910	By-elections
ENGLAND AND WALES (cont.)										
Glamorgan	Gower	over 20%	L	L	L	L	L	L-L	Lab	1888: L
Staffordshire	Lichfield	,,	L	L	LU	L	L	L	L	1896: L
Warwickshire	Nuneaton	,,	L	C	C	C	C	L-L	Lab	
Gloucestershire	Forest of Dean	,,	L	L	L	L	L	L	L	1887: L / 1911: L
Cumberland	Cockermouth	over 10%	C	L	L	L	C	L	C	1906: C
Northumberland	Hexham	,,	L	L	L	L	L	L	L	1907: L
Durham	Sunderland (2 Members)	,,	L	L	L	L	C	L	C	
			L	L	L	L	C	C	Lab	
	South Shields	,,	C	C	L	L	LU	U	U	1898: LU
	Durham City	,,	L	L	L	L	L	L	U	1893: L
	Gateshead	,,	L	L	L	L	L-L	L	L	1904: L-L
Yorkshire	Barkston Ash	,,	C	C	C	C	C	C	C	1905: L
	Wakefield	,,	C	C	LU	LU	C	C	L	1902: C
	Attercliffe	,,	L	L	L	L	L	Lab	Lab	1909: Lab
Derbyshire	South Derbyshire	,,	L	L	C	C	L	L	L	
Nottinghamshire	Rushcliffe		L	C	L	L	L	L	L	
	Bassetlaw	,,	C	C	C	C	L	C	C	
	West Nottingham	,,	L	L	LU	L	L	L	L	
Lancashire	Radcliffe	,,	L	L	L	L	L	L	L	
	Ashton-under-Lyne	,,	C	C	C	C	C	C	C	
	Eccles	,,	C	L	L	L	L	L	L	
	Chorley	,,	C	C	C	C	C	C	C	1890: L

County	Constituency	Mining Vote (1910)	Electoral History								By-elections
			1885	1886	1892	1895	1900	1906	1910	1910	
Flintshire	Flintshire	over 10%	L	L	L	L	L	L	L	L	
Glamorgan	South Glamorgan	,,	L	L	L	C	C	L-L	L	Lab	1890: L
Carmarthenshire	East Carmarthenshire	,,	L	L	L	L	L	L	L	L	1912: L
Breconshire	Breconshire	,,	L	L	L	L	L	L	L	L	
Staffordshire	Hanley		L	L	L	L	C	L-L	Lab	Lab	1912: L
	Stoke-on-Trent	,,	L	L	L	LU	C	L-L	L-L	L-L	1890: L
	Newcastle under Lyme	,,	L	LU	L	L	LU	L	L	L	
Warwickshire	Tamworth	,,	C	C	C	C	C	C	C	C	1909: C
Somersetshire	Frome	,,	L	C	L	C	L	L	L	L	1896: L
SCOTLAND	West Fife	over 50%	L	L	L	L	L	L	L	Lab	1899: L
	West Lothian	over 30%	L	L	L	L	L	L	L	L	1893: LU 1913: L
	NE. Lanarkshire	,,	L	L	L	L	L	L	L	L	1901: LU 1904: L 1911: L
	Mid Lanarkshire	,,	L	L	L	L	L	L	L	L	1888: L 1894: L 1912: U
	Midlothian	over 20%	L	L	L	L	L	L	L	L	
	Falkirk Burghs	,,	L	LU	L	LU	LU	L	L	L	
	South Ayrshire	,,	L	LU	L	LU	LU	L	L	L	
	South Lanarkshire	,,	L	C	C	C	C	L	L	L	1913: U
	Stirlingshire	,,	L	L	L	L	L	L	L	L	
	East Lothian	over 10%	C	L	C	L	L	C	L	L	1911: L
	NW. Lanarkshire	,,	L	LU	LU	LU	LU	LU	L	L	1899: L
	N. Ayrshire	,,	L	LU	LU	LU	LU	LU	L	L	1911: U

INDEX

PRINTED IN GREAT BRITAIN
AT THE UNIVERSITY PRESS, OXFORD
BY VIVIAN RIDLER
PRINTER TO THE UNIVERSITY